Mass Media and Political Communication in New Democracies

This book examines how political communication and the mass media have played a central role in the consolidation of emerging democracies around the world.

Covering a broad range of political and cultural contexts from Eastern and Southern Europe, Latin America, Asia and Africa, this new volume investigates the problems and conflicts arising in the process of establishing an independent media and competitive politics in post-autocratic societies. Considering the changing dynamic in the relationship between political actors, the media and their audience, the authors of this volume address the following issues:

- Changing journalistic role perceptions and journalistic quality.
- The reasons and consequences of persisting instrumentalization of the media by political actors.
- The role of the media in election campaigns.
- The way in which the citizens interpret political messages and the extent to which the media influence political attitudes and electoral behaviour.
- The role of the Internet in building a democratic public sphere.

This book will be of great interest to all those studying and researching democracy and democratization, comparative politics, political communication, journalism, media and the Internet.

Katrin Voltmer is Senior Lecturer of Political Communication at the Institute of Communication Studies, University of Leeds, UK.

Routledge/ECPR studies in European political science

Edited by Thomas Poguntke, *University of Birmingham, UK* and Jan W. van Deth, *University of Mannheim, Germany on behalf of the European Consortium for Political Research*

The Routledge/ECPR Studies in European Political Science series is published in association with the European Consortium for Political Research – the leading organization concerned with the growth and development of political science in Europe. The series presents high-quality edited volumes on topics at the leading edge of current interest in political science and related fields, with contributions from European scholars and others who have presented work at ECPR workshops or research groups.

Mass Media and Political Communication in New Democracies

Edited by Katrin Voltmer

Routledge
Taylor & Francis Group
LONDON AND NEW YORK

First published in 2006
by Routledge
2 Park Square, Milton Park, Abingdon, Oxon, OX14 4RN

Simultaneously published in the USA and Canada
by Routledge
605 Third Avenue, New York, NY 10017

Routledge is an imprint of the Taylor & Francis Group, an informa business

Typeset in Baskerville by Wearset Ltd, Boldon, Tyne anel Wear

British Library Cataloguing in Publication Data
A catalogue record for this book is available from the British Library

Library of Congress Cataloging in Publication Data
A catalog record for this book has been requested

ISBN13: 978–0–415–33779–3 (hbk)
ISBN13: 978–0–415–45971–6 (pbk)

Contents

Illustrations

Figures

Tables

Contributors

Carlos Barrera is Professor in the Department of Public Communication of the University of Navarra, Spain. Since July 2004 he has been Vice Chair of the IAMCR History Section. He is the author of more than sixty books, chapters and articles. He has conducted various research projects on the press during the Spanish transition to democracy.

Kees Brants is director of the MA programme in European Communication Studies and Senior Fellow at the Amsterdam School of Communications Research, both at the University of Amsterdam. He holds a Special Chair in Political Communication at Leiden University.

Arnold S. de Beer is Emeritus Professor in the Department of Journalism, Stellenbosch University, South Africa. Recent publications deal with global journalism; media and elections; public relations in developing democracies; war and media; the Internet in Africa; media coverage of HIV/AIDS; and journalism skills. De Beer is editor of *Ecquid Novi* and on the editorial board of *Journalism Reviews*.

Hedwig de Smaele is a Postdoctoral Fellow of the Fund for Scientific Research, Flanders (Belgium) and lecturer in Politics and Mass Media at Ghent University, Department of Communication. She also heads the subgroup 'Social and Political Studies' of the Centre for Russian, International, Socio-political and Economic Studies (CERISE) in Ghent. She has published mainly on Russian mass media and (Central and Eastern) European audiovisual policy.

Roberto Espíndola is Senior Lecturer in Politics and Acting Director of the Centre for European Studies, where he also directs the Marie Curie Training Site on Europeanisation. His research and publications focus on electoral campaigns and political parties with particular reference to new democracies in Latin America and Europe. Dr Espíndola sits on the editorial board of several international journals, including *Global Society* and the *Journal of Political Marketing*.

Natalya Krasnoboka is a Ph.D. candidate and research assistant at the University of Antwerp, Belgium. Her research focuses on problems of media in transitional societies, the relationship between traditional and new media, and the role of the Internet as an alternative medium.

Ming-Ying Lee is a Ph.D. candidate in Sociology at the University of Warwick, UK. He is currently completing his thesis on the public understanding of democracy and the application for e-government in Taiwan. His major research interests include political socialization and the information society, particularly in its political dimensions.

Ian McAllister is Professor of Political Science in the Research School of Social Sciences at the Australian National University. His research interests are in the areas of comparative political behaviour, political parties, voters and electoral systems. His most recent book, with David M. Farrell, is *The Australian Electoral System* (University of NSW Press, 2005).

Ellen Mickiewicz is Professor of Political Science and Director of the DeWitt Wallace Center for Communications and Journalism at Duke University. Much of her work has focused on prospects for media and transition. She is author or editor of numerous journal articles and books including her most recent *Changing Channels: Television and the Struggle for Power in Russia* (Oxford University Press, 1997). She also serves on the editorial boards of the *International Journal of Press and Politics* and *Political Communication.*

Sarah Oates is a lecturer in Politics at the University of Glasgow and has written extensively on the Russian mass media and elections. Currently, she is studying the framing of the terrorist threat in Russian and US elections through a grant from the Economic and Social Research Council.

Gary Rawnsley is Senior Lecturer in Politics, and Director of the Institute of Asia-Pacific Studies, University of Nottingham. His most recent publications are *Political Communications in Greater China* (edited with Ming-Yeh Rawnsley, RoutledgeCurzon, 2003) and 'Treading a Fine Line: Democratisation and the Media in Taiwan', in *Parliamentary Affairs*, 57:1 (2004). He is currently completing a book on political communication and democracy for Palgrave.

Rüdiger Schmitt-Beck is Professor of Political Science at the University of Duisburg-Essen, Germany. His research interests are in the field of comparative politics, especially on topics of political communication, electoral behaviour, political culture, social movements and political participation.

Katrin Voltmer is Senior Lecturer of Political Communication at the Institute of Communications Studies at the University of Leeds, UK. Her research interests include the role of the media in transitions to democracy, the quality of political news, and the media's impact on individual attitudes and participation.

Silvio Waisbord is Senior Program Officer at the Academy for Educational Development, Washington, DC. Previously, he was Associate Professor in the Department of Journalism and Media Studies at Rutgers University, USA. He has written about media globalization, journalism, and development. His most recent coedited book is *Global Media, Latin Politics* (with Elizabeth Fox; University of Texas Press, 2002). He is currently working on a book about development communication.

Herman Wasserman, D.Litt. is a Senior Lecturer in the Department of Journalism of the University of Stellenbosch, South Africa, and Deputy Editor of *Ecquid Novi*, a South African journal for journalism research. His research interests include African perspectives on media ethics, media and the construction of post-apartheid identity and the use of ICTs for social activism.

Stephen White is Professor of International Politics and a member of the School of Central and East European Studies at the University of Glasgow, UK. His recent books include *Russia's New Politics* (Cambridge University Press, 2000) and *The Soviet Political Elite from Lenin to Gorbachev* (with Evan Mawdsley, Oxford University Press, 2000).

Ricardo Zugasti is Assistant Professor at the School of Public Communication, University of Navarra, Spain. In his doctoral thesis he examined the political characterization which the Spanish press attributed to King Juan Carlos I and his monarchy during the transition to democracy.

Series editor's preface

After a hopeful start, the 'third wave' of democratization seems to have lost its momentum. Many emerging democracies reached a 'stand-off' or 'cease fire' between democratic and non-democratic forces, resulting in hybrid forms of illiberal democracy. Elected governments defend free multi-party elections, but frequently fail to regulate or take control of powerful groups in society. Yet the spread of democracy around the world continues. In its Annual Report of 2004, *Freedom House* concludes that since the beginning of global action against terrorism in autumn 2001, 51 countries showed overall progress in their attempts to improve democracy, while 27 slid back. Most improvement has been made in central and eastern Europe, and in east Asia; least in the Middle East, north Africa, and central Asia. After the initial enthusiasm, then, emerging democracies struggle with the further development of democracy – and some of them are much more successful than others.

Despite the fact that the crucial importance of mass media for the endurance and improvement of every democracy is hard to overlook, the role of the media has not drawn major attention from the scholarly community dealing with democratic transformations. Modern political communication strategies increasingly rely on the use (and manipulation) of media presentations of candidates and their characteristics and backgrounds. The contributors to this volume differ in their research interests, study designs, selected material, and the scope of the analyses presented, but they all deal with the impact of mass media in emerging democracies around the world. Furthermore, they reject the conventional metaphor of the role of the mass media as a 'marketplace of ideas'. Instead, an interactionist approach is used based on the recognition that mass media, political actors, and the audience all produce, receive, and interpret political messages. The organization of the volume in three parts reflects this attention for (i) mass media and journalistic practice, (ii) political parties and governments, and (iii) the audience. In this way, the relationships between political communication and democratization are analysed from different perspectives without losing sight of their interdependencies.

Before the specific analyses are presented, Katrin Voltmer summarizes the major questions and approaches in her introduction to this volume by discussing the advantages of an interactionist approach for the study of political communication in emerging democracies (Chapter 1). The five consecutive contributions address mass media and journalistic practices in several countries. Carlos Barrera and Ricardo Zugasti examine how the majority of Spanish newspapers supported the transition to democracy in the late 1970s (Chapter 2). Results from a detailed analysis of the potentially antagonistic relationships between press freedom and democracy in Russia are presented by Hedwig de Smaele (Chapter 3). Herman Wasserman and Arnold de Beer focus on the significant changes in South African mass media after the successful transformation to democracy, and the continuous difficulties of repositioning the media in accordance with the new social and political situation (Chapter 4). The role of the mass media as a 'watchdog' and the need for apolitical and fact-based journalism are critically evaluated by Silvio Waisbord in a study of the decline of trust in media in Latin America in the last two decades (Chapter 5). The opportunities for new media in new democracies are studied by Natalya Krasnoboka and Kees Brants in their study of the considerable differences between newspaper and Internet publications in Ukrainian elections (Chapter 6). The next four contributions deal with political actors and electoral campaigning. Roberto Espíndola discusses the role of mass media in political campaigning in democratic consolidation processes in Argentina, Chile, and Uruguay (Chapter 7). A very different situation is analysed by Gary Rawnsley who focuses on the professionalization of election campaigning after Taiwan's transition from a single-party system to a regular democracy (Chapter 8). The last two contributions in this part direct the attention towards the role of television and Internet communication in new democracies. Sarah Oates argues convincingly that Russian media do not only promote parties, but create them as well (Chapter 9). Ming-Ying Lee shows that, although the Taiwanese government embraced e-government, no expansion of democratic participation can be observed (Chapter 10). The final part of the volume consists of three contributions on the role of citizens. The first two chapters deal, again, with the very interesting Russian case. Ellen Mickiewicz points out the specific discourses and framing processes used by Russian citizens confronted with state-controlled news programmes (Chapter 11), whereas Stephen White and Ian McAllister concentrate on the advantages for incumbents in situations where the media are controlled by the very same political actors (Chapter 12). Katrin Voltmer and Rüdiger Schmitt-Beck compare the impact of mass media on the development of democratic orientations in Bulgaria, Hungary, Chile, and Uruguay, showing clearly that the extent of media impact depends on the historical development of the political system in specific countries (Chapter 13). Finally, Katrin Voltmer returns to the major problems and prospects in her concluding chapter. While the various chapters concentrate on specific countries or regions, the concluding chapter focuses on thematic topics (Chapter 14).

The results obtained from an interactionist approach to the study of the close relationships between political communication and the problems of ongoing democratization used in this volume underline the need for differentiated and careful interpretations and considerations. From a global perspective, democracy is certainly on the rise. Yet emerging democracies are faced with very serious obstacles that are closely related to their specific historical experiences. Spain is not Russia, and Taiwan is not South Africa. What these emerging democracies have in common, however, is the crucial role the mass media plays in processes of political communication. Establishing free elections opens the door for sophisticated campaign strategies and the use of mass media that do not only have the long-term benevolent consequences presumed by most observers of Western democracies. Only if a balance can be found between the interests of political actors, the mass media, and the citizenries in specific countries will emerging democracies have a chance to survive and to overcome the transitory phase of illiberal democracy.

Jan W. van Deth, Series Editor
Mannheim, April 2005

Preface

This book originated in a workshop on 'Political Communication, the Mass Media, and the Consolidation of New Democracies' which I conducted with Slavko Splichal at the 2002 Joint Session of Workshops of the European Consortium for Political Research (ECPR) in Turin. All authors have extensively revised and updated their papers for publication. In addition, in order to achieve a broad range of both issues and countries additional contributions have been included that were not presented at the Turin workshop. I wish to thank the European Consortium for Political Research for having made this workshop and its publication possible. I would also like to thank Rebecca Reid for her meticulous assistance in editing this volume.

Katrin Voltmer
December 2004

1 The mass media and the dynamics of political communication in processes of democratization

An introduction

Katrin Voltmer

The unexpected magnitude of the 'third wave' of formerly autocratic countries establishing, or beginning to establish, democratic institutions over the last decade of the twentieth century has triggered an unprecedented interest in processes of social and political change. In fact, the study of transition to democracy, which used to be a specialized niche of students of particular areas, such as Southern Europe and Latin America (Gunther *et al.* 1995; Linz and Stepan 1996), has become something like a growth industry, with an enormous output of publications.

Transitions to democracy are social experiments that affect virtually all aspects of a society. They therefore provide a unique opportunity for deepening both theoretical and empirical understanding of the functioning of democratic institutions in different cultural and political contexts. The development of recently emerging democracies shows that democracy is a highly contingent enterprise, the success of which is not only dependent on the 'right' institutional design, but also on a multitude of other factors that need to be taken into account if we are to understand the conditions under which new democracies work. While some new democracies have successfully adopted the institutions and procedures of their Western role models (for example the east-central European countries that joined the European Union in May 2004), many others fall short of any standards of a viable democracy. In order to explain the apparent variation, many authors have argued that research on democratization needs to broaden its conceptual scope by taking organizations and processes into account that are not directly related to governmental decision-making but nevertheless might have a significant impact on the quality of democratic institutions and the way in which they operate (Grugel 2002; Merkel 1998).

The mass media are one such organization that has been largely ignored by mainstream democratization studies in spite of the fact that their performance is believed to have a pivotal impact not only on the functioning of other democratic institutions but also on the viability of the democratic process as a whole. However, many scholars in the West have argued that the media's ability to promote democracy is limited and have even held them responsible for many of the deficiencies from which established democracies appear to suffer (Entman 1989; Patterson 1998). This book aims to explore the role of the media in emerging democracies and the reasons for their success, or failure, in contributing to the consolidation of the new political order. More specifically, the chapters of this volume analyse how the media position themselves in the new political circumstances, and how other participants – such as governments, political parties and citizens – respond to the changing media environment. The book provides a unique comparative perspective on the issue by contrasting the experience of a broad range of new democracies from Africa, Asia, Eastern Europe and Latin America. While most of the chapters focus on one particular country, they address similar questions and thus collectively make it possible to draw more generalized conclusions about the expectations, problems and conflicts arising as the media alter their role from an instrument of autocratic power to an independent voice in the political debate.

This introductory chapter seeks to lay out the general theoretical foundation for studying the role of the mass media in transitions to democracy and the consolidation process thereafter. In the first part of this chapter I will present the normative arguments that establish the media as a democratic institution. Starting with a discussion of first principles is important for clarifying the underlying standards on which any evaluative judgments about the media's contribution to strengthening, or undermining, the viability of new democracies can be based. However, as this chapter suggests, the normative claims about the media's democratic role suffer from various inconsistencies that are bound to cause conflicts and misunderstandings in processes of democratizing the media. The second section of this chapter presents a heuristic model of political communication as a system of interaction that places the media in a broader context of the political process, and thus helps to organize theorizing on the role of the mass media in new democracies. This model serves to better understand the interdependence of mass communication and democratic politics and the consequences this may have on the way in which political messages are conveyed and employed in different political and cultural contexts. As yet, we lack a thorough understanding of whether – and, if so, how – political communication in new democracies differs from the situation in established democracies, which is the reason why much of the literature referred to in the following paragraphs relates to Western democracies. Hence, it remains an open empirical question how far these approaches can be applied to countries outside the western world. The chapters of this volume seek to provide some answers to this question.

The mass media as a democratic institution

From the early beginnings of democratic thought in the eighteenth century, political philosophers have recognized the crucial role of uninhibited public debate and free speech, which was later extended to the demand for a free press (Keane 1991). Several arguments have been brought forward to justify freedom of the press, the most common idea being that the media provide for a free 'marketplace of ideas' where contradicting voices compete for public recognition without the interference of the state.[1] The notion of a 'marketplace of ideas' is based on the liberal belief that no single agency be allowed to have the last say on the course of politics. Rather, it is through public exchange of argument and counter-argument that the 'truth' eventually emerges (Mill 1859, reprinted 1974). From the perspective of the 'marketplace of ideas' argument, the media are usually assigned a more passive role, serving as a forum where a variety of groups and individuals are given the opportunity to express their views. In many respects the situation in new democracies appears quite similar to the struggle for an autonomous public sphere in the eighteenth century. In order to encourage the development of a vivid civil society and to overcome the autocratic dominance of political elites, it is of crucial importance that alternative views have access to the forum of the media, regardless of the validity of their truth claims.

Albeit central to the liberal understanding of media in democracy, the premises of the 'marketplace of ideas' have been criticized for several reasons. In particular, it has been questioned whether the confrontation of competing views is really the best way of revealing 'the truth', as it may in fact contribute to confusion and the aggravation of conflicts. In the worst case, it might not be the best argument that prevails but rather that of those who are able to voice their views most effectively (Gutmann and Thompson 1996). Another disputed aspect of the 'marketplace of ideas' argument is whether and to what extent the media themselves may actively contribute to the public debate by promoting a particular point of view. In other words, are partisan media a legitimate part of the 'marketplace of ideas', or is their role confined to that of a neutral conveyor of the views of other actors? The distinction between internal and external, or vertical and horizontal, diversity acknowledges that there are different possible ways of establishing a vital 'marketplace of ideas' (McQuail 1986; Napoli 1999; Voltmer 2000). Internal, or vertical, diversity denotes to a situation where the full range of relevant views is represented within a particular media outlet, whereas external, or horizontal, diversity emerges as the aggregate of a variety of biased media. Thus, the meaning of diversity and the way in which a 'marketplace of ideas' can be brought about are not self-evident, and are likely to be disputed between the state, societal groups and the media in the course of transition to democracy.

While the 'marketplace of ideas' argument places political actors and their need to make themselves heard at the centre of concern, the notion of an information function focuses on the individual citizen as the main beneficiary of public communication. In a political system where political power is allocated on the basis of popular decision-making, the competence and rationality of the citizens is of utmost importance. In fact, without the citizens' ability to make informed choices the legitimacy of democratic elections would be seriously flawed (Dahl 1989). Hence, the quality of democratic decision-making is closely linked to the quality of information provided by the media. The two roles of the media – forum and information provider – are not mutually exclusive, but neither are they necessarily identical. What serves the publicity needs of political actors is not automatically the kind of information that fosters understanding and rational decision-making on the side of the citizens, and vice versa.

However, defining the exact meaning of 'information quality' is an almost impossible task as individuals differ in terms of their abilities and needs. Comprehensiveness seems to be an obvious feature. Yet, with the increasing complexity of political issues selectivity, meaningful simplification and, to some extent, interpretation of otherwise incomprehensible issues and events are equally important. One way of reducing the complexity of the political world is biased information that organizes the ongoing debate on the background of particular value preferences. Lemert (1989) argues that media which are committed to a particular cause offer 'mobilizing information' that has the potential to strengthen political identities and encourages participation.[2] Evidently, there is a trade-off between the ideal of comprehensive and neutral information that presents all sides of a controversy, and politicization that mobilizes citizens to take part in the political process.

Information quality and the need for orientation are probably of even more significance in new democracies, especially during the period immediately following the breakdown of the old regime. While in established democracies citizens acquire their political knowledge over a long period of time, usually without making a particular effort to learn about political issues, citizens in new democracies have to cope with a large range of hitherto unknown institutions and procedures. In addition, it can be assumed that, in a situation where traditional agencies of socialization – such as political parties and trade unions – have lost their credibility or even ceased to exist, the media are left as the main source where citizens can obtain the information they need to take part in public life.

A third argument for the media as a democratic institution is the idea that they act as a 'watchdog' or 'fourth estate' that keeps political authorities accountable by monitoring their activities and investigating possible abuses of political power (Curran 1991). The concept of a 'fourth estate' is related to the principle of division of powers that developed during the eighteenth century as an attempt to curb the then all-powerful absolute state. Some authors even argue that the control function of the media is more important than their information function because it protects citizens from state interference into individual freedom (Kelley and Donway 1990).

In the context of transition to democracy, the watchdog role of the media cannot be overstated, as one of the main tasks of democratization is to establish mechanisms that hold political elites accountable and responsive to the people. However, the relationship between the media and the state in new democracies is more complex. Undoubtedly, it is essential for the emancipation of society that state authorities are challenged. Yet, at the same time, the legitimacy of the new regime is often highly fragile and there is a risk of overstretching the capacities of the new government, especially when faced with mounting economic problems or the collapse of public security. Furthermore, the media themselves are often unable to survive without state subsidies, which might severely impair their ability to criticize political power holders. Paradoxically, the media's ability to safeguard democratic accountability eventually depends on the degree to which political institutions have adopted democratic structures and procedures (Morris and Waisbord 2001; Price *et al.* 2002).

The three sets of arguments that established the normative justification of the political role of the media in Western democracies – diversity and the 'marketplace of ideas', information and enlightened citizenship, and public watchdog and government accountability – have in common their aim to protect the objectives and interests of the individual vis-à-vis the state. What these classical concepts largely ignore, though, is the notion of a public interest that exists over and above the mere aggregation of particularistic interests. McQuail (1992: 66–78) in his normative theory of media performance therefore includes 'social order' alongside 'freedom' and 'equality' as one of three basic communication values that need to be implemented in media organizations and journalistic practice. However, there is no objective standard as to how to balance particularistic and collective communicative needs. Consequently, established democracies have found very different solutions to this problem, with a particular mix of journalistic rights, on the one hand, and obligations imposed on the media, on the other. The tension between freedom and the public interest can be expected to be a central conflict in new democracies. These societies are frequently faced with fragile identities, deep social divisions and unfinished nation-building, making integration and unity of overriding importance. At the same time, there is the risk that governments instrumentalize the need for collective identity and consensus to justify the oppression of dissonant views and opposition.

Much of the existing literature on the media in new democracies has focused on problems of media policy: how the normative standards discussed above have been implemented in the structure of post-authoritarian media systems, and whether existing political and economic conditions in particular countries foster or inhibit the media's ability to fulfil their democratic role (Curran and Park 2000; Downing 1996; Paletz *et al.* 1995; Splichal 1994). However, important as this research may be for the study of the media in new democracies, it does not investigate the implications of the media's actual performance for the democratic consolidation process. Technically speaking, the media are treated as a dependent variable, subjected to political interference or market forces, rather than an independent variable that affects the way in which other political actors operate. In other words, the media in new democracies are not only subjected to change, they are also actively taking part in the process of democratization by shaping the orientations and actions of other participants.

This perspective has only recently entered the academic debate. For example, Mughan and Gunther suggest a more complex approach that conceptualizes the role of the media in processes of political change as a 'reciprocal relationship between the media and the politics of democracy and democratization' (2000: 2). According to the authors, this interactive relationship is to be understood as an interplay of macro-level conditions (such as institutional structures and formal regulation), and micro-level variables (such as the values and beliefs of the actors involved). In a similar vein, Pfetsch argues that, if we are to understand the way in which politics is represented in the public domain, we have to consider not only the institutional conditions of the political system and the media system, but also the cultural dimension of political communication which involves 'the subjective action orientations, attitudes, and norms of actors in professional political communication roles' (2004: 345).

Understanding the dynamics of political communication – an interactionist approach

This volume pursues and further develops a similar line of argument by taking a process-oriented perspective on the relationship between mass communication and democratization. The main emphasis of the chapters of this book lies not on structural changes but on the day-to-day practices of political communication and on the production and reception of political messages. The overall structure of the book is based on a model that conceptualizes political communication as a system of dynamic interaction between political actors, the media and audience members, each of whom is involved in producing, receiving and interpreting political messages (Blumler and Gurevitch 1995). Viewing political communication as a system of interaction implies that all three sets of actors are dependent on the performance of the other actors of the system as a resource for achieving their own interests and objectives. As a result of the high degree of mutual interdependence, all these actors – but particularly politicians and the media – are constantly involved in a complex web of interactions and negotiations over aims, procedures and, ultimately, control of the public agenda. Not surprisingly, these interactions are frequently characterized by conflicts and disruptions, but equally by the compromises and cooperation that are required to maintain the relationship.

This model can be employed as a heuristics to guide the analysis of political communication in any political context. Because of its emphasis on change, it seems particularly suited to the study of political communication processes in new democracies. The basic assumption of a systems theoretical approach is that any change in one component of the system causes changes in the behaviour and orientations of other actors who try to adapt to the new conditions by redefining their communication strategies. In addition, systems of political communication respond to changes in the broader environment in which they operate, which can be triggered by political and economic developments, repercussions of international crises, or the emergence of new communications technologies such as the Internet.

Transitions from authoritarian rule to democratic governance require radical new role orientations and rules of interaction within the political communication system, although in many cases the actors involved are the same organizations – even the same individuals – as under the old regime. This process of renegotiating the power balance between governments and the media can be expected to be significantly determined by the nature and trajectories of the old regime and its practices of political propaganda even long after the implementation of democratic institutions. It is important to keep in mind that non-democratic regimes differ in many respects – not only in terms of their power structure, but also in the way they deal with the media, resulting in specific configurations and conflicts after the demise of the old regime.

Another important conclusion to be drawn from conceptualizing political communication as a system of interaction is that success and failure are systemic rather than the result of the performance of one particular actor (Blumler and Gurevitch 1995: 4). Hence, the quality of mediated politics depends on both politicians and journalists, and the way in which they address the citizens. Any lack of diversity in the 'marketplace of ideas', low quality of information or absence of critical discussion are not, therefore, an isolated problem of the media, but a result of the specific constraints evolving from the media's relationships with politicians and the audience. Similarly, the way in which politicians package their messages to voters is as much a response to the demands and needs of the citizens as a function of the routines of the media. And finally, citizens' understanding of political matters and the way in which they fulfil their own role as the ultimate sovereign of the democratic process is to a large extent a response to the content, form and quality of the messages they receive from politicians and the mass media. This is not to say that journalists, politicians and citizens do not bear any responsibility for their own actions. But understanding the interdependencies between these actors helps to explain why, in some cases, the media are more successful in meeting the standards of democratic public communication than in others.

The following sections will briefly discuss each of the three sets of actors, and their objectives, strategies and specific dependency on other components of the system. Each concludes with a brief summary of the chapters of this volume that focus on that set of actors and their problems in adopting a democratic role in the political communication process.

The mass media

Arguably the mass media serve as the main link between governments, political parties, candidates, etc. and voters, as the opportunities for direct communication between citizens and their representatives are extremely limited both in terms of the scale of the audience reached and the scope of the issues covered. However, the media are not just channels conveying the messages politicians want them to communicate to voters. They are also active participants in the creation of political messages (Cook 1998). Even though most of the time the media are not the immediate origina-tors of these messages, they have a significant impact on what is communi-cated in the public sphere, and what is omitted, thereby setting the agenda of the political debate (Dearing and Rogers 1996; McCombs *et al.* 1997). Equally important is how political matters are presented by the media. Dramatization, personalization and eye-catching visuals are examples of what journalists regard as the makings of a good story. Another important journalistic device is adherence to a pro–contra format of presenting political conflicts, something that Tuchman (1972) identi-fies as a 'strategic ritual' journalists use in order to protect themselves from any accusations of distorting the 'truth'. The whole package of jour-nalistic rules – the routines of collecting information, criteria of selection and the style of presentation – has been termed 'media logic' and signific-antly differs from other modes of public communication, for example the openly persuasive style of 'party logic', especially during election cam-paigns (Mazzoleni 1987).

Media logic can be understood as a strategy the media use to maintain their relationship with a mass audience on which they depend for their economic survival. Since for most viewers and readers politics plays only a marginal role in everyday life, they are looking out for easy-to-consume, 'low salience' information (Neuman 1986). The way in which the media present politics meets these needs in a perfect manner, even up to a point where the boundaries between political information and entertainment become blurred. With regard to the media's relationships with political actors, media logic is bound to cause conflicts over the selection and framing of political issues. However, since the media depend on high-ranking politicians as a reliable source of stories with high news value, they have to strike a delicate balance between sticking to their own rules of the game and making concessions to their sources in order to maintain good working relationships. In some instances the media might even give up their own logic to some degree and form alliances with political actors. In these cases the media exchange loyalty to particular parties or the government for privileged, often exclusive, access to 'their' news sources.

Media logic and its specific components cannot be assumed to be uniform across time and culture. While some of the presentation formats evolve from the nature of specific media technologies – for example television's reliance on visuals – others seem to be rooted in cultural value systems and are hence more open to contextual circumstances. It therefore remains an open question as to what extent the media in new democracies adopt the news values that govern Western journalism, and to what extent they continue to follow the traditions that exist in the indigenous political culture of their own country. Equally, whether or not the media form alliances with particular parties or subscribe to particular ideologies is influenced by the constellations within the political communication system. Most media were closely related to particular political actors during the old regime: either as propaganda instruments of the government or ruling party, or as clandestine media in the hands of opposition groups. Maintaining these relationships after transition might provide the media with a distinct editorial identity and even economic support. However, with changing audience expectations this strategy is not without risks, as partisan media may be perceived as less trustworthy than neutral outlets.

It is a matter of great concern, not only in new but also in established democracies, whether or not media logic is compatible with the normative standards of a democratic public sphere. To some extent, one can argue that democratic benefits evolve as a by-product of professional news reporting. For example, including opposing viewpoints when covering current events satisfies the media's preference for conflict as a central news factor. More often than not, this results in a rather mechanistic pro–contra format of reporting that disguises the complexity of political controversies. Yet the confrontation of different opinions is arguably a way of achieving plurality in the 'marketplace of ideas' and of challenging any claims to absolute truth. Further, simplification and the presentation of politics as storytelling is an important contribution to providing comprehensible information that enables all citizens, not only political experts and the well-educated, to become involved in political affairs. Finally, the media's preference for deviance encourages investigative reporting. Since politicians try to keep dubious practices, misjudgements and failures out of the public light by all means, the media's interest in scandals and breaking news is a strong driving force for unravelling what is going on behind the scenes.

However, the same elements of news reporting have frequently been blamed for the apparent crisis of political communication in Western democracies. Instead of connecting citizens with the world of politics, it is believed that the trivialization of political reporting and the predominance of entertainment, especially in television, are responsible for the growing apathy of citizens and their abstinence from even basic participation such as voting (Putnam 1995). Further, as Patterson (1993) argues, the confrontational style of election coverage has brought about an image of politics that resembles horse races and game shows rather than a rational debate about policy alternatives. At the same time, the media's search for scandals has been accused of increasingly deteriorating into witch hunts for the sake of scandals which often seem to be of little relevance to substantial political issues (Thompson 2000). It seems that the compatibility of media logic with the democratic mission of public communication is a sliding scale that is to a large extent determined by the nature and extent of market constraints, legal restrictions and political pressures to which the media are subjected.

The chapters in Part I of this volume address problems of the democratic performance of the media in new democracies from different perspectives and in different cultural and political circumstances. Barrera and Zugasti provide a historical account of the early days of the now well-consolidated Spanish democracy. They show that, in the highly fragile situation after Franco's death, the media placed themselves on the side of the democratically minded elites and acted in the interest of democratic values and national integration. De Smaele explores the relationship between the media and government in today's Russia which is characterized by an extreme degree of mutual mistrust and hostility. The situation in South Africa after the end of the apartheid regime bears interesting similarities and differences. Wasserman and de Beer analyse the relationship between the media and the newly elected government in the light of the dispute over the democratic role of the media, captured in the notions of 'national interest' versus 'public interest'. The chapters by de Smaele and Wasserman and de Beer show how first principles are used by the opposing sides to renegotiate the rules that govern public communication. Waisbord's chapter shifts the focus to the relationship between the media and their audience. He argues that most Latin American media do not subscribe to the Western model of journalistic objectivity. Rather, they seek to win audiences by promoting and reinforcing particular political views. From this perspective, the emergence of a strong partisan press can be explained by the media's response to audience needs rather than political dependencies. The last chapter in this section, by Krasnoboka and Brants, turns to the Ukraine, a country that at the time of writing had made only minimal progress in the implementation of democratic structures. The authors show that, in a situation where the government still holds absolute control over the media of mass communication, new communications technologies such as the Internet gain crucial importance in the democratization of public communication.

Political actors

In Western mass democracies, political actors – in particular governments and political parties – have become highly dependent on the mass media. During election campaigns a party's or candidate's media strategy is now the pivotal cornerstone for electoral success. This reliance on the media is not entirely new: as Seymour-Ure (1974) points out, the development of mass-based political parties during the nineteenth century was closely related to the emergence of a popular mass circulation press capable of politicizing and mobilizing large segments of society, most notably the working class. However, the extent to which the media have become an indispensable part of party strategy, or even function as a substitute for an efficient party organization (Polsby 1980), is arguably a recent phenomenon.

As far as established democracies are concerned, several factors have contributed to this development, the most important being the decline of party identification and an increasingly volatile electorate. With a growing number of floating voters and shrinking turnout rates, ever more effort has to be invested into persuading the undecided. At the same time, parties have lost much of their traditional communication resources. The number of active party members who volunteer to distribute campaign material and carry out door-to-door canvassing has dropped, and traditional alliances with intermediary organizations, such as trade unions and churches, have weakened over the last decades. Recent election campaigns have therefore seen an unprecedented modernization and professionalization of electioneering, often referred to as 'Americanization' of campaign communication (Swanson and Mancini 1996). The new campaign strategies are centred on effective manipulation of the media agenda by tailoring political messages in a way that mimics media logic in an almost perfect manner. Political consultancies that specialize in designing media campaigns for political actors have become a worldwide growth industry, with star 'spin doctors' like Dick Morris, Peter Gould and Saatchi and Saatchi selling their products all over the world, and attracting clients from many new democracies, including Russia, South Africa and South Korea (Plasser and Plasser 2002).

One reason for the high demand for political consultants in new democracies is that 'Americanized' campaigning seems to be tailor-made for political parties in post-authoritarian systems. Although there are significant differences across countries, many parties in new democracies enter the democratic contest without having any effective communication resources at their disposal. Post-transition parties are often typical examples of Panebianco's (1988) 'electoral-professional parties' that lack any significant membership and are almost exclusively built on the activities and ambitions of elite figures (see also Diamond and Gunther 2001; Hofferbert 1998). Without effective access to the media, these parties would be unable to mobilize sufficient popular support to win elections. The problems of uncertain electoral support and weak party organizations do not necessarily fade with subsequent elections. Many new democracies, especially in Eastern Europe, have experienced enormous shifts in voter preferences, to the effect that parties that won a comfortable majority in one election were wiped out from the political landscape in the next one (Klingemann *et al.* 2000). Governments therefore tend not to give up control over the media, especially television, ironically using very similar methods of news manipulation as their authoritarian predecessors. However, what might appear as bad habits dying hard is in fact a consequence of the specific structural problems of electoral politics in new democracies. Political parties and candidates are rational actors who employ any available means to achieve their goal of gaining and maintaining power. The more they lack political channels of mobilization, such as loyal constituencies, strong grassroots membership and societal alliances, the more they are likely to instrumentalize the media for their own purposes.

The situation is somewhat different in countries where structures of organized pluralism could hibernate to some extent during authoritarian rule, either because pre-existing parties were not entirely eliminated or because strong opposition movements developed which were subsequently able to form new democratic parties with solid popular support. Further, politicians and parties that are embedded in the informal structures of social life can employ these social ties as a mobilization resource in electoral contests. In the absence of strong ideological cues, political parties may reinvigorate cultural symbols retrieved from, for example, religious, regional or ethnic identities in order to compete for the support of voters. If parties can rely on these kinds of traditional communication resources they are unlikely to adopt the full scale of 'Americanized' campaign strategies. Rather, specific hybrid forms of communicating to voters may develop that combine 'home-grown' styles with professional marketing techniques.

If we understand campaign strategies and political marketing as part of the interactions taking place in the political communication system, then the responses of the other participants in this process have to be taken into account. The development of political communication in Western democracies shows that wherever candidates or political parties subscribed to the new package of modern campaigning, the media were more than willing to join the game because of the perfect match between the messages they received from their sources and their own logic of operation. Well-planned pseudo-events, telegenic candidates, juicy 'sound bites' and the right dose of emotional messages makes the input fed in by an efficient campaign machine almost irresistible to the media. However, the media quickly realized that they were at risk of losing their autonomy, and with it their credibility, if they were too willing to convey fabricated campaign messages. They therefore started to make 'spin' a topic of news coverage, thereby unmasking the messages as purposeful and manipulative. 'Disdaining' the news in this way helps the media to regain some of the independence they have lost to professional communication consultants (Esser *et al.* 2001; Semetko *et al.* 1991). In this light, the extremely aggressive reporting style that can be observed in many new democracies might be not so much an indicator of an overambitious media striving to fulfil their watchdog function, but rather a strategy of the media to prove their independence from political power-holders.

How do the voters respond to the ever-faster armament race of electioneering? Some scholars have raised concerns about the increasing muck-raking between the opposing camps, arguing that negative campaigning depresses voter turnout (Ansolabehere and Iyengar 1997) – although this has been disputed and empirical evidence does not provide a clear-cut picture (Brians and Wattenberg 1996). In spite of the apparent deficiencies of modern campaigns, empirical research has shown that they fulfil their democratic function surprisingly well. Campaign communication is able to activate latent party alignments and even contributes to voters' political knowledge (Farrell and Schmitt-Beck 2002; Finkel 1993; Huckfeldt *et al.* 2000). However, doubts remain as to the democratic virtues of political marketing and electioneering for a rational public debate on contested policies. Modern campaign techniques might help political parties and candidates to win majorities in a volatile environment, but they seem to be frightfully void of fresh ideas and imaginative policy solutions. The strategy of avoiding ideological cues and clear policy commitments in order not to put off floating voters may eventually strip the public marketplace of any ideas altogether.

The chapters in Part II of this volume explore how political actors in as different political contexts as Latin America, Taiwan and Russia communicate to citizens, especially during election campaigns. Espíndola's comparative analysis of recent election campaigns in Latin America underlines the crucial importance of efficient party organizations. He shows that while 'Americanized' electioneering has been widely employed, extensive grassroot campaigning has proven the more successful strategy for winning elections in these countries. Rawnsley's chapter turns to recent campaigns in Taiwan and comes to similar conclusions. Even though in this Asian country party organizations and party ideologies play a less important role, candidates employ strategies that combine modern campaign techniques and reliance on traditional patterns of communicating to voters. In both the Latin American and the Taiwanese case the media are but one channel of communication that complements, but has not yet replaced, conventional campaign communication. The situation is dramatically different in Russia. Oates' analysis of recent Russian presidential and parliamentary elections shows how control of the media has replaced party organizations as an instrument for mobilizing electoral majorities. Finally, Lee returns to Taiwan and explores political communication beyond election campaigns. He analyses how the government employs the Internet to communicate with citizens. The chapter identifies the advantages and shortcomings of e-government and discusses how citizens in Taiwan have responded to the opportunities opened up by online communication with their elected representatives.

The citizens

Turning finally to the third component of the political communication system, the citizens, it seems that their impact on what is publicly communicated is rather limited. In contrast to politicians and the media, the voice of the people is rarely heard in public unless they succeed in organizing themselves for effective collective action such as citizens' movements or large-scale public demonstrations. This is not to say that the citizens are irrelevant for the formation of public communication. On the contrary: since mobilizing popular support is the ultimate goal of the communication activities of media and political actors alike, citizens' preferences shape the way in which political messages are communicated in the public sphere. Yet the citizens are clearly more at the receiving end of the political communication process than actively involved in creating and disseminating political messages. Blumler and Gurevitch (1995: 12) therefore distinguish between the horizontal interactions that take place between political institutions and the media, on the one hand, and a vertical, top-down flow of communication between these actors and the citizenry, on the other hand. Hence, the crucial question is whether the political information provided by political actors and the media contributes to an 'enlightened' and participatory citizenry.

The extent to which political messages affect citizens' political orientations and choices has been of major concern in political communication research from as early as the 1940s when a group of researchers around Paul Lazarsfeld conducted the first empirical research into political propaganda and the role played by the media during election campaigns (Lazarsfeld *et al.* 1944, reprinted 1968). From the very beginning, media effects research has faced significant methodological and conceptual difficulties, resulting in contradicting and often disappointingly weak empirical evidence for the existence of communications influences (Bartels 1993).

One important conclusion to be drawn from the large body of literature in this field is that media messages rarely affect their audience in a direct and immediate way, as they are filtered through complex cognitive processes of perception and interpretation. When encountering political messages, individuals use existing cognitive schemata and beliefs to decode and evaluate what they read or watch (Livingstone 1996; Zaller 1992). Furthermore, these processes are embedded in social processes of interaction with other people in the social environment to which individuals belong. Most people talk to family members, friends or co-workers about political issues they regard important, so that the interpretation of political messages is filtered through shared interests and group norms (Huckfeldt and Sprague 1995; Schmitt-Beck 2003). The finding that media effects are not uniform across time, issues and groups of audiences has led to the concept of the active audience (Biocca 1988). The central assumption of this approach is that communication effects depend as much on the characteristics of the audience members and how they process information as on the actual content of a message.

That said, it has to be emphasized that the contingent nature of media effects (and communication effects in general) does not imply that political messages do not have any impact on citizens' political attitudes and behaviour. For example, empirical research has produced strong evidence for the power of media agenda-setting and framing, whereby the salience of particular issues on the media agenda primes individuals' evaluation of political objects (Iyengar and Kinder 1987). Even though the media and political campaigns might not be able to shape individual vote choices directly, the process of making particular issues and aspects of issues more accessible to what people take into consideration and talk about to other citizens can eventually have a significant impact on the outcome of an election. Furthermore, partisan cues in the media, especially when in line with the norms of the social environment of an individual, have proved an important factor in mobilizing political affiliations and participation in elections (Dalton *et al.* 1998), while exposure to cross-cutting information – i.e. media bias that contradicts an individuals' own predispositions – can increase voting volatility among citizens with low levels of party identification (Brynin and Newton 2001).

All these findings stem from established Western democracies, and as yet there is only very little empirical research on the impact of mass communication and political campaigning on citizens in new democracies. Although similar cognitive and social mechanisms can be assumed to be at work in both new and old democracies, the specific conditions under which citizens encounter and respond to political messages during periods of political transition might differ significantly from the Western context where the relationship between voters, the media and political actors is relatively stable. For a considerable period of time after the demise of the old regime, citizens in new democracies experience an extraordinarily high level of uncertainty. Not only can the future no longer be expected to be a continuation of the *status quo*, but many of the values and practices citizens have acquired during their life under autocratic rule have become inadequate for mastering the new situation in an effective way.

When it comes to elections, most citizens in new democracies, with the probable exception of supporters of the previous ruling party or those who took part in an opposition movement against the old regime, make their choices without being able to rely on longstanding beliefs and political affiliations. One could therefore hypothesize that the role of the media in new democracies goes far beyond reinforcing and mobilizing existing preferences, but to a significant degree involves shaping and changing citizens' orientations and behaviour. However, the extent to which this is the case depends on the dynamics within the political communication system as a whole, and the performance of the actors involved under the new conditions. In countries where political parties managed to preserve at least some of their organizational structure and pre-authoritarian values and traditions, they are likely to defend their position as main agents of political socialization. If this is not the case, the media may step into the resulting vacuum of orientation, provided they enjoy sufficient trust and credibility among their audience to be accepted as opinion leaders in political matters.

The chapters in Part III of this volume present unique empirical material that helps to understand the power and the limitations of the media in moving public opinion in new democracies. Mickiewicz' contribution further elaborates the notion of an active audience and shows how Russian citizens perceive and interpret what they encounter in the media. Her findings support the 'negotiated nature of information reception' that denies any simplistic notion of media effects. White and McAllister remain in Russia and analyse the effects of television in recent parliamentary elections. Using data from focus groups and representative surveys they show that vote choice for Kremlin-supported parties was significantly influenced by television, whereas preference for the Communist Party remained largely unaffected by media exposure. Finally, Voltmer and Schmitt-Beck move beyond electoral politics and address the question as to whether the media foster or undermine democratic citizenship and support of democracy. Their data include survey results from four new democracies – two Eastern European and two Latin American – allowing for a comparison between different situational and institutional contexts of political communication.

The final chapter of the book sets out to discuss the issues outlined in the introduction in a comparative perspective by bringing together the main findings of the individual chapters of this volume. Possible explanations for the similarities and differences between countries will be explored in an attempt to broaden our understanding of the interaction between the mass media, political actors and citizens in emerging democracies.

Notes

1 The 'marketplace' metaphor does not necessarily imply a market structure of private media ownership. In the context of the media's democratic role, the

meaning of 'marketplace' is better captured by the notion of the marketplace as a public space in a community, such as the *agora* in Athenian democracy.

2 Another form of simplifying information is arguably tabloidization and infotainment. More often than not, tabloid formats lead to a marginalization of politics and hence might not provide any meaningful information that is related to democratic citizenship. However, it has to be noted that empirical findings on the significance of the tabloid press are ambiguous (Baum 2003; Franklin 1997).

References

Ansolabehere, S. and Iyengar, S. (1997) *Going Negative. How Political Advertisements Shrink and Polarize the Electorate*, New York: Free Press.

Bartels, L.M. (1993) 'Message received. The political impact of media exposure', *American Political Science Review*, 87: 267–85.

Baum, M.A. (2003) 'Soft news and political knowledge. Evidence of absence or absence of evidence?' *Political Communication*, 20: 173–90.

Biocca, F.A. (1988) 'Opposing conceptions of the audience. The active and passive hemisphere of mass communication theory', in J.A. Anderson (ed.) *Communication Yearbook*, vol. 11, Newbury Park, CA: Sage, 51–80.

Blumler, J.G. and Gurevitch, M. (1995) *The Crisis of Public Communication*, New York: Routledge.

Brians, C.L. and Wattenberg, M.P. (1996) 'Campaign issue knowledge and salience. Comparing reception from TV commercials, TV news and newspapers', *American Journal of Political Science*, 40: 172–93.

Brynin, M. and Newton, K. (2001) 'The national press and party voting in the UK', *Political Studies*, 49: 265–85.

Cook, T.E. (1998) *Governing with the News. The News Media as a Political Institution*, Chicago, IL: Chicago University Press.

Curran, J. (1991) 'Mass media and democracy. A reappraisal', in J. Curran and M. Gurevitch (eds) *Mass Media and Society*, London: Arnold, 82–117.

Curran, J. and Park, M.J. (eds) (2000) *De-Westernizing Media Studies*, London: Routledge.

Dahl, R. (1989) *Democracy and its Critics*, New Haven, CT: Yale University Press.

Dalton, R.J., Beck, P.A. and Huckfeldt, R. (1998) 'Partisan cues and the media. Information flows in the 1992 presidential election', *American Political Science Review*, 92: 111–26.

Dearing, J.W. and Rogers, E.M. (1996) *Agenda Setting*, London: Sage.

Diamond, L. and Gunther, R. (eds) (2001) *Political Parties and Democracy*, Baltimore, MD: Johns Hopkins University Press.

Downing, J.D.H. (1996) *Internationalizing Media Theory. Transition, Power, Culture. Reflections on Media in Russia, Poland and Hungary, 1980–1995*, London: Sage.

Entman, R.M. (1989) *Democracy Without Citizens. Media and the Decay of American Politics*, New York: Oxford University Press.

Esser, F., Reinemann, C. and Fan, D. (2001) 'Spin doctors in the United States, Great Britain, and Germany. Metacommunication about media manipulation', *Press/Politics*, 6(1): 16–45.

Farrell, D.M. and Schmitt-Beck, R. (2002) *Do Political Campaigns Matter? Campaign Effects in Elections and Referendums*, London: Routledge.

Finkel, S.E. (1993) 'Reexamining the "minimal effects" model in recent presidential campaigns', *Journal of Politics*, 55: 1–21.

Franklin, B. (1997) *Newzak and the News Media*, London: Arnold.

Grugel, J. (2002) *Democratization. A Critical Introduction*, Basingstoke: Palgrave.

Gunther, R., Diamandouros, N. and Puhle, H.-J. (eds) (1995) *The Politics of Democratic Consolidation. Southern Europe in Comparative Perspective*, Baltimore, MD: Johns Hopkins University Press.

Gutmann, A. and Thompson, D. (1996) *Democracy and Disagreement*, Cambridge, MA: Harvard University Press.

Hofferbert, R. (ed.) (1998) 'Party structure and party performance in new and old democracies', *Political Studies*, 46 (special issue).

Huckfeldt, R. and Sprague, J. (1995) *Citizens, Politics and Social Communication. Information and Influence in an Election Campaign*, Cambridge, UK: Cambridge University Press.

Huckfeldt, R., Sprague, J. and Levine, J. (2000) 'The dynamics of collective deliberation in the 1996 election. Campaign effects on accessibility, certainty, and accuracy', *American Political Science Review*, 94: 641–52.

Iyengar, S. and Kinder, D. (1987) *News That Matters. Television and American Opinion*, Chicago, IL: University of Chicago Press.

Keane, J. (1991) *The Media and Democracy*, Cambridge, UK: Polity Press.

Kelley, D. and Donway, R. (1990) 'Liberalism and free speech', in J. Lichtenberg (ed.) *Democracy and the Mass Media*, Cambridge, UK: Cambridge University Press, 66–101.

Klingemann, H.-D., Mochmann, E., and Newton, K. (eds) (2000) *Elections in Central and Eastern Europe. The First Wave*, Berlin: Sigma.

Lazarsfeld, P.F., Berelson, B. and Gaudet, H. (1944, reprinted 1968) *The People's Choice. How the Voter Makes up His Mind in a Presidential Campaign*, New York: Columbia University Press.

Lemert, J.B. (1989) *Criticizing the Media. Empirical Approaches*, Newbury Park, CA: Sage.

Linz, J. and Stepan, A. (1996) *Problems of Democratic Transition and Consolidation. South Europe, South America, and Post-Communist Europe*, Baltimore, MD: Johns Hopkins University Press.

Livingstone, S. (1996) 'On the continuing problem of media effects', in J. Curran and M. Gurevitch (eds) *Mass Media and Society*, 2nd edn, London: Arnold, 225–42.

McCombs, M., Shaw, D. L. and Weaver, D. (1997) *Communication and Democracy. Exploring the Intellectual Frontiers of Agenda-setting Theory*, Mahwah, NJ: Erlbaum.

McQuail, D. (1986) 'Diversity in political communication. Its sources, forms and future', in P. Golding, G. Murdock and P. Schlesinger (eds) *Communicating Politics. Mass Communications and the Political Process*, Leicester: Leicester University Press, 133–49.

—— (1992) *Media Performance. Mass Communication and the Public Interest*, London: Sage.

Mazzoleni, G. (1987) 'Media logic and party logic in campaign coverage. The Italian general election 1983', *European Journal of Communication*, 2: 81–103.

Merkel, W. (1998) 'The consolidation of post-autocratic democracies. A multi-level model', *Democratization*, 5(3): 33–67.

Mill, J.S. (1859 reprinted 1974) *On Liberty*, London: Penguin.

Morris, N. and Waisbord, S. (2001) *Media and Globalization. Why the State Matters*, Lanham, MD: Rowman & Littlefield.

Mughan, A. and Gunther, R. (2000) 'The media in democratic and nondemocratic regimes. A multi-level perspective', in R. Gunther and A. Mughan (eds) *Democracy and the Media. A Comparative Perspective*, Cambridge, UK: Cambridge University Press, 1–27.

Napoli, P.M. (1999) 'Deconstructing the diversity principle', *Journal of Communication*, 49(4): 7–34.

Neuman, R.W. (1986) *The Paradox of Mass Politics. Knowledge and Opinion in the American Electorate*, Cambridge, MA: Harvard University Press.

Paletz, D., Jakubowicz, K. and Novosel, P. (1995) *Glasnost and After. Media and Change in Central and Eastern Europe*, Cresskill, NJ: Hampton.

Panebianco, A. (1988) *Political Parties. Organizations and Power*, Cambridge, UK: Cambridge University Press.

Patterson, T.E. (1993) *Out of Order*, New York: Knopf.

—— (1998) 'The media's limitations as an instrument of democracy', *International Political Science Review*, 19(1): 55–67.

Pfetsch, B. (2004) 'From political culture to political communication culture. A theoretical approach to comparative analysis', in F. Esser and B. Pfetsch (eds) *Comparing Political Communication. Theories, Cases, and Challenges*, Cambridge, UK: Cambridge University Press, 344–66.

Plasser, F. and Plasser, G. (2002) *Global Political Campaigning. A Worldwide Analysis of Campaign Professionals and Their Practices*, Westport, CT: Praeger.

Polsby, N.W. (1980) 'The news media as an alternative to party in the presidential selection process', in R.A. Goldwin (ed.) *Political Parties in the Eighties*, Washington, DC: American Enterprise Institute for Public Policy Research, 50–66.

Price, M.E., Razumilowicz, B. and Verhulst, S.G. (2002) *Media Reform. Democratizing the Media, Democratizing the State*, London: Routledge.

Putnam, R.D. (1995) 'Bowling alone. America's declining social capital', *Journal of Democracy*, 6: 65–78.

Schmitt-Beck, R. (2003) 'Mass communication, personal communication and vote choice. The filter hypothesis of media influence in comparative perspective', *British Journal of Political Science*, 33: 233–59.

Semetko, H.A., Blumler, J.G., Gurevitch, M. and Weaver, D.H. (1991) *The Formation of Campaign Agendas. A Comparative Analysis of Party and Media Roles in Recent American and British Elections*, Hillsdale, NJ: Erlbaum.

Seymour-Ure, C. (1974) *The Political Impact of Mass Media*, London: Constable/ Sage.

Splichal, S. (1994) *Media Beyond Socialism. Theory and Practice in East-Central Europe*, Boulder, CO: Westview.

Swanson, D.L. and Mancini, P. (eds) (1996) *Politics, Media, and Modern Democracy. An International Study of Innovations in Electoral Campaigning and their Consequences*, Westport, CT: Praeger.

Thompson, J.B. (2000) *Political Scandal. Power and Visibility in the Media Age*, Cambridge, UK: Polity.

Tuchman, G. (1972) 'Objectivity as strategic ritual. An examination of newsmen's notions of objectivity', *American Journal of Sociology*, 77: 660–79.

Voltmer, K. (2000) 'Structures of diversity in press and broadcasting systems. The institutional context of public communication in Western Democracies', *WZB Discussion Papers*, FSIII 00–201, Berlin: Wissenschaftszentrum Berlin für Sozialforschung.

Zaller, J.R. (1992) *The Nature and Origins of Mass Opinion*, Cambridge: Cambridge University Press.

Part I

The mass media and journalistic practice

Normative dilemmas, professionalization and political instrumentalization

2 The role of the press in times of transition

The building of the Spanish democracy (1975–78)

Carlos Barrera and Ricardo Zugasti

From the strictest political–institutional point of view, the transition to democracy which took place after the death of General Franco in November 1975 ended in December 1978, when the new democratic constitution was approved by referendum. At the centre of these political changes was the Law for Political Reform in December 1976, which dissolved the francoist parliament and called for the free election of a new parliament whose job would be to draft a constitution. The Centre Democratic Union (*Unión de Centro Democrático*) won the elections on 15 June 1977 and, only a few months later, the parliament decreed a total amnesty that included crimes involving bloodshed. This period was complicated by attempts by terrorist groups of the extreme right and left and the Basque separatist movement to destabilize the young democracy, as well as by resistance from some factions within the military.

The Spanish model of democratic transition presents a series of peculiarities with respect to other similar processes. Especially noteworthy were its negotiated nature and the absence of a call to hold authorities within the dictatorship politically and criminally responsible for their actions (Barahona *et al.* 2001; Colomer 1998: 10–18; Resina 2000: 17–28, 83–95). Both King Juan Carlos I, designated by Franco as his successor, and his second government, presided over by Adolfo Suárez and beginning in July 1976, were institutions whose legitimacy was rooted in the dictatorship and its laws. Both held the reins of political reform, a fact received with certain prejudice on the part of the democratic opposition who had been excluded from the decision-making process. These parties demanded a complete break from the past rather than mere reforms (and, although conceived as reform, the final result of the process was, indeed, a break).

From the end of 1976 onwards, negotiations between the government and opposition parties were very frequent. A sort of tacit pact guided the attitude and behaviour of almost all the political forces involved in the process. The final objective was the same for both government and opposition: to avoid holding the opposition parties criminally responsible for their past activities against the regime, in order to provide a fresh start. Stated another way, it was an attempt to begin anew with a clean slate, through a deliberate policy of forgetting the past as a way to promote national reconciliation. In the back of the minds of the principal political actors of the period of transition was the memory of the two Spains that confronted each other during the Civil War of 1936–39 (Aguilar Fernández 1996: 226–61). These sentiments were generally shared by the citizens of Spain. Similarly, the majority of the press acted in an extremely responsible manner, recognizing the need to sometimes sacrifice their own ideological position in order to work toward the long-term objective of the citizens and their representatives – a new, democratic political system in which everyone could take part.

When Franco died in 1975, Spanish newspapers were already enjoying some degree of press freedom. Nevertheless, those margins became progressively broader in the following years (Alférez 1986; Barrera 1995; Chuliá 2001). The ultimate legal recognition of freedom of information came with the Constitution of 1978, in which Article 20 stated: 'Every Spaniard has the right to freely communicate or receive true information by any means.'

By 1984, there were approximately 115 newspapers in publication – and only half of these had existed in 1975, which gives an idea of the transformations that the sector was experiencing (Iglesias 1989: 436–44). In 1976, two new dailies appeared in Madrid, the country's principal newspaper market: *El País* and *Diario 16*. Both were of the centre-left and were destined to play important roles during the transition process. In two areas with an important nationalist (separatist) sentiment, Catalonia and the Basque Country, nationalist newspapers were founded: *Avui* (which was published entirely in the Catalan language) in 1976, and the Basque titles *Deia* and *Egin* in 1977. In 1978, the newspaper *El Periódico de Catalunya* was founded as a more modern and centre-left alternative to the conservative *La Vanguardia*. Meanwhile, many of the more established newspapers, such as *ABC* and *Ya* in Madrid, and *La Vanguardia, El Correo Catalán* and *El Noticiero Universal* in Barcelona, fell into crisis. Some were able to survive but others ended up closing their doors in the 1980s or 1990s. The circulation of daily newspapers in the principal Spanish markets between 1975 and 1978 is shown in Table 2.1.

These data indicate that the fastest growing newspapers were those of the extreme right (*El Alcázar* and *El Imparcial*) and those of the centre to centre-left (*El País* and *Diario 16*). The first group took advantage of a feeling of nostalgia for the francoist era to criticize the social, economic and political instability of the transitional period. The other two newspapers, for their part, worked successfully to give voice to the new political, social and cultural sectors as they became part of mainstream Spanish public life. Similar tendencies were seen in the Catalan and Basque press.

Table 2.1 Circulation of Spanish national and regional daily newspapers (1975–78)

		Year of first publication	Circulation			
			1975	1976	1977	1978
Madrid	*ABC*	1903	187,484	171,382	145,162	126,952
	Pueblo	1940	182,220	142,607	90,590	72,346
	Ya	1935	168,756	154,446	129,448	120,595
	Informaciones	1922	72,145	64,106	44,172	36,305
	El Alcázar	1936	13,119	26,724	63,646	66,104
	El País	1976		116,600	137,562	12,931
	Diario 16	1976			73,073	47,672
	El Imparcial	1977				51,962
Barcelona	*La Vanguardia*	1881	222,685	211,736	196,886	187,240
	El Noticiero Universal	1888	78,866	67,197	51,622	44,055
	El Correo Catalán	1876	67,001	60,720	48,796	40,075
	Tele/eXprés	1964	35,631	33,584	22,663	–
	Diario de Barcelona	1792	28,743	30,311	25,842	–
	Avui	1976		55,727	40,036	33,946
	Mundo Diario	1968		34,003	47,528	49,187
Basque Country	*El Correo Español–EPV*	1910	86,479	88,790	80,578	69,128
	La Gaceta del Norte	1901	85,557	77,779	66,230	54,301
	Deia	1977				50,485*
	Egin	1977				47,031

Source: *Oficina para la Justificación de la Difusión* (Audit Bureau of Circulations).

Note
*Circulation first audited in 1979.

Analysing Spanish newspapers' presentation of the transition to democracy

Most of the literature dealing with the Spanish transition underlines the importance that consensus in basic democratic values played in both politics and society. In this context, through their mediating role, the press acted as a link between political elites and citizens. This chapter aims to demonstrate how the majority of newspapers supported the main guidelines of political reform and the strategy of consensus led by the main political parties. It presents the results of several studies, based on both quantitative and qualitative content analysis of the daily press, which provide answers to a variety of questions about the relationship between the press and other political actors, how the values proper to a democratic political culture were introduced and presented by the press, and finally the role that the press played in the success of the political transition process.

It is important not to forget that, as in the case of politicians, there were numerous newspapers that had supported the francoist dictatorship but nevertheless decided to follow the path toward democracy rather than attempt to disrupt the process (Aguilar 1982; Santos 1995). There were only a couple of exceptions, fundamentally from the extreme right and Basque nationalist sectors.

The analysis was undertaken through a double sampling of daily newspapers and political events. We took sample editorials from 12 newspapers (*ABC, Pueblo, Ya, El Alcázar, El País* and *Diario 16* from Madrid, *La Vanguardia, El Correo Catalán* and *Avui* from Barcelona, and *El Correo Español, La Gaceta del Norte* and *Deia* from the Basque Country), examining references to a total of 21 events that historians generally consider to have been milestones of the transition period. Since the amnesty and the subject of autonomy affected some regions more than others, with the effects being particularly strong in Catalonia and the Basque Country, we selected a range of newspapers that included both national publications and newspapers from those two regions.

We chose to use a combination of quantitative and qualitative methods because in our experience quantitative analysis does not succeed in capturing all the information and nuances of the data. The analysis of how editorials presented the introduction of new democratic values takes into account both the number of times these values were mentioned and the arguments that newspapers used to refer to them.

In addition, as supplementary information, we will show some interesting results obtained from the quantitative analysis of news published on the newspapers' front pages and also a particularly interesting case study (coverage of the general amnesty granted in October 1977), which will provide more in-depth understanding of how that consensus functioned.

The common objective is to demonstrate how the press influenced political change in two ways: through the selection and categorization of the news provided to the readers, and through the editorial commentary directed more specifically to the political elites. We have attempted to balance the news and editorial aspects of the newspapers since both of them reflect and help to define a newspaper's position. The news analysis allows us to identify which newspapers gave increased coverage to the growing opposition groups, while the editorials help us to discover the arguments used to support the political changes while providing, at the same time, an interpretation of the recent history of Spain.

'Democratic values' in editorials

The concept of 'democratic values' embraces: first, the elements that are normally associated with democracy as a political system; second, values that are characteristic of a transition period from an authoritarian regime or dictatorship to a parliamentary democracy; and, finally, those considered to be consequences of the democracy-building process (Mainer and Juliá 2000: 31–51). We distinguished between these three types of value in our analysis.

Thus, in the analysis of the newspaper editorials, we first sought explicit references to 'democracy', 'liberty' and/or 'freedom', 'amnesty' and 'regional autonomy', because these were the principal demands from the sectors of the population working for profound political and institutional change. The presence and frequency of these keywords helped to reveal the degree of involvement in the democratic process on the part of the newspapers.

With regard to the second type of value, we paid attention to explicit mentions of values that could be considered as representations, supports or consequences of democracy: 'concord' and 'reconciliation' (as a way of forgetting the past and building a future through consensus, cohabitation and negotiation); the maintenance of 'authority' and 'social order' (necessary to avoid the process getting out of hand in moments of difficulty or as a result of provocation by extreme reactionaries or revolutionaries); and 'elections' and 'referenda' (as effective achievement of citizen participation in the political process and representative of the return of sovereignty to the people).

Finally, because the transition process took place in a very specific political context, we also examined references to the immediate and remote past, that is to say Franco and/or francoism and the Civil War. Several studies have already demonstrated that the historic memory of both periods acted as a conditioning element of the democratic process (Aguilar Fernández 1996; Reig 1999; Resina 2000).

Quantitative analysis

As a necessary first step, we were interested in discovering how often the key concepts of democracy, liberty, amnesty and autonomy were addressed. In the case of the concept of democracy, we only accepted the explicit appearance, in adjectival, substantive or adverbial form, of the term. Within the concept of liberty we accepted explicit mention as well as all its concrete representations, which is to say, the civil rights of association, expression, assembly, demonstration, etc. In the case of the concept of amnesty, we also accepted mention of pardons or any synonyms. We did the same with autonomy, where we accepted its distinct variations: regionalism, nationalism, rights of the people, etc.

As Table 2.2 shows, the concept of democracy appeared in more than two-thirds of the 441 editorials. This is not surprising since it is the term that obviously best encompasses what we have referred to as 'democratic values'. The topic of civil liberties appeared quite often – in almost half of the editorials – while amnesty and autonomy also appeared, but much less frequently. From the point of view of chronological development of the events of the transition, it seems logical that the principal emphasis was placed on the first two concepts, since the other two would normally follow as consequence.

Table 2.2 Frequency of specific references to democracy, civil liberties, autonomy and amnesty, and to values and topics associated with democracy and the transitional process in 441 Spanish newspaper editorials published at 21 key points between 1975 and 1978

	Frequency (%)
Democracy	69.8
Civil liberties	46.0
Autonomy	32.9
Amnesty	18.8
Elections, referenda	59.4
Concord, reconciliation, etc.	54.6
Authority, order	27.0
Franco, francoism and/or the Civil War	57.6

The results of our analysis of references to other values or topics that might represent, support or result from the new democratic political culture – and references to the past that connect directly with significant values such as concord and reconciliation – are also shown in Table 2.2. This reveals that there were numerous references to the need for concord, consensus and accord as unavoidable conditions for the building of a new democratic regime. These values were mentioned in more than half the editorials: a level very similar to that of references to Franco, francoism and the Civil War. Indeed, these are like two sides of the same coin in that they both involve starting over with a clean slate (leaving behind war and division) in order to establish a new order founded on peace and reconciliation.

The frequency with which authority and/or public order were mentioned might be considered surprising. The explanation lies in the fact that stable peace required the maintenance of social order, and therefore the presence of authority. These values, which might be considered more characteristic of the Franco dictatorship, were nevertheless soon incorporated into the 'democratic package', especially when events or the actions of extreme groups posed a potential threat to the success of the reform process. Many newspapers explained that, especially after amnesty, there would emerge a democracy based on law and order whose future must be ensured by the government.

Up until now, we have presented the newspapers as a single block, which has allowed us to point out characteristics common to all. However, even with quantitative approaches it is possible to reveal differences in editorial treatment. To do this, we investigated how frequently each newspaper referred to certain concepts as a percentage of overall editorial content.

Two classifications were especially revealing of the distinct sensitivities of the newspapers analysed: those relating to mentions of francoism and of amnesty. These two topics hold special meaning because they involve ways of understanding the history of the recent past. The results are shown Table 2.3.

At the top of both lists are the same five newspapers: four new titles (the Madrid-based *El País* and *Diario 16*, and the nationalist *Deia* and *Avui*) and *El Alcázar*. This last newspaper, loyal to francoism, continued to vigorously defend the regime from growing criticism and to consider the amnesty an unjust relegation of the Civil War to the past. For their part, the new newspapers were characterized by fewer ties to the past and a stronger attachment to the new political situation. Their frequent references to the previous regime were almost always negative in nature, and they tended to promote amnesty, which they saw as necessary if the country was to make a clean break with the past.

In contrast, the more conservative and traditional newspapers (*ABC*, *Ya*, *El Correo Español*, *La Vanguardia* and *La Gaceta del Norte*) either consciously or unconsciously made far fewer references to the recent past. The state-controlled *Pueblo* and the moderate *El Correo Catalán* were somewhere in between.

Somewhat different results are obtained when we take a look at editorial references to the subject of autonomy. As Table 2.4 shows, there are clearly great quantitative differences from one newspaper to the other with regard to this issue, considered by many to be the great novelty of the Spanish transition to democracy. The newspapers that gave the most editorial attention to autonomy were the six published in the Basque Country and Catalonia. Prominently heading the list are the two nationalist newspapers *Avui* and *Deia* – but even the most conservative titles, such as

Table 2.3 Frequency with which individual newspapers referred to francoism and amnesty in editorials published at 21 key points between 1975 and 1978

Francoism		Amnesty	
Newspaper	Frequency (%)	Newspaper	Frequency (%)
Deia	77.8	Deia	33.3
El Alcázar	73.7	Avui	29.2
Diario 16	72.6	Diario 16	24.2
El País	66.0	El Alcázar	21.1
Avui	62.5	El País	20.8
El Correo Catalán	52.1	El Correo Español	18.8
Pueblo	50.0	Pueblo	18.4
La Gaceta del Norte	44.4	Ya	16.0
La Vanguardia	39.6	ABC	15.9
El Correo Español	28.1	El Correo Catalán	14.6
Ya	26.0	La Vanguardia	12.5
ABC	22.7	La Gaceta del Norte	11.1
Mean	48.8	Mean	18.8

Table 2.4 Frequency with which individual newspapers referred to autonomy in editorials published at 21 key points between 1975 and 1978

Newspaper	Frequency (%)
Avui	79.2
Deia	66.7
El Correo Catalán	52.1
La Gaceta del Norte	44.4
El Correo Español	43.8
La Vanguardia	41.7
El País	32.1
Diario 16	22.6
Ya	20.0
ABC	18.2
Pueblo	15.8
El Alcázar	5.3
Mean	32.9

La Gaceta del Norte, El Correo Español and *La Vanguardia*, proved themselves sensitive to the resurgence of regionalist or nationalist movements. In the seventh and eight positions are the two new Madrid newspapers of the centre-left, *El País* and *Diario 16*. The older Madrid newspapers follow, with *El Alcázar* at the end of the list. The extremely low proportion of editorial references to autonomy in this publication comes as no surprise when one considers its long-standing aversion to anything that might threaten the national unity of Spain.

Qualitative analysis

Very few newspapers dared to speak of 'democracy' explicitly and openly even after the first official speech of the new King on 22 November 1975. *Informaciones* and *El Correo Catalán* were the most notable exceptions, while *Ya* and *La Vanguardia* also alluded to democracy but in a more measured form. However, almost all made extensive use of the term after the famous speech made by the King before the United States Congress and Senate in June 1976. In this speech the King himself used the term, stating: 'The Monarchy will ensure that, under the principles of democracy, the social peace and political stability will be maintained in Spain'. This seemed to end the reticence on the part of the press, which until then had been extremely cautious in its opinions. In a sense, many newspapers (especially the most traditional ones) were pulled along by the King's initiative instead of themselves pressing for change.

On more than one occasion, the newly founded newspapers revealed their sceptical attitude towards the idea that it was possible to forge a democracy out of dictatorial institutions. Newspapers such as *El País* and *Avui* campaigned in favour of abstention in the referendum campaign for approval of the Law for Political Reform in December 1976, although they admitted that the path would ultimately lead to the establishment of a democratic regime. With a stronger dose of pragmatism, *Diario 16* advocated the affirmative vote, explaining: 'The referendum is a step but still one within the francoist framework. But ... after it we will be a little closer to democracy and surely further from the dictatorship' ('En peligro', 14 December 1976: 4).

A young democracy, recently stung by the whip of terrorism, needed the strength to ensure public order. Although order and authority were characteristics more closely associated with decades of dictatorship, the majority of the newspapers considered them essential to build a solid democracy. Even the centre-left and nationalist press demanded them. *Diario 16* considered them to be 'the first condition of democracy' ('Sí, pero más', 27 January 1977: 4). The general amnesty of October 1977 was another opportunity for the majority of the newspapers to declare, as did *ABC*, that, 'from this moment forward, there cannot be allowed, for any reason, breaches of public disorder under the banner of amnesty' ('Por abrumadora mayoría, punto y aparte', 15 October 1977: 2).

With the exception of *El Alcázar*, all the newspapers in our sample considered amnesty to be a necessary step along the road to national reconciliation. There were disagreements throughout the transition process about the various partial amnesties, which were granted before the final amnesty was agreed by all the political parties in Parliament in October 1977. Some considered the partial amnesties inadequate because they did not include crimes involving bloodshed.

'Concord' and 'reconciliation' were two of the words most often repeated by the newspapers, consistent with the guidelines of the King's initial message. All of the newspapers, except for *El Alcázar*, continued to call for concord and reconciliation on many occasions. The King continued in his role as guarantor of concord, and the other political and social actors, mainly the Government and the political parties, gradually adopted similar positions. With the passing of time, related terms – such as consensus, cohabitation, pact and negotiation – also began to appear in the journalistic discourse.

Among the historical events analysed were two that stood out as special landmarks in the path to concord: the King's speech in the first session of the democratic Parliament on 22 July 1977, and the approval by referendum of the Constitution on 6 December 1978. In the first of these events, reconciliation was clearly visible in the gathering on the parliamentary floor of representatives of the two Spains that had faced each other in the Civil War. The Constitution, for its part, was criticized only in two of the newspapers: the extreme-right *El Alcázar* and the Basque nationalist *Deia*. The latter emphasized the high degree of abstention registered in the referendum, especially in the Basque Country. This was felt to reflect a lack of authentic consensus because 'there exist more than two Spains' (8 December 1978: 15) – and these were not recognized by the constitution.

The radicalism of the extreme right and left was seen as the greatest enemy of the democratic process, and therefore the desire for a mutual reconciliation was adopted by most political actors. When, in January 1977, a wave of kidnappings and assassinations put the transition in danger, the editors of all the Madrid newspapers agreed to publish the same editorial, entitled 'For the Unity of Everyone'. This agreement represented a historical milestone in favour of concord and unity during the transition, carried out by the press as a collective actor – even *El Alcázar* included the editorial. In one of its paragraphs was stated:

> Whoever started this machinery is the enemy of everyone, the enemy of the Spanish people. Their scheme is clear: try to impede the establishment of civil formulas of open and structured cohabitation to which the Spanish have a right. In facing such a challenge, all political and social forces are obligated to join forces, leaving to one side their differences, proclaiming their decision to complete the journey down the road to democracy through free elections.
>
> (All Madrid newspapers, 29 January 1977)

With respect to the question of autonomy, the press was initially cautious. In his first message, the King referred to the need to recognize the 'regional peculiarities'. In those days, only *El Correo Catalán* was brave enough to state: 'the Catalan people – like all the other peoples of Spain – have to see their identity legally recognized' ('Los pueblos de España', 28 November 1975: 11). It was not until after the Suárez government had made a statement on 16 July 1976 that most of the editorials explicitly used the term 'autonomy'. However, it was the newly founded *Avui* that went the furthest in its claims, calling for the statute of autonomy enjoyed in the years prior to the Civil War:

> Our people, together with the others which form part of the Iberian community, demand not only recognition of their regional peculiarities but also, by way of the statute, insist on the restoration of their historic liberties.
>
> ('Que els fets abonin les paraules', 18 July 1976: 1)

Months later, there began to appear in various newspapers the term 'nationalities', riskier than 'regions' when it came to referring to the different lands included within the Spanish geography. *Avui* requested the recognition of a 'plurinational Spanish state' ('Balanç de dotze mesos', 20 November 1976: 1) and, motivated by the *Diada* (Catalan National Day, celebrated on 11 September) of 1977, went so far as to state 'the right of the peoples to self-determination is beyond discussion' (13 September

1977: 1). It was from that moment that the Catalan newspaper with the largest circulation, the liberal-conservative *La Vanguardia*, began to use the adjective 'national' to refer to the realities of the region: 'Democracy in Spain can be firmly established through recognition of national and regional differences' ('Un papel digno', 11 September 1977: 5). In contrast to its usual restraint, *La Vanguardia* made a clear turn toward Catalan nationalism. Although all the newspapers, with exception of *El Alcázar*, accepted the restoration of the Government of Catalonia in September 1977, the more conservative *ABC* expressed reservations: 'The re-establishment, in itself, we view as correct, convenient, and acceptable. But only as long as it is understood never to be contrary to the unquestionable unity of Spain' ('Ante el restablecimiento de la Generalitat provisional', 30 September 1977: 2).[1]

All the newspapers, except for *El Alcázar*, offered undeniable and explicit support for the political reforms, since they viewed parliamentary democracy as the best political system for Spain. However, this fundamental and shared support of the democratization process did not mean that all of them evaluated francoism negatively. On the contrary, some viewed its legacy favourably, especially with regard to social and economic progress.

According to the way they treated the francoist regime, we can distinguish different groups of newspapers. First, *El Alcázar* was fully apologetic toward francoism, based mainly on a comparison of its material achievements with those achieved with the advent of democracy and political liberties. Then, there were some newspapers that readily alluded positively to Franco's regime, especially to its accomplishments, while stating that this position was not incompatible with democracy-building. The positive references to the francoist regime on the part of these newspapers gradually diminished as the process of democratization advanced.

Lastly, there were those newspapers that offered frequent blanket criticism of francoism. *El País*, *Diario 16* and *El Correo Catalán* were the first to refer openly to francoism as a dictatorship, and to those were added the voices of the nationalist newspapers *Avui* and *Deia*. *Diario 16* even referred to what it called the 'original sin' of the monarchy of King Juan Carlos, speaking of the paradox of 'the King of the francoists on the road to convert himself into the King of all Spaniards' ('Monarquía: un año', 22 November 1976: 4). The turn toward nationalism that *La Vanguardia* took in the autumn of 1977 was also accompanied by the appearance of criticisms of the francoist regime, something never before seen in that newspaper.

The memory of the Civil War as a collective failure was palpable during the first years of the transition. The message of the majority of the Spanish press about this critical event in the contemporary political life of the nation can be summarized in four essential and shared points: (i) historical experience should make it less likely that the errors committed at that

time would be repeated; (ii) with the transition process, historical preju-
dices regarding the ability of Spanish people to organize themselves in a
democracy were being eliminated; (iii) pardon and amnesty were necessary for the reconciliation of the Spanish people through the forgetting of
the past; (iv) the new Constitution meant the opposite to the mutual
revenge or resentment of those who fought in the Civil War or their ideological heirs.

Considered as a whole and with occasional exceptions, the newspapers
maintained a more or less shared discourse with regard to the principal
objectives of political change. These basically consisted of a democratic
system, based on the return of sovereignty to the people and the restoration of fundamental civil rights, which would be achieved through
reconciliation and the forgetting of the past and through the establishment of self-governing institutions for the regions.

Throughout the three-year period from the death of Franco until the
ratification of the Constitution, this shared journalistic discourse was
enriched by new values derived from the different steps in the political
evolution of the transition. While concord and reconciliation were concepts that may have been internalized early on in the process, this was not
the case with the 'democratic recuperation' of other values, such as order
and authority. On the other hand, the different historical traditions of the
newspapers – or lack of tradition in the case of the new publications –
influenced their respective discourses. Newspapers such as *ABC, Ya, La
Vanguardia,* and *El Correo Español* generally exhibited more cautious attitudes with regard to political reform, and were more respectful of the past
than *El País, Diario 16, Avui* and *Deia. El Alcázar* continued to march to its
own drum, its extreme-right stance in permanent disagreement with virtually every step of the transition process.

Political news and new actors on the front pages

From news – the raw material of newspapers – emerge the editorials and
the columnists' commentaries. The front page is an example of the
ongoing policy of selection and categorization of the news carried out by
every newspaper, and the place where reality is framed in a manner consistent with editorial policies and principles. For these reasons, we under-
took a quantitative analysis of the news published on the front page of the
main Spanish newspapers in 1976 and 1977, the period in which the most
important political and institutional changes took place. In the study of
1976 we took the first ten days of each month as a sample, identifying
5,272 pieces of news. For 1977 we considered the first seven days as sufficient to safeguard the statistical validity of the sample, and found 3,451
items. Therefore, the total sample consisted of 8,723 items. For this analysis, we only used newspapers with national circulation in order to safeguard the balance among the kind of news items presented to readers. In

addition to the six newspapers included in the previous analysis, we also looked at coverage in *Informaciones* and *Arriba.* (The latter does not appear in Table 2.1 because its circulation was not audited by the *Oficina para la Justificación de la Difusión.*)

We established a series of basic variables, which permitted us to determine the importance given to the 'national political news'. Under this heading we included news that referred to activities instigated by official institutions (government, parliament, etc.), by opposition parties or groups (illegal until the beginning of 1977) and, finally, as a result of social or labour protests, including disturbances of public order and terrorist attacks.

Such political news fully dominated the front pages of the national newspapers and, over the one-year period between increased by nearly three percentage points (from 53.9 to 56.8 per cent). In addition, there was a notable growth in news referring to the opposition and to protest, increasing jointly from 21 to 28.2, to the detriment of coverage of the official activities, which dropped 4.3 points to reach 28.6. The difference between these two blocks, which was 11.9 points in 1976, fell to a mere 0.4 in 1977. Thus, news of official political activities diminished almost to the point of reaching the level of reporting of those that perhaps better represented the new Spain: the political groups and opposition trade unions which, at the time, were the cause of much of the public protest and disorder. Two other factors influenced the increasing newsworthiness of the 'other Spain': the legal recognition of the parties and labour unions in 1977 and the fact that, after the first elections, the government no longer monopolized the political initiative in the way that it had before.

When describing the behaviour of each newspaper it is especially interesting to examine which played the most important role in disseminating the three different types of political news. Thus, we calculated the percentage of official, opposition and protest news that each paper carried on their front pages in proportion to all the political news published by each. Table 2.5 summarizes our findings.

Generally speaking, some newspapers tended to provide greater coverage of the activities of the opposition groups while at the same time dedicating less coverage to official activity. While these newspapers tended to be situated more toward the left of the political spectrum (*Informaciones, El País* and *Diario 16*), the most representative of the extreme right, *El Alcázar*, was also in this group. In fact, in 1977, there was a larger percentage of opposition and protest news in these newspapers than official information. Given their political orientation, it would seem logical that the three leftist newspapers would report this type of news more than those newspapers that were more closely aligned with power (the state-run *Arriba* and *Pueblo*, and the Christian Democratic *Ya*). In the case of *El Alcázar*, it must be said that a large part of the news about the opposition referred either to groups of the extreme right, towards whom the

Table 2.5 Proportions of different types of political news published in Spanish national newspapers in 1976 and 1977

	% of political news, by type					
	Official		Opposition		Protest	
	1976	1977	1976	1977	1976	1977
El Alcázar	60.8	43.2	26.0	32.0	13.2	24.8
ABC	69.2	58.7	9.7	17.9	21.1	23.4
Ya	56.2	49.8	12.9	15.1	30.9	35.1
Arriba	66.1	60.7	13.1	17.4	20.8	21.9
Pueblo	71.4	55.1	7.2	17.6	21.4	27.3
Informaciones	54.1	45.1	20.4	20.1	25.5	34.8
El País	51.6	43.6	22.8	27.1	25.6	29.3
Diario 16	37.1	43.2	45.4	29.5	17.5	27.3
Mean	61.0	50.4	16.5	21.8	22.5	27.8

newspaper was more sympathetic, or the communist party, in which case the news was almost always negative and intended to harm the party's public image.

Journalistic coverage of the General Amnesty of 1977

One of the most representative events, if only for its symbolic nature, was the general amnesty of October 1977, a measure that looked to the past in an attempt to forget and to the future in order to build. The amnesty eliminated the penalties for political crime, including those for terrorism, in order to construct a system for everyone except those who decided to opt out voluntarily. It was not the only amnesty granted since the death of Franco and was, as a matter of fact, the least inclusive. It was, however, the most significant because it included crimes involving bloodshed and was overwhelmingly approved by the Parliament, which had been elected just four months earlier. The three other measures of forgiveness had been: the pardon granted by the King after his proclamation of 25 November 1975, in which 8,903 prisoners were released; the amnesty conceded by the first Suárez government on 30 July 1976, which resulted in the release of 287 prisoners; and that announced on 14 March 1977, in which 1,940 prisoners were liberated. (In contrast, the general amnesty of 1977 only affected 89 prisoners.)

In this case, we analysed a total of 11 newspapers, six with national circulation and published in Madrid (*ABC, Pueblo, Ya, El Alcázar, El País* and *Diario 16*), *El Correo Español, Egin* and *Deia* from the Basque Country, and *Diario de Navarra* and *El Pensamiento Navarro* from Navarra – a region bordering the Basque Country and France that Basque nationalists considered part of their nation. In this manner we attempted to include the full range of political attitudes and ideologies, both at the national level and with regard to the two regions most affected by the amnesty, given that the majority of the released prisoners were members of the Basque terrorist group, ETA (*Euskadi Ta Askatasuna*). From the news coverage of 1–18 October, we obtained a total sample of 879 items of news, editorials, articles and other kinds of text.

The three Basque newspapers (*El Correo Español, Egin* and *Deia*) carried the most thorough coverage, providing 38.2 per cent of the total information. The four with the least coverage were, perhaps significantly, two from the extreme right (*El Alcázar* and *El Pensamiento Navarro*), the state-controlled *Pueblo* and the conservative *ABC*.

In order to define the frame of the news disseminated by the different newspapers, we examined three variables: their specific contents, the geographic origin of the texts, and the individuals, political parties or other organizations from which they originated. For example, the texts referring to the discussion, negotiation and approval of the amnesty law was only 51.6 per cent of the total, while the sum of those referring to street demonstrations, terrorist acts and prison disorder represented 41 per cent, and the remaining 7.4 per cent referred to the immediate consequences of the law. This means that the newspapers recognized (to varying degrees) the important role played by the groups demanding amnesty in influencing those drafting the legislation.

A great plurality was found in the personal or partisan sources of the news or commentaries regarding amnesty.[2] Within the principal group of social and political actors there was a clear majority of nationalist or leftist groups or organizations, a faithful reflection of the social pressure being exerted in favour of amnesty. The degree to which these groups appeared in the press depended, as one might expect, on the ideological perspective or geographical origin of the newspapers. For example, the three Basque newspapers, taken together, accounted for more than 50 per cent of the news items relating to parties of the extreme left (59.3 per cent), Basque Nationalist Party (50.9 per cent), other leftist Basque nationalist parties (58.2 per cent), ETA (50.2 per cent), prisoners (70 per cent) and the pressure groups *Gestoras Pro-Amnistía* and/or COPEL (55.8 per cent).[3] The mere mention of these political or social forces came to demonstrate how these newspapers became more sensitive toward news originating from such strongly pro-amnesty sectors.

The Madrid newspapers, in step with the greater relevance given to news concerning negotiation, approval and discussion of the law, proved themselves more receptive towards news generated by the larger, nationally significant political parties. However, the two newly founded newspapers of the centre-left, *El País* and *Diario 16*, used them significantly less than the others and were more disposed to seek other sources. In fact, they were as or more likely to use the *Gestoras Pro-Amnistía* and COPEL than the Basque newspapers.

As to the general background common to almost all the newspapers, a qualitative approach shows that the five most often repeated ideas were that amnesty: (i) meant reconciliation and a fresh beginning for Spain, overcoming the differences that divided the two Spains of the Civil War; (ii) was broad and beneficial for future political stability of the nation; (iii) was reached as a result of political negotiation among all the parties present in the newly elected parliament, as a reflection of people's opinion; (iv) was an exceptional act and, as such, unrepeatable; and (v) should positively influence the aspirations of the Basque people and even aid in the elimination of separatist terrorism.

Remaining well outside the central discussion were the newspapers located on the political extremes. Thus, *El Alcázar* considered the amnesty to be an illegal act, the product of the government's 'bastard exchange of partisan political convenience' (11 October 1977: 3).[4] On the other side, *Egin* wrote that amnesty would only make sense 'when change, with respect to the previous political situation, is complete' ('Amnistía: beste pauso motx bat', 1 October 1977: 14), something that it did not yet feel had taken place in Spain.

The 'ability to forget', a concept essential to amnesty, was a key requirement. *El País* and *Diario 16* made forgetting the past the centrepiece of their pro-amnesty campaign – but this did not mean forgetting the 40 years of francoist dictatorship, which was referred to as 'a long, dark period of Spanish life in which violence originated mainly from the political power' (*El País*, 15 October 1977: 1). Pages later, *El País*'s editorial emphasized the fact that the historical memory of a people should serve to 'nourish pacific projects of cohabitation towards the future, not to nurture resentments regarding the past' ('Amnistía, al fin', 15 October 1977: 6).

The newspapers generally supported amnesty, converted into a necessary condition for the continuity of the new democratic regime. However, that journalistic discourse, while dominant, was not at all uniform, in as much as each newspaper framed the issue in accordance with its own ideological principles.

Conclusions

The period from 1975 to 1978 demonstrated how both politics and press, each acting in its own field, sought convergence in the final objective: a democracy accepted by everybody, negotiated through general consensus, with no exclusions except for violent or extremist groups. The press was one element more to call for moderation and also for firmness in the face of potentially destabilizing provocation. In this sense, the press served as a support and as one more ally to the government, King Juan Carlos and the consensus-building strategy sought by the principal political forces. The press promoted the three basic fundamentals of democratic political culture in Spain during the transition: liberty, amnesty and autonomy. These were the same main objectives that people claimed in the street demonstrations of the time.

This did not mean that opinion was unanimous about the political issues of the time, since there were differences and discrepancies in the nuances presented by the various newspapers. We can distinguish four areas of disagreement: their initial approaches; the arguments they used in support of the reform measures; their plans for reaching the established objectives; and their fundamental perspectives regarding the recent past and the near future. Despite these differences, a spirit of political realism prevailed, which resulted in the sacrifice of individual positions in favour of working for the main collective objectives. In spite of the ideological differences among them, there was a conscious effort to focus on their areas of agreement rather than their differences. Their conduct and messages showed reasonable moderation, instead of demagogical demands or pointless agitation: they did not, for example, use their different views of the past as political weapons against one another. This was another apparent similarity with the behaviour of the politicians.

The new democratic values and their consequences were internalized by the majority of the journalistic actors, although to varying degrees. They all understood the need for a broad amnesty but there were differing interpretations as to whom amnesty should or should not apply. All recognized the need to channel the desires for greater self-government in the regions but they differed as to the best procedure and the timescale for its introduction. The political milestones by which the liberty of the Spaniards became reality (elections, referenda, etc.) were interpreted more as collective triumphs of the Spanish people than as victories of the centrist governments of Suárez, although at the same time his indisputable political leadership was recognized. Only a few newspapers of the extreme right or the Basque nationalists did not join in the general consensus.

An important contribution of the press to the pluralism of the political debate was the progressive introduction of the new political actors into the public arena. Over a period of time, the press worked hard to ensure that the various groups of the democratic opposition, until then clandestine or merely tolerated, had a voice in public matters affecting Spain in 1976 and 1977. The press, particularly the newly founded newspapers, often became their principal spokesman due to the lack of other viable channels of communication. By reporting their activities during the initial years of the transition, the press contributed significantly to the normalization of the image of such parties as political actors.

The relationship between politicians and journalists throughout the period in which contemporary Spanish democracy was created was somewhat unusual. In general terms, there was a high level of mutual understanding and even complicity between them to share common objectives and present them to society as those most appropriate for the new social order which was evolving. Certainly the editors of the main newspapers were invited by the government in 1976 to deal very carefully with information about the King, the militaries and the Spanish unity in order not to destabilize the incipient democratic process (Chuliá 2001: 209). But there was no need to repeat those warnings due to the internal assumption of those premises by the majority of journalists.

The functions carried out by the politicians and journalists were different although complementary. The governments generally carried out the political initiative, especially when Suárez was named Prime Minister in July 1976. After a short period in which Suárez was received with suspicion and even with hostility by the public, a tacit agreement between politicians and journalists was begun with regard to the policy of multi-party consensus which would govern the constituent process.

Some Spanish newspapers became the critical conscience of the democratic reforms and acted to accelerate the transition process. On the other hand, the newspapers that quietly coexisted with francoism but also supported the transition process also played an important role. It is worth reflecting on how deep their support was of the reform process and how much of this support represented political, journalistic and commercial convenience. There was a sort of 'democratic conversion' of companies and editorial staff, which took place in a scarcely traumatic manner. Finally, only a few newspapers preferred to remain faithful to the ideological and political principals of francoism.

It can be said that, during the first years of the transition, the press generally supported the objectives of the government. It was a voluntary, not imposed, collaboration, based on common objectives shared by political and journalistic actors, both of them forming part of the general elite consensus in that time. From 1979, with the normalization of political life and the subsequent partisan fight for reaching the power, this exceptional 'journalistic consensus' disappeared.

Notes

1 The *Generalitat* was the name of the historic Catalonian self-government demanded by the majority of Catalonian political parties. Other newspapers offered a similar discourse. See *El Correo Español*, 1 October 1977: 23 ('Ha desaparecido un fantasma'), *Ya*, 30 September 1977: 5 ('La Generalidad, restablecida') and *Pueblo*, 30 September 1977: 3 ('España, siempre una').

2 We recorded, in each text, up to a maximum of three protagonists. In the present commentary all were considered together, independently of order of appearance in the text.

3 The Basque Nationalist Party (*Partido Nacionalista Vasco*, PNV), founded by Sabino Arana at the end of the nineteenth century, represented the moderate wing of the Basque nationalist groups and was, in the Basque Country, the most successful party in the elections of 1977. The terrorist group ETA was founded in 1959 by a group of young radical PNV members. Its first mortal attack was

carried out in 1968. The *Gestoras Pro-Amnistía* sought to put pressure on the Government and accelerate the concession of a total amnesty, especially for the Basque prisoners. COPEL (Coordinated Prisoners in Struggle) was an active organization promoting disorder in Spanish prisons.

4 Jato, D., 'Compraventa de amnistías', *El Alcázar*, 11 October 1977: 3.

References

Aguilar, M.A. (1982) *El Vértigo de la Prensa*, Madrid: Mezquita.

Aguilar Fernández, P. (1996) *Memoria y Olvido de la Guerra Civil Española*, Madrid: Alianza.

Alférez, A. (1986) *Cuarto Poder en España. La Prensa desde la Ley Fraga*, Barcelona: Plaza & Janés.

Barahona de Brito, A., González-Enríquez, C. and Aguilar, P. (2001) *The Politics of Memory. Transitional Justice in Democratizing Societies*, New York: Oxford University Press.

Barrera, C. (1995) *Sin Mordaza. Veinte Años de Prensa en Democracia*, Madrid: Temas de Hoy.

Chuliá, E. (2001) *El Poder y la Palabra. Prensa y Poder Político en las Dictaduras. El Régimen de Franco ante la Prensa y el Periodismo*, Madrid: Biblioteca Nueva/UNED.

Colomer, J.M. (1998) *La Transición a la Democracia: El Modelo Español*, Barcelona: Anagrama.

Iglesias, F. (1989) 'Las transformaciones de la prensa diaria', in J.T. Álvarez (ed.) *Historia de los Medios de Comunicación en España. Periodismo, Imagen y Publicidad (1900–1990)*, Barcelona: Ariel.

Mainer, J.C. and Juliá, S. (2000) *El Aprendizaje de la Libertad, 1973–1986*, Madrid: Alianza.

Reig, A. (1999) *Memoria de la Guerra Civil. Los Mitos de la Tribu*, Madrid: Alianza.

Resina, J.R. (ed.) (2000) *Disremembering the Dictatorship. The Politics of Memory in the Spanish Transition to Democracy*, Amsterdam: Editions Rodopi B.V.

Santos, F. (1995) *Periodistas*, Madrid: Temas de Hoy.

3 'In the name of democracy'

The paradox of democracy and press freedom in post-communist Russia

Hedwig de Smaele

> It is not enough to merely defend democracy. To defend it may be to lose it, to extend it is to strengthen it. Democracy is not property; it is an idea.
> (Hubert H. Humphrey, US Democratic Vice-President, 1 October 1942)

The twentieth century has commonly been labelled 'the century of democracy' (Freedom House 2000; Sen 1999). Following the first, slow wave of democratization from 1828 to 1926, the century experienced a second (1943–64) and third (1974–90) wave of democratization (Huntington 1993). As a result, 121 of the world's 192 governments are called democracies (Karlekar 2003: 8). Post-Soviet Russia, which shed authoritarian rule only in the last wave of democratization, is one of them. Article 1 of the 1993 Russian Constitution names the Russian Federation a 'democratic, federal, rule of law state'.

The worldwide spread of democracy has been accompanied by the expansion of press freedom (Sussman 2003: 13). Hence, a free press is assumed to be an essential feature of democracy. A free press operates as a check on politics and as a link between the citizens and their political representatives: it is an instrument for holding governments accountable, and for citizens to get informed, communicate their wishes and participate in the political decision-making. In all dissident movements in Eastern Europe the demand for democracy was accompanied by the demand for a free press. In Russia, Mikhail Gorbachev stressed the importance of *glasnost* (not the equivalent of press freedom but a step in that direction) as a *sine qua non* for democratic reform (Gorbachev 1987: 91). Later, Boris Yeltsin affirmed that he could not conceive of a democratic society 'without the freedom of expression and the press' (radio address cited in *Moskvosky Komsomolets*, 15 March 1997: 1), while Vladimir Putin has also emphasized the relationship: 'without a truly free media, Russian democracy will not survive' (statement to the Russian Parliament, 8 July 2000, cited in Mereu 2000). The principles of freedom of mass information and the inadmissibility of censorship were formalized in the Russian Law on Mass Media (27 December 1991) and the 1993 Constitution.

So much for the good news. The labels given to Russia – ranging from formal democracy (Kaldor & Vejvoda 1999) to authoritarian (Sakwa 1998), delegated (Remington 1999; Weigle 2000), manipulative (Delyagin 2000) or totalitarian democracy (Goble 2000) – suggest a congruence with the democratic model which is at best superficial and imperfect. This comment about Russia coincides with more general observations. 'If we look beyond the form of democracy', Diamond (1996: 31) writes, 'we see erosion and stagnation'. He calls this 'one of the most striking features of the "third wave" [of democratization]' (1996: 23): the gap between so-called electoral and liberal democracy or, in other words, the stagnation of liberal democracy.

Similarly, (Russian) press freedom is not absolute. The American organization Freedom House went as far as to lower the status of Russian mass media from 'partly free' in 2002 to 'not free' in 2003. Again, Russia is not an isolated case. Freedom House observes that, worldwide, 'the presence of a minimum standard of electoral conduct does not automatically lead to other attributes of mature democracy, such as strong civic institutions, an independent judiciary, and vibrant and free media' (Karlekar 2003: 8–9). The overall trend towards democracy does not prevent 'increased state-directed pressure on the media and a global decline in press freedom', nor therefore 'rising levels of violations of press freedom by democratically elected regimes' (2003: 8–9).

Amartya Sen hands us at least a partial explanation for the divergent observations of 'more democracy' but at the same time also 'less democracy', and 'more press freedom' but simultaneously 'no press freedom'. Democracy is a word with a highly positive emotional value that 'while not yet universally practised, nor indeed uniformly accepted, in the general climate of world opinion, has achieved the status of being taken to be generally right' (Sen 1999: 5). Like democracy, press freedom is increasingly expected by world culture and international organizations, stimulating countries to have, at least in name, both a democratic regime and a free press.

Moreover, while the general theoretical assumption remains that press freedom and democracy are strongly connected and mutually reinforcing, the process of democratization (in so-called 'new democracies' like Russia) or the protection of democracy (in so-called 'old democracies' like those of Western Europe) is often eagerly seized upon as a justification to (more or less severely) *limit* press freedom, thus creating a kind of paradoxical relationship between democracy and press freedom.

This chapter will discuss the paradoxical relationship between press freedom and democracy in post-communist Russia. Post-communist Russia represents a unique historical and socio-political setting, which does not readily allow for generalization. Nevertheless, observations on Russia can contribute to our understanding of the connection between press freedom and democracy in other contexts, especially those of the so-called 'new democracies'. Before looking at the Russian situation – from the sides of the politicians, the media and the public – let us begin with a general discussion on press freedom in relation to democracy.

Press freedom and democracy

At a minimum, democracy is a political system based on free, competitive and regular elections. This 'electoral' democracy presumes space for political opposition movements and political parties that represent a significant range of voter choice and whose leaders can openly compete for and be elected to positions of power in government (Schumpeter 1943). The concept of 'liberal' (Diamond 1996) or 'substantial' democracy (Kaldor and Vejvoda 1999) extends the key element of free competition with a range of political and civil rights (freedom of speech, freedom of association, freedom of religion, etc.) and the notions of the rule of law, inclusive citizenship and civil society. The concept of substantial democracy cannot easily be reduced to a set of procedures and institutions but is described as 'a way of regulating power relations in such a way as to maximize the opportunities for individuals to influence the conditions in which they live, to participate in and influence debates about the key decisions that affect society' (Kaldor & Vejvoda 1999: 3–4). Democracy should not be thought of as an either–or category, but rather as a continuum. The choice is not between democracy or no democracy, but between more or less democracy, which comes down very often to 'old' and 'new' democracies (Mayer 1989: 72). Linz and Stepan (1996) distinguish 'consolidated' and 'transitional' democracies: consolidation is attained when democracy has become 'the only game in town', constitutionally as well as behaviourally and attitudinally (1996: 5–6).

A free press is a cornerstone of democracy. Far from being a kind of 'bonus' of liberal democracy, it is the 'basis' of electoral democracy. In order to be able to vote consciously and freely, citizens need to be aware of all the options and have access to all the relevant information. Providing this information is the *raison d'être* of the press. An essential precondition to fulfil this task is its separation from state and political institutions, and its freedom from inhibiting forms of economic, political or other dependency.

The stress on freedom is not self-evident, nor universally accepted. It might be true that 'traditional free press theory lacks a prescriptive character', as 'it does not in its simple and most basic form say anything of what the press ought to do' (McQuail 1976: 9). But free press theory has had its critics: from the mid twentieth-century Hutchins Commission to the late twentieth-century advocates of public/civic journalism. Central to their criticism is the stress on (social/press) responsibility linked to, or even taking priority over, freedom. John Merrill observes a paradigm shift taking place in the second half of the twentieth century: 'the shift is basically from the press to the people (or to national rulers) – from press libertarianism to press responsibility' (2002: 17).

Rights carry responsibilities. Thus, naturally, the press does not only have to be free but (professionally) responsible: 'It is their [the media's] responsibility to maximize the opportunities for citizens to make political decisions and cast ballots on the basis of informed choice – retrospectively, about the extent to which the government has kept its promises in office, and prospectively, about how rival candidates will act if (re)elected to office' (Gunther & Mughan 2000: 422). This is not a small responsibility: making the best of the information flow necessary for the good functioning of democracy. But for some critics this task is not sufficient in itself, and they want to pass onto the press the responsibility for enhancing/protecting democracy *an sich*. Cohen-Almagor puts this strongly: 'It is for the media to take a firm stand to defend democracy whenever it is threatened' (2001: 90).

The performance of the media, then, is no longer measured in terms of fullness, completeness or fairness of information but in terms of rightness of information. Hence, full information can undercut rather than promote the reforms undertaken by a democratic government. Frances Foster calls this 'the defence of democracy theory' – a theory that 'views democracy as an established system of power besieged by hostile forces intent on its destruction' (1996: 99). This view is not without danger because it is morally loaded. When democracy is morally 'good', assumed critics of democracy have to be morally 'bad'. A 'responsible press' then is made a moral judge, allowed to silence inconvenient ('bad') views: ones that may slow down the process of democratization or that doubt the legitimacy of democracy without necessarily being a threat to it. Press freedom plays at a loss; but so does democracy. Thus, democracy needs dissent.

When is it allowed to put into operation what Cohen-Almagor (2001: xvi) has called the 'self-defence mechanisms to safeguard and protect democracy'? And when does the phrase 'press responsibility' simply become 'a code word for restrictions on the news media short of censorship' (Sussman 2003: 23)? In every country and at every moment, fierce debates take place about the borders of press freedom. Free press is in delicate balance with other competing values which spur limitations on press freedom – in order to prevent a threat to public order, or protect the security of the state or of third parties (such as minors). But, while some of the 'competing' goals are clearly defined (for example the protection of privacy), the goal of 'enhancing democracy' is too all-embracing and morally loaded to be workable.

The paradox of democracy and press freedom

The politicians' side

The process of democratization in Russia, paradoxically, became a justification to curtail press freedom and keep the media instrumentalized. The instrumental use of the mass media in post-communist Russia is a continuation of the communist past and an expression of the collectivist nature of society. The Soviet media were indeed free from the profit motive, but in no sense free from external goals (the building of a communist society, class homogenization) and external control and pressures (from the Communist Party and the government). Although the external (societal) goal has changed from the construction of a communist society to the provision of support for a new democratic society, the mobilization of the mass media as a means to a goal has remained largely unchanged (de Smaele 2001).

Gorbachev (president from 1985 to 1991) considered the mass media major instruments in promoting his politics of *glasnost* and securing support for his reforms. As before, the mass media mobilized people for the ideology of socialism – but now in a more dynamic way. Yassen Zassoursky, Dean of the Faculty of Journalism of the Moscow State University, has labelled the media model during this period as, successively, the 'glasnost model' (1997: 3) and the 'instrumental model' (1998: 16, 1999: 29–30). The former expresses an element of change, namely the break with the previous 'administrative–bureaucratic model'; in the latter, the aspect of continuity is brought to the fore.

Zassoursky describes the first years of Yeltsin's presidency (which ran from 1991 to 2000) as the era of 'the fourth power model'. Expectations, however, were pitched too high, and he suggests that from 1995–96 onwards the situation is best described by an 'authoritarian–corporate model', as continuity again triumphed over change (Y. Zassoursky 1997, 1998, 1999). Yeltsin was the self-appointed patron of democracy and press freedom. While it is obvious that he 'allowed' the press more freedom than any of his predecessors, he never questioned his presumed right to grant such freedom. In exchange, he expected the mass media to support his reforms loyally. Yeltsin embodied the belief that, in order to improve democratic procedures, one has to step 'beyond' these very procedures. In the name of democracy – and following the anti-Gorbachev coup d'état of August 1991, Yeltsin banned a number of newspapers that did not detach themselves explicitly from the coup. In the name of democracy, Yeltsin fired upon Parliament in October 1993 and again banned opposition newspapers. In the name of democracy, Yeltsin ruled largely by decree, ignoring a whole series of 'horizontal checks'. In the name of democracy, Yeltsin blatantly expected the mass media to support and arrange his re-election in 1996. In the name of democracy, Yeltsin presented his 'heir' to the voters/media consumers of Russia in the autumn of 1999.

Like Gorbachev and Yeltsin before him, Vladimir Putin (2000–) tends to seek in the unique socio-political setting of Russia and its process of democratization a justification to curtail media autonomy. In the name of democracy, Putin launched the fight against the independent television stations NTV and TV-6 in 2000 and 2001. In the name of democracy, Putin limited the information flow on terrorism-related topics. Much quoted is the comment of his spokesman Sergej Yasterzhembsky to journalists from the daily *Nezavisimaya Gazeta*: 'The media should take into account the challenges the nation is facing now. When the nation mobilizes its strength to achieve a goal, this imposes obligations on everybody, including the media' (see Whitmore 2000). Although uttered in the specific context of the Russian war against separatist rebels in Chechnya, the statement testifies to a view of media as instruments and to the prioritization of responsibility above freedom.

The means to pressure the media and keep them instrumental are numerous. The president and the executive have *direct* control over the media via the appointment (and dismissal) of media functionaries, especially the chairmen of the national television channels ORT (*Obshchestvennoe Rossiskoye Televidenie*, Russian Public Television, known more recently as *Pervyi kanal*, the First Channel), RTR (Russian Television and Radio) and *Kul'tura* (Culture). Another means of direct control are the state organizations directly subordinated to the executive. In addition to the Media Ministry (which has changed name and structure four times since the origin of the independent Russian Federation), these include *ad hoc* institutions such as Yeltsin's 'Federal Information Centre of Russia', which was actuated by the crisis between the Russian Parliament and the president and which existed parallel to the Ministry of Press and Information from December 1992 to December 1993, and the 'Russian Information Agency', created in 1999 to control press coverage of the war in Chechnya. Institutions which may appear to have less direct authority over the media can also play a role. The Security Council, formed in 1992 mainly as a discussion forum and consultative body, was turned by Putin into a more important policy instrument; the 'Commission on Information Security', for example, deals extensively with mass media policy.

The possibilities for *indirect* control are even greater. There is the financial dependency of the media on (state) subsidies or (corporate) sponsorship, either open or secret. There is the dependency on state facilities such as printing houses, transmitters and satellites, and on state organs instead of independent organs for the issuance of licenses. Expensive court cases (especially concerning slander and libel) scare off 'nasty' media, and the (all but transparent) accreditation procedure of journalists and even the use of violence against them can be seen as effective control mechanisms. To this we can add the legal insecurity due to the rapid succession of presidential and governmental decrees and orders, that often include contradictory measures, as well as the unpredictable changes in policy and practice of, for instance, tax collection (massively allowed tax evasion followed by strict enforcement).

The side of the media

It does not appear fair, however, to pass the responsibility for this system exclusively onto the authorities. Are the media – in the terms of Merrill *et al.* (1990: 59) – 'forced' or 'free' partners of the authorities? The question of guilt is inappropriate. We can only observe and conclude.

In the early years of the Russian Federation (1992–93), which were marked by the conflict between president and parliament, 'most of the Russian media appeared to adopt a strongly pro-government stance' (Benn 1996: 472). A content analysis of central television programmes in the run-up to the referendum of 25 April 1993 showed 'the obtrusive partisanship of state television' (Mickiewicz and Richter 1996: 119). The majority of the media *voluntarily* opted for the new – and hence democratic – partiality. Their leaders approached Yeltsin on their own initiative to request protection (of press freedom) and promised loyalty (meaning partiality) in return (Chugaev 1992).

The presidential elections of 1996 are a well-documented case in this sense. Again, the majority of journalists and media professionals rallied behind Yeltsin and *voluntarily* agreed with the mobilization function of the media. As Shevelov, vice-president of television channel ORT, stated: 'you can only refer to pressure if there is resistance. There is none' (cited in Lange 1996: 15). The journalists adhered to partisanship not only for material reasons but also out of normative considerations. Igor Malashenko, then president of the private television station NTV, joined the Yeltsin re-election campaign in April 1996 as chief media advisor and explained this logic as follows: if the private media had provided 'unbiased, professional, and objective' campaign coverage, Zhuganov would have won the election and journalists would have lost their freedom permanently. Better, he argued, to become a temporary 'instrument of propaganda' in the hands of the Kremlin. *Partijnost'* was justified for the protection of democracy and consequently press freedom. In the name of democracy journalists voluntarily gave up their autonomy and their freedom (Belin 1997; European Institute for the Media 1996: 8; I. Zassoursky 1999: 105).

In general, and outside the election context, empirical research has confirmed the voluntary alliance between journalists and authorities (for example Juskevits 2000; Kuzin 1996; Manaev 1995; Svitich and Shiryaeva 1997). The average Russian journalist does not reject the paternalistic character of power and therefore accepts its tutelage in mass communication. The concept adhered to is that of the active or participant journalist, as described by the Hungarian writer Janos Horvat (in Gross 1996: 111): someone who wants to influence politics and audiences according to his or her political beliefs. The restriction of their activity to the presentation of mere facts is indeed often regarded as a devaluation of the profession of the journalist (Voltmer 2000: 478).

The attitude of the individual journalist suits the media owners, who, under the 'protective banner of freedom of press' (Foster 1996: 100), protect their own freedom and their particular interests. Since the majority of media holdings are part of larger financial–industrial groups and money in Russia is still made through political connections, political, economic and media interests go closely together. Political and economic elites try to secure via the media their own wealth, status and influence. Boris Berezovsky and Vladimir Gusinsky are the classic – although nowadays disgraced – examples of political–economic media oligarchs. When Gusinsky's media outlets became the target of prosecution, he immediately declaimed that press freedom and, by extension, democracy was endangered. His alarm was taken up by other journalists in Russia as well as in foreign countries (the USA in the first place). There were, however, also sceptical voices. Robert Coalson (2000) wrote in a column in *The Moscow Times*: 'Gusinsky has shown very little genuine concern for press freedom. Like the other oligarchs, he only appears when his own interests are directly at risk'. In the same way Sergej Markov (2001: 24) noted with reference to a rally on freedom of speech: 'all speeches by NTV stars were about NTV's freedom. Such egoism could not inspire champions of freedom of expression'. 'The concept of freedom of speech has become hackneyed after Gusinsky and somewhat awkward to use', concludes the not entirely neutral General Director of Gazprom-Media, Alfred Kokh (2001: 20).

And the public?

As Price and Krug (2000: 4) state: 'for free and independent media to "work", the community in question must value the role that the media play'. Much of the Russian population, however, seems either hostile or indifferent to independent journalism. It is telling that 'independent' media in Russia are identified with 'opposition' media. Media independence is considered illusory, and partisanship the norm. The Russian audience – which Mickiewicz (2000: 115) calls 'exceptionally media-literate' – responds to mass media information not by asking 'is this true' but '*komu eto vygodno?*' (who might benefit from it?). News is interpreted in function of the source of news, be it Berezovsky's, Gusinsky's or the government's channel, or Potanin's, LUKoil's or the Communist Party's newspaper. In addition, state-controlled media are trusted more than private ones (Coalson 2001). The view of media as instruments of support (president, government, 'the system') is commonly accepted, as polls throughout the 1990s and early 2000s have repeatedly shown. 'In today's Russia, media freedom is . . . not the most fashionable and popularly supported notion', declared television presenter and journalist Evgeny Kiselev in an interview with Jeremy Drukker (*Transitions Online*, 10 July 2000). Elena Androunas points to the absence of 'freedom as a state of mind' (1993: 35).

The result: 'genuinely pluralistic unfree media'

The result is a pluralist but not an independent press. In the sense of the representation of a broad range of political expressions, opinions and interests, post-communist Russia is hardly less pluralistic than older democracies and probably even more so. In his book on media policy in Western Europe, Peter Humphreys (1996: 312) points at a systematic decline of pluralism in the twentieth century, caused by a de-ideologization of traditional politics and a commercialization, standardization and concentration of the media. While the Russian media system is also characterized by a high degree of concentration, this concentration is not at all linked with de-politicization. As Alexei Pankin says: 'money in the CIS is still made through connections in the government, and in this game it helps to own newspapers and stations as instruments of political influence' (1998: 33). Ivan Sigal (1997) has called Russian news coverage 'a part of politics'. 'In such circumstances', says *Izvestiya* journalist Sergej Agafonov, 'a free independent press is doomed, but an unfree and dependent press can flourish' (cited in Banerjee 1997: 59). Pankin speaks of a unique result: 'genuinely pluralistic unfree media' (1998: 30). However, a pluralism that derives the right to exist from the presence of different power groups in society is an uncertain pluralism. Hence, when the different power groups join forces because they feel threatened in their positions, as was the case in the 1996 presidential elections, this pluralism dies.

Any opinion that is presented claims to be the 'right' opinion. Every side in the power struggle claims to be on the 'right' side – and thus to have democracy on its side. In the power struggle at the beginning of the 1990s, both Yeltsin and the Russian Parliament pictured the opponent as an 'antidemocratic force', while justifying their own action as a defence of democracy. Ten years later, both Putin and Gusinsky equally consider their opponent an enemy of democracy. The pluralism present in the Russian press is not only an uncertain pluralism, but also a highly opinionated and morally loaded pluralism. The greatest victim of this kind of pluralism is (factual) information. Every newspaper and every television channel brings its own *versiya* of the facts. In order to get an accurate picture of what happened, one has to read some six newspapers and watch several television stations daily, claims Andrei Fadin (1997). But who does?

On the one hand, the presentation of information with the in-built intention of promoting 'democracy' (national security, personal interests, etc.) is a distortion of the 'pure' information function of mass media – 'what has happened and why did it happen?' To be able to fulfil their information function, media need to be free from external goals and clearly separated from external (political and economic) power groups. On the other hand, press freedom presumes that, although independent, the press is not shielded from government and industry. A necessary precondition for the media to function autonomously is their guaranteed access to (political and economic) information and transparency of governance. Worldwide, a correlation can be seen between press freedom and transparency, and between transparency and democracy:

> Information gathering is a vital component of freedom of information. Without access to information, journalists are engaged primarily in the presentation of opinions. And while openness in the statement of opinions is an important element of democratic society, it is not sufficient for its development and maintenance. The possibility for an informed citizenry depends on the ability of journalists to have access to sources. Without this kind of journalistic effectiveness, a society can have free and independent media, but their utility toward advancement of democratic institution-building might be severely limited.
>
> (Price and Krug 2000: 19)

Access to information in Russia

A climate of open access to information clings to the principle of information as a universal *right*, adjudged to everyone on an equal basis according to laws and procedures (universalism), whereas a culture of secrecy approaches information as a *privilege*, dependent on position or connections (particularism). Russia has always been characterized by a culture of secrecy rather than transparency. In the Soviet Union, journalists had extremely limited access to information in the first place, and the information acquired had to pass through several strict (mainly political–ideological) filters before appearing in the news. A limited flow of information was the norm. In addition, information was not available to everyone on the same conditions. Access to news sources depended on one's hierarchical (Party) position. The privileges of the *nomenklatura*, or 'first-class' citizens (Novosel 1995: 11–12), not only encompassed material benefits (such as housing, food, health care and education) but also enhanced access to information, ranging from access to 'forbidden' films or books (those that were not considered suitable for general distribution – see, for example, Benn 1992: 9) to the receipt of special foreign news bulletins, put together on a daily basis by TASS and distributed in different colours according to the degree of detail and intended readership (Lendvai 1981: 129–31). Although highly placed officials could obviously claim access to more information, they too received information only on a 'need-to-know' basis (Bauer *et al.* 1959: 43). The overall result was an information deficit. Information was one of the most sought after commodities in the Soviet Union (Ellis 1999: 6). Informal networks, oral communication and rumours filled the vacuum (Banai 1997: 252; Bauer and Gleicher 1964; Inkeles and Bauer 1959: 163–5).

In the transition to a free market economy, privileged access to information played a crucial role in the process of privatizations which became known as 'insider privatizations'. Privileged information remains important in post-communist Russia, where the right to information and inadmissibility of censorship are included, nevertheless, in the 1993 Constitution (Article 29) and in the 1991 Russian Federation Law on the Mass Media (Article 1). The Law on Mass Media assigns the right to receive information directly only to the mass media: Russian citizens have the right to receive true information on the activities of state organs, public organizations and officials *via* the mass media (Article 38.1). State officials, in their turn, are obliged to inform the media about their activities: on demand, but also actively via press conferences and the distribution of statistical and other materials (Article 38.2). Refusal to provide information is allowed only in case of state, commercial or other law-protective secrets (Article 40.1), and this has to be clearly communicated (Article 40.2). The Penal Code (Article 144) fixes high penalties for unlawful refusal to provide information and for hindering the professional activity of journalists.

The notion of 'state and other law-protective secrets', including commercial secrets, thwarts and subverts the general right to information as written down in the 1993 Constitution and the 1991 Law on Mass Media (de Smaele 2004). The broad interpretation of secret information allows for a large measure of control. The panellists that the International Research and Exchanges Board brought together to discuss the media situation in Russia agreed unanimously that 'access to some publicly relevant information is not free: authorities continue to view information as their property, and want to control access' (2001: 196). In the annual overviews of violations of journalists' rights, compiled by the Glasnost Defence Foundation since 1993, violation of the journalists' right to information – namely denial of information to journalists, refusals of journalists' accreditations and refusals to admit journalists to press conferences and certain locations – remains a frequently quoted problem (www.gdf.ru/monitor/). Surveys cited by Svitich and Shiryaeva (1997: 157) confirm this finding as well as a deterioration in journalists' rights of access to information throughout the 1990s. Especially difficult to obtain are bare facts, figures and documents. Little has changed in this respect since Soviet times. The executive has the worst reputation with regard to openness of information, followed by the security services, commercial companies, state companies and financial companies (Svitich and Shiryaeva 1997: 154–60).

Journalists do not receive rights by laws, but by the personal preference of (state) officials and press services, observes Vladimir Ermolin (2002: 7). By law, the media are equal – but, by preference, some are more equal than others. Code words in the process of information-gathering in Russia remain 'trust, relations, and integration' (Banai 1997: 242). Authorities have relations with some media professionals who enjoy 'privileges' to receive information unavailable to the rest of the media. Among the 'privileged media' in the Yeltsin era were, according to Gulyaev (1996: 14), news agencies such as ITAR–TASS and Interfaks, daily newspapers such as *Kommersant* and *Izvestiya*, and weeklies such as *Argumenti i fakty*. The most important private channel, NTV, has had various relationships with the president and his administration, having been a 'neutral' or 'opposition' channel in 1994–95, a 'supporting' channel in the presidential elections of 1996 and, again, an 'opposition' channel in 2000. With each phase, the levels of access to information shifted accordingly. In the early years, when NTV adopted an oppositional stand, NTV journalists were on occasion denied access to the Kremlin (*Omri Daily Digest*, 13 February 1996). In September 1996, however, the 'collaborating' channel received its broadcast license for the entire fourth channel by presidential decree, and enjoyed privileges such as the same transmission rates as the state channels and increased access to information. When it began to act again as an opposition channel, NTV saw its privileges, and ultimately its future, disappear. A more recent illustration is the way in which the Kremlin handled the disaster with the sunken submarine Kursk in the summer of 2000. Media coverage of the disaster was restricted, with only one journalist from the state-controlled television channel RTR granted full access to the disaster scene. Ivan Konovalov (2002: 51) says that the Kursk disaster was crucial in dividing journalists into 'ours' (*svoi*) and 'others' (*chuzhikh*). Journalists of state media, like RTR, belong to the category 'ours' and consequently enjoy an enhanced access to information. Konovalov then ranks the television stations, in order of declining closeness to the Kremlin, as: RTR, ORT, NTV, TV-Centre.

Very few journalists or media organs claim their right to receive information before court (Svitich and Shiryaeva 1997: 160). Maintaining privileged relations is the preferred means of overcoming the information barrier, with the main alternative being to bribe officials or openly purchase information from them. Finally, according to the Presidential Judicial Chamber for Information Disputes and the Union of Russian Journalists, 'if these methods are beyond them, they resort to fabrication and conjecture' (from the 1995 Joint Recommendation on the Freedom of Mass Information and the Responsibility of Journalists, cited by Price *et al.* 2002: 339–42). Indeed, the Recommendation passes on responsibility for the dissemination of untruthful information in the media to the closed administration, recording that 'Unreliability, incompleteness, and distortion of information very often results from the inaccessibility of sources of information' (Price *et al.* 2002: 341).

Conclusions

We started from the common understanding that press freedom and democracy are closely associated concepts. Neither concept, however, is unequivocally defined. Democracy implies participation of the citizens in the decision-making process, or at least in the election of the government – but gradations are legion. Press freedom implies media autonomy: freedom from external goals and controls. Again, gradations are numerous. Having said that, the correlation seems to exist: in the sense that there was 'no democracy' and 'no press freedom' in the Soviet Union and there is only 'partial democracy' and 'partial press freedom' in post-communist Russia. A third concept should be added, that is crucial to both press freedom and democracy, namely the right to know or the right to information coupled with transparency of governance and administration. Information has to be considered a key concept in democracy and, at times, an antidote to opinion. Rather than 'in the name of democracy' the media should report 'in the name of the people's right to know'.

The close integration of democracy with press freedom and, by extension, of politics with mass media has to be seen not only in terms of manipulation and force but also in terms of sharing a common political and information culture. The concept of culture suggests some commonality of values: politicians, media workers and the public share the same political culture and, in addition, the same information and communication culture. The concept of culture also suggests some continuity over time: not only throughout the communist and post-communist period but also dating back to the time of the czars. Culture is not unchangeable, but high expectations about the role of the media as triggers of democracy are doomed to fail. The media and society develop together and in coherent patterns.

References

Androunas, E. (1993) *Soviet Media in Transition. Structural and Economic Alternatives*, London: Praeger.

Banai, M. (1997) 'Children of the System. Management in Russia', in T. Clark (ed.) *Advancement in Organizational Behaviour. Essays in Honour of Derek S. Pugh*, Aldershot, Brookfield: Ashgate.

Banerjee, N. (1997) 'Big business takes over. A budding independent press returns to the old ways', *Columbia Journalism Review*, Nov–Dec; 59–61.

Bauer, R.A. and Gleicher, D.B. (1964) 'Word-of-mouth communication in the Soviet Union', in L.A. Dexter and D.M. White (eds) *People, Society and Mass Communications*, New York: The Free Press of Glencoe.

Bauer, R.A., Inkeles, A. and Kluchkhohn, C. (1959) *How The Soviet System Works. Cultural, Psychological, and Social Themes*, Cambridge, MA: Harvard University Press.

Belin, L. (1997) 'Politicization and self-censorship in the Russian media', paper presented at the national conference of the American Association for the Advancement of Slavic Studies, Seattle, WA, November 1997. Online. Available HTTP: <http://www.rferl.org/nca/special/rumediapaper/index.html> (accessed 4 June 1998).

Benn, D.W. (1992) *From Glasnost to Freedom of Speech. Russian Openness and International Relations*, London: Pinter.

——(1996) 'The Russian media in post-Soviet conditions', *Europe–Asia Studies*, 48(3): 471–9.

Chugaev, S. (1992) 'Boris El'tsin. Budu zashchishchat' svobodu i dostojnstvo Rossijskoj pressy', *Izvestiya*, 17 July.

Coalson, R. (2000) 'Media watch. Uniting to protect media', *The Moscow Times*, 19 May. Online. Available HTTP: <http://www.themoscowtimes.ru/19-May-2000/stories/story40.html> (accessed 19 May 2000).

——(2001) 'Russia. Managing the messengers', *CPJ Press Freedom Reports from around the World*. Online. Available HTTP: <http://www.cpj.org/Briefings/2001/Russia_coalson/Russia_coalson.html> (accessed 10 February 2004).

Cohen-Almagor, R. (2001) *Speech, Media and Ethics. The Limits of Free Expression. Critical Studies on Freedom of Expression, Freedom of the Press and the Public's Right to Know*, Basingstoke: Palgrave.

Delyagin, M. (2000) *Russia Reform Monitor*, 742; 31 January.

de Smaele, H. (2001) *Massamedia in communistisch en postcommunistisch Rusland (1917–2000). Factoren van continuïteit of van verandering?* Gent: Universiteit Gent.

——(2004) 'Limited access to information as a means of censorship in post-communist Russia', paper presented at the EURICOM Colloquium on Censorship and Democracy, Piran, 15–17 April 2004.

Diamond, L. (1996) 'Is the third wave over?' *Journal of Democracy*, 7(3): 20–37.

Ellis, F. (1999) *From Glasnost to the Internet. Russia's New Infosphere*, London: Macmillan.

Ermolin, V. (2002) 'Pressa i silovye vedomstva. Vzaimoterpimost' kak forma sotrudnichestva', in M. Pogorelyj and I. Safranchuk (eds), *Sovremennaya rossijskaya voennaya zhurnalistika. Opyt, problemy, perspektivy*, Moscow: Gendal'f.

European Institute for the Media (1996) *Media and the Russian Presidential Elections. Preliminary Report, 4 July 1996*, Düsseldorf: EIM.

Fadin, A. (1997) 'Media profile. In Russia, private doesn't mean independent. Bankers and oil tycoons use the media as a business weapon', *Transitions*, 4(5): 90–2. Online posting: fsumedia@sovam.com (accessed 8 October 1997).

Foster, F. (1996) 'Information and the problem of democracy. The Russian experience', *American Journal of Comparative Law*, 44: 243; reprinted in M.E. Price, A. Richter and P.K. Yu (eds) (2002) *Russian Media Law and Policy in the Yeltsin Decade. Essays and Documents*, The Hague: Kluwer Law International.

Freedom House (2000) *Democracy's Century. A Survey of Global Political Change in the 20th Century, Freedom House Report*. Online. Available HTTP: <http://www.freedomhouse.org/reports/century.html> (accessed 6 March 2002).

Goble, P. (2000) 'Toward totalitarian democracy?' *RFE/RL Report*, 21 February.

Gorbachev, M.S. (1987) *Perestroika i novoe myshlenie dlia nashei strany i dlia vsego mira*, Moscow: Izdatel'stvo polit. lit-ry. [Published in Dutch as *Perestrojka. Een nieuwe visie voor mijn land en de wereld*, Utrecht: Het Spectrum; in English as *Perestroika. New Thinking for our Country and the World*, London: Collins.]

Gross, P. (1996) *Mass Media in Revolution and National Development. The Romanian Laboratory*, Ames, IO: Iowa State University Press.

Gulyaev, M. (1996) 'Media as contested power in post-glasnost Russia', *Post-Soviet Media Law and Policy Newsletter*, 29; 12–16.

Gunther, R. and Mughan, A. (2000) 'The political impact of the media. A reassessment', in R. Gunther and A. Mughan (eds) *Democracy and the Media. A Comparative Perspective*, Cambridge: Cambridge University Press.

Humphreys, P.J. (1996) *Mass Media and Media Policy in Western Europe*, Manchester: Manchester University Press.

Huntington, S.P. (1993) *The Third Wave. Democratization in the Late Twentieth Century*, Norman, OK: University of Oklahoma Press.

Inkeles, A. and Bauer, R.A. (1959) *The Soviet Citizen. Daily Life in a Totalitarian Society*, Cambridge, MA: Harvard University Press.

International Research and Exchanges Board (2001) *Media Sustainability Index 2001. The Development of Sustainable Independent Media in Europe and Eurasia*, Washington, DC: IREX. Online. Available HTTP: <http://www.irex.org/publications-resources/msi_2001/index.htm> (accessed 2 February 2002).

Juskevits, S. (2000) 'The role of the journalist in transition', paper presented at the 6th ICCEES World Congress, Tampere, 29 July–3 August 2000.

Kaldor, M. and Vejvoda, I. (1999) 'Democratization in Central and East European countries. An overview', in M. Kaldor and I. Vejvoda (eds) *Democratization in Central and Eastern Europe*, London: Pinter.

Karlekar, K.D. (2003) 'Press Freedom in 2002', in K.D. Karlekar (ed.) *Freedom of the Press 2003. A Global Survey of Media Independence*, New York: Rowman & Littlefield. Online. Available HTTP: <http://www.freedomhouse.org/research/pressurvey.htm> (accessed 17 March 2004).

Kokh, A. (2001) 'Gusinsky has made "freedom" a bad word', *Russia Watch*, 6; 19–20.

Konovalov, I. (2002) 'Voennaya telezhurnalistika. Osobennosti zhanra', in M. Pogorelyj and I. Safranchuk (eds) *Sovremennaya rossijskaya voennaya zhurnalistika. Opyt, problemy, perspektivy*, Moscow: Gendal'f.

Kuzin, V.I. (1996) 'Kto i kogda postroit bashnyu? Vospominaniya o proshlom s sovremennym kommentariem', in *Fakul'tet Zhurnalistiki. Pervye 50 let. Stat'I, ocherki*, St Petersburg: Izdatel'stvo Sankt-Peterburgskogo Universiteta.

Lange, Y. (1996) 'The media and the Russian presidential election', *The Bulletin*, 13(3): 13–15.

Lendvai, P. (1981) *The Bureaucracy of Truth. How Communist Governments Manage the News*, London: Burnett Books.

Linz, J.J. and Stepan, A. (1996) *Problems of Democratic Transition and Consolidation. Southern Europe, South America, and Post-Communist Europe*, Baltimore, MD: John Hopkins University Press.

McQuail, D. (1976) *Review of Sociological Writing on the Press*, London: Her Majesty's Stationery Office.

Manaev, O. (1995) 'Rethinking the social role of the media in a society in transition', *Canadian Journal of Communication*, 20(1): 45–65.

Markov, S. (2001) 'Russian media in a revolutionary period', *Russia Watch*, 6: 22–5.

Mayer, L.C. (1989) *Redefining Comparative Politics. Promise versus Performance*, Newbury Park, CA: Sage.

Mereu, F. (2000) 'Is this the current view of freedom of the press?', *The Russia Journal*, 3(39): 7–13 October.

Merrill, J.C. (2002) 'Chaos and order. Sacrificing the individual for the sake of social harmony' in J.B. Atkins (ed.) *The Mission. Journalism, Ethics and the World,* Ames, IO: Iowa State University Press.

Merrill, J.C., Lee, J. and Friedlander, E.J. (1990) *Modern Mass Media,* New York: Harper & Row.

Mickiewicz, E. (2000) 'Institutional incapacity, the attentive public, and media pluralism in Russia', in R. Gunther and A. Mughan (eds) *Democracy and the Media. A Comparative Perspective,* Cambridge: Cambridge University Press.

Mickiewicz, E. and Richter, A. (1996) 'Television, campaigning, and elections in the Soviet Union and post-Soviet Russia', in D.L. Swanson and P. Mancini (eds) *Politics, Media, and Modern Democracy. An International Study of Innovations in Electoral Campaigning and their Consequences,* Westport, CT: Praeger.

Novosel, P. (1995) 'The iron law of communication', in D.J. Paletz, K. Jakubowicz and P. Novosel (eds) *Glasnost and After. Media and Change in Central and Eastern Europe,* Cresskill, NJ: Hampton Press.

Pankin, A. (1998) 'Economic constraints on media independence and pluralism in Eastern and Central Europe', *Balkanmedia,* 7(1): 27–34.

Price, M.E. and Krug, P. (2000) *Enabling Environment for Free and Independent Media;* a report prepared by Oxford University Programme in Comparative Media Law & Policy. Online. Available HTTP: <http://pcmlp.socleg.ox.ac.uk/enablingenvironmentgallery.htm> (accessed 26 February 2004).

Price, M.E., Richter, A. and Yu, P.K. (eds) (2002) *Russian Media Law and Policy in the Yeltsin Decade. Essays and Documents,* The Hague: Kluwer Law International.

Remington, T.F. (1999) *Politics in Russia,* New York: Longman.

Sakwa, R. (1998) 'Russian political evolution. A structural approach', in M. Cox (ed.) *Rethinking the Soviet Collapse. Sovietology, the Death of Communism and the New Russia,* London: Pinter.

Schumpeter, J.A. (1943) *Capitalism, Socialism and Democracy.* London: Allen & Unwin. [Published in Dutch as *Kapitalisme, Socialisme en Democratie,* 3rd ed. (1979), De Haan, Haarlem: Unieboek BV Bussum.]

Sen, A. (1999) 'Democracy as a universal value', *Journal of Democracy,* 10(3): 3–17.

Sigal, I. (1997) *A Survey of Russian Television.* Prepared for USAID, in collaboration with the staff of Internews Moscow. Online. Available HTTP: <http://www.internews.ras.ru/report/tv/> (accessed 6 April 1997).

Sussman, L.R. (2003) 'Press freedom, the past quarter century. The vile and the valiant', in K.D. Karlekar (ed.) *Freedom of the Press 2003. A Global Survey of Media Independence,* New York: Rowman & Littlefield. Online. Available HTTP: <http://www.freedomhouse.org/research/pressurvey.htm> (accessed 17 March 2004).

Svitich, L.G. and Shiryaeva, A.A. (1997) *Zhurnalistskoe obrazovanie. Vzglyad sotsiologa,* Moscow: IKAR.

Voltmer, K. (2000) 'Constructing political reality in Russia. *Izvestiya* – between old and new journalistic practices', *European Journal of Communication,* 15(4): 469–500.

Weigle, M.A. (2000) *Russia's Liberal Project. State–Society Relations in the Transition from Communism,* Pennsylvania, PA: Pennsylvania State University Press.

Whitmore, B. (2000) 'No more heroes. New Russia asserts old press controls', *International Press Institute Report,* 1. Online. Available HTTP: <http://www.freemedia.at/publicat.html> (accessed 16 August 2002).

Zassoursky, I. (1999) *Mass-Media vtoroj respubliki*, Moscow: Izdatel'stvo Moskovskogo Universiteta.

Zassoursky, Y.N. (1997) 'Media in transition and politics in Russia', paper presented at the International Conference on Media and Politics, Brussels, 27 February–1 March 1997.

——(1998) 'Changing media and communications', in Y.N. Zassoursky and E. Vartanova (eds) *Changing Media and Communications*, Moscow: Faculty of Journalism, IKAR.

——(1999) 'Open society and access to information. The role of Russian media', in Y.N. Zassoursky and E. Vartanova (eds) *Media, Communications and the Open Society*, Moscow: Faculty of Journalism, IKAR.

4 Conflicts of interest?

Debating the media's role in post-apartheid South Africa

Herman Wasserman and Arnold S. de Beer

The transition of South Africa from an authoritarian state under oligarchian white-minority rule to a constitutional democracy formally occurred on 27 April 1994, when all the country's citizens were allowed to cast their ballots in the first democratic elections. This election marked the culmination of a democratization process that was initiated in 1990, when, after decades of increasing pressure from within the country and internationally, then president F.W. de Klerk announced the unbanning of the liberation movements and the release of all political prisoners, including future president Nelson Mandela. As could be expected, these events set into motion processes that have reconfigured the political and social landscape. In 2004, ten years after the election of the first democratic government, these processes were far from completed. One of the areas in which the transformation process is still underway, amid much debate, is that of the media. This chapter will give an outline of some of the most significant changes that have taken place in the media sector since democratization, and explore some of the salient issues and conflicts arising from these developments.

The chapter aims to indicate the developments of the past decade with regard to the media, and how these developments relate to ongoing debates about the media's role in democratic South African society. Through these different focus points, we will attempt to show that, although legacies of the past remain, it would not be an exaggeration to say that the decade has been, and continues to be, marked by one operative word: change.

The chapter will consequently give an overview of the following developments:

- ownership changes;
- changes in the prevailing normative frameworks;
- broadening of the media sphere;
- conflicts between the mainstream media and the post-apartheid government; and
- the different value systems that gave rise to friction between the media and government.

Changing hands: ownership and political transition

The mainstream media landscape under apartheid was largely white. The white media were split along ideological lines, with the English language liberal press tied to mining capital tolerated by the government, while the apartheid state had a largely subservient Afrikaner nationalist press at their service (Jacobs 2004: 106; Tomaselli and Dunn 2001). The broadcasting sector (see Tomaselli *et al.* 1989) was almost exclusively under the control of the South African Broadcasting Corporation (SABC), owned by the apartheid state. There were alternative media, but they operated under constant threat.

During the 1990s this situation changed significantly, both as far as ownership and editorial composition are concerned. While the alternative media (see Switzer 1997; Tomaselli and Louw 1991) dwindled in the early 1990s as external funding dried up (Jordan 2004), two big ownership transfers to so-called black empowerment consortiums (namely Johnnic and Nail) brought some of the biggest newspaper titles under black ownership. In another notable development, the Irish Independent group gained control of a series of newspaper titles, thereby opening up the South African media for global competition.

Broadcasting became more diversified – the SABC was restructured to reflect racial diversity in its programming and staffing, and its top administration was opened up to public scrutiny (Jacobs 2004; Tomaselli 2000). After 1994, a new private free-to-air broadcaster, e.tv, was introduced, which provided competition for the public broadcaster's entertainment and news programming. The commercial subscription television service M-Net, in operation since the late 1980s, entered the satellite television market through its sister company MultiChoice in 1995, and now offers satellite television subscription to more than 50 countries, dominating the African market (Jacobs 2004: 140). Community radio stations have also been introduced as a result of new legislation that broadened the access to mass media.

Tabloid newspapers have appeared on the market since 2000. While some commentators (Addison 2003) see them as providing black communities in particular with self-help information such as health and life skills advice columns, others (Jacobs 2004: 148–9) point to their right-wing political stance and sensationalist approach. Their arrival marked the start of circulation wars. The heightened commercial pressure of an increasingly competitive media market (both in South Africa and globally, as a result of technological advances in globalizing media) also resulted in a 'tabloidization' of all – but especially print – media: a reduction of staff, a 'juniorization' of newsrooms, a preference for commercial imperatives in making editorial judgements, and the erosion of specialized reporting (Harber 2002; Jacobs 2004: 149). The dearth of journalistic skills was also noted in an audit among junior journalists commissioned by the South

African National Editors' Forum (Sanef) in 2002 (De Beer and Steyn 2002).

As part of the restructuring of media institutions to start to reflect the demographics of South African society, the racial composition of newsrooms started to change dramatically, with more black journalists writing for and editing mainstream publications. The integration of black and white journalists was formalized in 1996 with the founding of Sanef. However, some critics have pointed out that, although the South African media has changed its hue as far as editorial and ownership patterns are concerned, it is still to a certain extent class-based and not sufficiently diverse (Tomaselli cited in Harber 2002; Duncan 2003; Haffajee 2004; Jacobs 2004; Jordan 2004).

Changing the rules: shifts in normative regimes

The media under apartheid was subject to strict control. While mainstream media often toed the party line (in the case of the Afrikaans media) or offered liberal criticism (in the case of the English language media), a number of alternative, anti-apartheid media outlets did exist (see Switzer 1997; Tomaselli and Louw 1991). These operated under the constant threat of state harassment or governmental control of different kinds, and in many cases fell victim to a government that did not take kindly to criticism. Journalists working for these publications were often harassed or jailed, and their publications often censored or banned under a barrage of restrictive laws, especially under the so-called States of Emergency that granted the government even more draconian powers. According to Hachten and Giffard (1984), more than a hundred laws were in place to control the media in one way or another. The almost exclusively state-owned broadcast media served as a propaganda tool for government (Jacobs 2004; Switzer and Adhikari 2000).

Television was only introduced in 1976, after long governmental resistance (Tomaselli *et al.* 1989). The opposition to the medium was supposedly a result of the corruptible cultural and moral influence it posed, although its greater vulnerability to outside criticism of the apartheid system was also feared (Hachten and Giffard 1984). The prevailing moral climate was stifling, inspired by a paranoid state which prohibited reference to imprisoned struggle leaders like Mandela or use of their photographs, and which enforced a narrow Calvinist doctrine on moral issues. Pornography, gambling and literature posing a threat to apartheid ideology – from Mao Zedong to Afrikaans novelists describing interracial romance – were prohibited. Because of the strict legislative environment, the media under apartheid were more concerned with not breaking the law than with engaging in discussions regarding their ethical duty towards society (Froneman 1994).

The normative regime underwent radical change with the start of the democratization process in the 1990s (see Giffard *et al.* 1997; Jackson 1993).[1] The repressive apartheid media laws were repealed and media freedom was entrenched in the new Constitution within a Bill of Rights guaranteeing not only media freedom but also freedom of expression and access to official information (although retaining certain limitations, such as those on the incitement to violence or racial hatred). The adoption of the Constitution can be seen as the most important formal legislative change impacting on the operation of the media in post-apartheid society (Oosthuizen 2002: 101; Retief 2002: 26). The scrapping of apartheid-era laws such as the Internal Security Act (Act 74 of 1982) enabled the media to, *inter alia*, quote members of previously banned parties like the African National Congress (ANC) and limited the powers of the government to interfere in editorial matters. (For an overview of the role of the South African media in important democratic political processes such as elections, see De Beer 2004.)

The Publications Act of 1974 was replaced with the Films and Publications Act (65 of 1996), in which restrictive laws were replaced by a liberal classification system (Oosthuizen 2002: 97, 103). A section (Section 205) of the Criminal Procedures Act (57 of 1977) remains on the statute books and can still (and has been) used to subpoena journalists to testify in court or to divulge their sources if this was 'deemed relevant to solve an alleged offence' (Oosthuizen 2002: 104). The persistence of apartheid-era laws is often objected against by media organizations such as Sanef, the Freedom of Expression Institute and the Media Institute of Southern Africa (see, for example, the latter's annual publication series: *So This is Democracy? State of the Media in Southern Africa*).

Whereas the media under apartheid was bound by strict legalistic measures, the emphasis since 1994 has been on self-regulation. Two watchdog bodies, the Press Ombudsman and the Broadcasting Complaints Commission of South Africa, replaced the South African Media Council, which was seen to have political baggage from the old order (Oosthuizen 2002: 72; Retief 2002: 237). These bodies hear complaints from the public and can reprimand media institutions that contravene their ethical codes. Many of the major publications and broadcasters now have their own codes of ethics, as do professional organizations such as the Freedom of Expression Institute, Sanef, the South African Union of Journalists and the Media Institute of Southern Africa. Such organizations can be seen to guard the public interest against interference from government, while the notion of 'public interest' – itself a contentious concept – has, in post-apartheid South Africa, been contested by the notion of the 'national interest', as will be discussed below.[2] While the Press Ombudsman and Broadcasting Complaints Commission deal primarily with the news media, a statutory body, the Film and Publications Board, was re-established to provide normative guidelines for the entertainment media and enforce age restrictions on entertainment products.

Changing audiences: broadening media access

As mentioned above, the South African media underwent important ownership changes during the democratization process. Media outlets that had previously been in white hands have been transferred to black owners in a range of so-called 'empowerment' deals.

While these ownership shifts have altered the face of the South African media, the establishment of new media outlets further diversified the media sphere. Foremost among the new developments, as far as the range of media on offer is concerned, is the change in the make-up of the broadcast sector. Since television and radio constitute the main news source for 96 per cent of South Africans (Davidson cited in Jacobs 2004: 134), these changes are of some significance. In a move that weakened state control over the public broadcaster, independent bodies were established to regulate licensing and ownership in the broadcasting sector.

In 1995, the Independent Broadcasting Authority (whose complaints and licensing functions were later divided between the Broadcasting Complaints Commission and the Independent Communications Authority) awarded licences to 80 new community radio stations. Although this number has subsequently dwindled to around 65 due largely to management and funding problems, it broadened access to the broadcasting media considerably. The licensing agreements stipulated that programming should be focused on community matters and assist in developing the quality of life of the specific community. By providing previously neglected geographical communities and communities of interest with media platforms, the broadcasting landscape was diversified radically.

The Media Development and Diversity Agency was subsequently established to assist in the development of community publications. This has met some resistance from the mainstream commercial media, who have to contribute to the agency's funding. While some of its critics pointed to the fact that, at least according to initial proposals (which were later modified), the agency would be open to government interference, others highlighted its tardiness in bringing new enterprises to fruition (Jordan 2004).

Further transformations to the radio sector included the sale of six of the SABC's regional stations to private investors and the reduction of government subsidies to the public broadcasting sector. This encouraged the SABC to look increasingly to advertising revenue to fund its public functions, a development with implications for its news and current affairs content (Jacobs 2003: 135). At the time of writing (September 2004), the SABC had asked the independent regulating body to relax its licensing agreements so that it could further commercialize some of its broadcasting services. As already mentioned, the television sector was broadened by the introduction of satellite television and a new free-to-air station. The SABC now provides free television services in all 11 official languages, as well as subscription services to other African countries as part of the satellite 'bouquet'. As a result, the broadcasting sector is now structured into three tiers: public, private/commercial and community.

The development of the Internet in the 1990s provided a further platform for the dissemination of news and the expansion of commercial media. Most of the major newspapers and magazines now have online versions, and the SABC and private commercial radio stations have a presence on the World Wide Web, ranging from programming information to news updates. The two big media conglomerates, Naspers and Independent, also have affiliated online news bulletin services (News24 and Independent Online, respectively).

By broadening the range of channels through which information can be distributed, the Internet can be seen as contributing to a more open society and as one of the developments in the post-apartheid South African media sphere that has the potential of strengthening democracy.[3] It has already started to play a role in political processes such as e-government and cyberactivism (Wasserman and De Beer 2004), although connectivity is still very low and unequally spread across the population. Because of the lack of access – despite governmental attempts to establish so-called 'telecentres' – its influence is likely to remain marginal as far as the broader population is concerned.

The more things change: friction continues

It would, given the discussion above, be fair to aver that the media sector in South Africa in the first ten years of democracy underwent some far-reaching changes as far as the ownership of the sector and the legislative and normative frameworks are concerned. In many ways, however, the media's relationship with the government remained uneasy. This can perhaps be seen as a result of different understandings of what the newly acquired right to freedom of speech meant (De Beer 2002; Fourie 2002; Shepperson and Tomaselli 2002).

Part of the friction between the post-apartheid government and the media also resulted from what can be called 'apartheid hangovers' – structural issues (such as ownership and staffing) and a deep-seated mistrust. This mistrust was dual in nature: the government did not trust the media to report fairly on it because it was predominantly still staffed by the same white males as had been the case during apartheid, while many members of the media industry[4] were cautious of possible threats to media freedom posed by the new government. This pessimistic expectation should be seen against the background of trends of governmental regulations in the region (Duncan 2003: 5), but has also been linked to 'racist and misplaced associations' of the new government with authoritarianism (Jacobs 2004: 132).

Friction between the media and the new government started early. On the eve of the April 1994 elections, Mandela painted a pessimistic picture of the South African media: 'With the exception of the *Sowetan*, the senior editorial staffs of all South Africa's daily newspapers are cast from the same racial mould. They are White, they are male, they are from a middle class background, they tend to share a very similar life experience' (Mandela 1994). He noted the 'one-dimensionality' of the media, since the 'principal players in the media' lacked knowledge of the 'life experience' of the majority in the country.

This criticism of the imbalances in the racial demographics of the media sector came to a head when the Human Rights Commission launched a full-scale investigation into alleged racism in the South African media in 1999–2000. This investigation did not improve levels of endearment between media and government. It was methodologically flawed, raised the ire of editors by subpoenaing them to testify and focused on superficial representations of racism in the media rather than scrutinizing the broader, more intricate power relations between racism, the market and the state (see *Rhodes Journalism Review* 1997; Krabill 2001).

Some of the positive results flowing from this inquiry were that Sanef took the lead in reassessing the nature, role and operation of the media in South Africa in 2001, in an attempt to overcome racial divides: a clear and conscious effort by the media to overcome racism (De Beer 2004). This included a special workshop on media ethics and a national audit on journalism skills (see De Beer and Steyn 2002). A special issue of the South African journal for journalism research, *Ecquid Novi*, was devoted to reactions by editors on the Human Rights Commission hearings (*Ecquid Novi* 2000: 21[2]).

The Human Rights Commission investigation followed on from the Truth and Reconciliation Commission's investigation of 1996, which included the media's role under apartheid[5] within its overall mandate of human rights abuses under apartheid. The hearings were initially aimed at state propaganda and spies in newsrooms, with the underlying assumption that the English-language press had contributed to the undermining of apartheid while the Afrikaans press supported the regime. These terms of reference were, however, broadened upon insistence by black journalists' organizations to also focus on treatment of black journalists in the English and alternative media. The Truth and Reconciliation Commission eventually also paid substantial attention to issues of press freedom and professional media institutions, but neglected aspects like programming and questions of political economy (Krabill 2001: 591–6). The Commission's inquiry into their role was not met with great enthusiasm among most mainstream media editors, and one media house, Naspers (save a number of its individual journalists, who defied company policy), refused to testify.

Whereas the media was the object of scrutiny under the Mandela presidency, it often clashed outright with Mandela's successor, Thabo Mbeki. Similar to the remarks made by Mandela regarding the skewed picture of

South Africa painted by the media were Mbeki's expressions of concern – even before he succeeded Mandela – at the 'major segment of political opinion' not being represented in the media (De Beer 2003: 104). Mbeki's relations with the media have been generally poor (Chotia and Jacobs 2002: 157). Maré (2003: 37) asserts: 'An intolerance of dissent marks Mbeki's style, with pressure on the media more consistent than was the case with Mandela's occasional outbursts'. The media, both local and international, has in turn also displayed antagonism towards Mbeki (Satgar 2002: 168). He has constantly come under fire from the media, on issues including his 'silent diplomacy' in the case of Zimbabwe, his HIV/Aids policy, alleged inadequate service delivery and what is perceived as his incessant overseas travel at the cost of local matters that are left unattended (Fourie 2002: 32).

Attempts were made to patch up the relations between Mbeki and the media, through a landmark meeting between the cabinet and the editors' forum Sanef in 2001 (the 'Sun City Indaba'). As part of the attempts to facilitate better communication between the government and the media, the idea of a Presidential Press Corps was suggested at the meeting. Two years later, after much debate about controversial selection procedures, this corps was established (Wasserman and Van Zyl 2003). Nevertheless, Mbeki and the media are still often at loggerheads. On more than one occasion, he has lashed out against the media, especially in his weekly letter on the ANC website (for example Mbeki 2003), accusing them of *inter alia* perpetuating colonial and apartheid stereotypes about Africans. These criticisms can be seen as arising from a difference in opinion as to what the media's role in society should be. This difference of opinion for a large part played out in a debate around two concepts: the public interest *versus* the national interest.

Changing loyalties: public *versus* national interest

The Sun City meeting between government and Sanef was organized after a number of statements by government voicing its concern about the media's apparent 'reluctance to embrace the concept of national interest'. In this debate it is worth noting that these terms could have been invoked by the respective role-players to disguise their own interests, in the name of some greater good. On the side of the government, the concept of 'national interest' might be used to mask the exercise of power; whereas the media might invoke the 'public interest' to defend decisions based in reality on the drive for audience figures or circulation. At the same time, the debate also took place at another level of discourse, namely normative arguments relating to the media's role in post-apartheid society. We will here try to map the main points of these discourses, bearing in mind that some overlap exists between descriptive and normative arguments.

The government put forward its position in the person of Joel Netshitenzhe, chief executive officer of the Government Communication and Information System. Netshitenzhe defined national interest as the 'aggregate of things that guarantee the survival and flourishing of a nation-state and nation' and, as such, defined by a democratically elected government (Netshitenzhe 2002). Some commentators, like the director of the Steve Biko Foundation, Xolela Mangcu, have viewed this concept positively: according to Mangcu (cited in Duncan 2003: 6), consensus can be reached on what the national interest means, as long as it is founded on constitutional values.

The media did not, however, accept the concept of 'national interest' as an adequate description of their role in post-apartheid South Africa. Instead, they asserted their role to be in service of the 'public interest'. In their submission on the Broadcasting Amendment Bill in 2003, the Media Institute of Southern Africa defined these two terms as follows:

> It is our contention that the use of the term 'national interest' in rela-tion to news gathering and dissemination is too restrictive and can have a narrow political connotation. Journalists work in the public interest, which is much wider. Politicians of a ruling party may decide that there should be secrecy over an issue 'in the national interest' – where the meaning of 'national interest' is defined by the politicians. Journalists work in the 'public interest', a sounder, much wider base that might override 'national interest'. Chapter Two of the (South African) Constitution protects the 'public interest'.
>
> (cited in Duncan 2003: 6)

As pointed out, this position, although apparently put forward as a norm-ative argument, could also be informed by the media's own interests regarding the prerogative to decide on the approach to news reporting. The defence of the 'public interest' could therefore be informed by a defi-nition of the 'public' which suits the media's orientation towards lucrative markets. On the other hand, the government's insistence on the 'national interest' as a principle for the media could stem from an attempt to limit criticism and exert power over the media. This could then be related back to the relentless criticism by the media on issues such as HIV/Aids policy and Zimbabwe.

Furthermore, the 'national interest' can be linked to a nationalist dis-course of identity, as could be seen in statements by Mbeki in which he castigated the media for being 'fishers of corrupt men':

> We should not, and will not, abandon the offensive to defeat the insulting campaigns further to entrench a stereotype that has, for cen-turies, sought to portray Africans as a people that are corrupt, given to telling lies, prone to theft and self-enrichment by immoral means, a people that are otherwise contemptible in the eyes of the 'civilized'.
>
> (Mbeki 2003)

Although these debates could be informed by the media and the government's need to protect their respective interests, they can also function, on another level, as a normative discourse pertaining to the essence of democracy, the role of the media, and the function of news reporting. These normative debates can then also be linked to broader discourses on the post-apartheid nation and divergent interpretations of the nature of the nascent democracy.

It is not only on the terrain of the media that the search for a 'national interest' steered policy debates and decisions in post-apartheid South Africa, as Vale (2003: 33) points out. Even on issues pertaining to the Southern African region, the role played by the newly democratic state beyond its borders was informed by the assertion of a new national identity within them.

The 'national interest' should also be seen against a tradition of debates around nationalism in the context of anti-apartheid discourse. The concept of 'nation' as used by the South African liberation movements was linked to a history of anti-colonial thought and struggles for self-determination, but contextualized and adapted for the South African context.[6] Post-apartheid critiques of the potential hegemonic potential of the concept 'national interest' should therefore also take cognisance of earlier attempts to define 'nation' in liberatory terms (see for instance Jordan 1988; Van Diepen 1988: 4). On the other hand, a narrowly defined Afrikaner nationalism provided the ideological underpinning of apartheid, and in the white community this form of nationalism was opposed to an English 'liberalism' (Jacobs 2004: 106).

In discussing the concept of 'national interest' in the context of the mass media, care should furthermore be taken not to equate the term willy-nilly with its use in other international contexts such as the United States, where it is used more in terms of measures to control the flow of information in the interest of state security (Acharya 2003). Given this history, it is perhaps understandable that attempts to foster national unity through refashioning concepts of nationhood would be met with some resistance from liberal democratic quarters.

With the establishment of democracy in South Africa in 1994, liberalism prevailed as the dominant political ethos, with an emphasis on individual rights and freedom. However, a contesting interpretation informed by black nationalism also exists (Johnson and Jacobs 2004). From the liberal point of view, individual rights are more important than allegiance to the 'nation' (Gouws 2003: 42), and concomitantly attempts to elicit the media's support for nation-building would be met with resistance from this perspective. Since freedom of the press is one of the central indicators (along with multi-party elections, separation of powers and economic growth) of liberal democracy (Gouws 2003: 42), claims by the post-apartheid government that the media should assist in nation-building were often read by critics of these proposals within the developmental framework (see McQuail 1983) and consequently viewed as attempts to limit media freedom (De Beer 2002). This reaction should in part also be understood against the backdrop of changing notions of citizenship in late modernity. Loyalty towards the nation-state has diminished more and more in favour of a notion of identity based on freedom of choice and loose communal bonds. At the same time, the autonomous nation-state itself has come under increased pressure from global capital networks (Robins 2003: 243, 245).

Both the terms 'national interest' and 'public interest' may be inadequate to describe the challenges facing the South African media ten years after democracy. Harber (2002) is of the opinion that both these schools of thought 'put their adherents into political corners where they tend to produce predictable and shallow journalism'. Habib (2004) points out that viewing the media's role to be the furtherance of the national interest rests on the incorrect assumption that the national interest is made up of a collective of individual interests and that the majority can correctly establish what is in the national interest.

The concept of 'public interest' assumes a homogeneity of a public, which is in fact divided along racial, ethnic and class lines. Critics such as former chairperson of Sanef, Mathatha Tsedu, and the ANC member of parliament (and, since 2004, minister of arts and culture) Pallo Jordan have also highlighted this problem inherent in speaking about the 'public interest' in South Africa. Tsedu noted that one could discern two 'publics' in South Africa – a vocal public, which is able to articulate and promote its own interests by means of the mass media, and a voiceless public, whose interests are marginalized (Duncan 2003: 6). Jordan (2004) argues that, since the mainstream media have racial, gender, class and regional biases, more attempts should be made to give members of this 'second public' access to the media.

Habib (2004) also suggests that the media's role in terms of reflecting the plurality of voices in South African society will only come about not only when media ownership is more pluralized, but also when the mainstream media asserts their independence from 'narrow commercial interests' to such an extent that the interest of the currently marginalized is also brought in the media spotlight. This is echoed by Ferial Haffajee, the editor of an influential (and, during apartheid, alternative) weekly, the *Mail and Guardian*. Quoting findings of a Konrad Adenauer Stiftung study that showed that the biggest threats to freedom of expression come from within – from the pressures brought about by advertisers, understaffing and advertorials masquerading as journalism – Haffajee suggested that the 'tortured debate' about the national versus public interest should give way to debate about how the public interest can be served, but without resorting to clashes between opposition and government (Haffajee 2004). For her, the challenge is to 'make a journalism that matters' by 'moving the epicentre of journalism' to the poor and marginalized.

Perhaps the crucial issue is therefore not whether the media should choose between serving the 'national interest' or the 'public interest', but how it conceives of 'nation' and 'public'. Who constitutes the 'public' in whose interest the mainstream claims to work? This is a question that warrants critical discussion.

Historical stages in news reporting

One way of dealing with the question posed above is to take a historical view of the role of the media in society.[7]

Societies experiencing conflict, especially racial conflict, and press reporting thereof, often face similar problems. Wilson and Gutiérrez (1995: 150) identify five stages experienced by the press in the US: exclusionary, threatening issue, confrontation, stereotypical selection and multi-racial coverage. As the following sections show, the present press situation in South Africa seems to reflect all five stages collapsed into one. They have become the latent or manifest press policy norm for South Africa.

Exclusionary phase

The history of apartheid news reporting is to a large extent that of racial exclusion. Even some liberal-minded newspapers treated black people as part of the 'native question' during the first half of the twentieth century, while the Afrikaans press promoted the idea of 'separate development'. Spokespersons for the black majority feel that in the new South Africa not enough news is being made available to and about the black community. On the other hand, many white (especially Afrikaans-speaking) South Africans experience a sense of exclusion from the new societal structures, and have interpreted their loss of power and privilege as a relegation to being '*bywoners in die land van hul geboorte*' (share-croppers in the land of their birth) (*Die Burger*, 7 January 1997).

Threatening-issue phase

While many arguments were offered for the implementation of apartheid, the perceived 'threat posed by black people' was grounded to a large extent in the fear the white minority felt in being surrounded by a majority of black Africans on the southern tip of the continent. This fear became apparent in especially the vast coverage given in the 1990s and early 2000s to conflict-ridden reports on crime. On the other hand, explicit racial polarization was to a large extent missing in the reporting leading up to the 2004 elections. Very little reporting continued to strengthen the perception of blacks being the cause for the tide of crime engulfing the country, while at the same time fuelling white fears and new racial strife. On the contrary, an overview of media reporting in the period 2003–4 showed that more and more news stories were published as news *per se* without an overt racial overtone overriding news decisions.[8]

Confrontation phase

While in the apartheid era black South Africans were left outside the political system, in post-apartheid South Africa the disillusionment with the outcome of political processes were not limited to whites having to come to grips with their new minority status, but also occurred among the unemployed black poor who felt that election promises were not being fulfilled. The finding of the Turner Commission in the US with regard to civil disorders of a press that 'has too long basked in a White world, looking out of it, if at all, with White men's eyes and a White perspective' (see Wilson and Gutiérrez 1995: 154) was also taken to the extreme in South Africa. As Mandela argued in 1994, the structure of the media meant that they generally upheld a white perspective on the country. With changes in ownership and editorial structure, an attempt was made to change this perspective, although the extent to which this was successful is still cause for debate.

Stereotypical selection phase

After racial confrontation over decades, a peaceful negotiated revolution was obtained in South Africa in 1994. Social order (see Wilson and Gutierrez 1995: 156–8) had to be restored, and a transition to a post-conflict period had to be made. While several critics have argued that the media is still not dealing with news topics that affect the black majority, the media catering for a white readership or audience often reported on white perceptions of crime and loss of job opportunities. However, the way the media reported on the 2004 elections showed a movement away from this phase of racial stereotyping towards a new emphasis on gender.

Multi-racial coverage phase

'Multi-racial news coverage is the earlier antithesis of exclusion' (Wilson and Gutiérrez 1995: 158–61). If it is to become the goal and policy of the (South African) news media, the last vestiges of prejudice and racism must be removed from the (news) gatekeeper ranks. The distinction between 'us' and 'them' will be less based on race, although the racial categories of apartheid might have to be upheld when necessary to deal with the inheritance of the past. Questions surrounding hegemony, resistance and 'race' arguably still need to form part of investigations into post-apartheid society, since they have been the master narratives during apartheid South Africa and their legacy cannot be dispensed with too easily (Distiller and Steyn

2004; Wasserman and Jacobs 2003: 17). Eventually, the ideal of multi-racial news coverage is that news will be reported from the perspective that 'us' represents all citizens (see Wilson and Gutiérrez 1995: 158–61).

For this point to be reached, affirmative action and black empowerment policies are seen as the main thrust towards the goal. However, the reality remains that the South African press is still very much divided, with, for example, Afrikaans newspapers, such as *Beeld* and *Die Burger*, emphasizing news important to their reader base, and black English-language newspapers, such as *Sowetan* and *New Nation*, almost exclusively covering news related to the black community. While large broadcast institutions like the SABC were being transformed to reflect the true demographic profile of the country (with a black majority), many whites were turning their radio and television receivers off or (when they could afford it) turning to privatized cultural channels such as the subscriber-only Afrikaans-language KykNET.

Conclusions

The media in South Africa today enjoys formal freedoms unheard of before democratization. These freedoms are constitutionally entrenched and it is unlikely that they will be tampered with at a statutory level. Much more likely, in the face of increased commercial competition, erosion of the journalistic skill-base and the structural make-up of the media sector, is that internal pressures in the industry will prevent it from adequately assessing its role in society and creatively repositioning itself with a view to the public at large. That this repositioning needs to be done remains important, however, if the media is to navigate a route for itself between the two narrow conceptions of a state-led national interest and a public interest that is defined on the basis of its profitability alone. A decade was too short for the completion of this arduous task.

Notes

1 This section draws on a more detailed discussion of post-apartheid ethical frameworks in Wasserman and Boloka (2004).
2 Some commentators (cited in Duncan 2003) have remarked that these regulatory bodies are not sufficient to ensure that the mainstream media are accountable to the broad public, and have called for the establishment of more non-commercial media outlets to serve the interests of communities and for the establishment of a so-called 'Fifth Estate' (i.e. the broader public) that would 'hold journalists at profit-driven media outlets accountable to the traditional democratic responsibilities of the media as "Fourth Estate"'.
3 In the light of the difficulties that the linguistic diversity of South Africa poses to especially the public broadcaster with its mandate of serving the whole of South African society, the Internet has also shown itself to be a suitable site for the creation of publication niches for Afrikaans, a language that suddenly after 1994 found itself in a minority position in the public media (Wasserman 2002).

4 As Duncan (2003: 5) points out, it is impossible to cite any set of responses as representing that of *the* media. References to the media here should therefore be seen as a broad assessment of the dominant discourse emanating from this sector, and not as a conclusive statement.

5 As Krabill (2001: 586) has pointed out, the South African media also played other roles in relation to the Truth and Reconciliation Commission outside the institutional investigation: as an observer and critic of the process and as a channel through which its work has been communicated to society at large.

6 Apartheid was, for instance, seen as a 'colonialism of a special type', where colonizer and colonized occupied the same territory. The applicability of colonialist terminology to define apartheid is a debatable topic, but such a discussion falls outside the scope of this chapter. It should be noted that nationalism in the context that it was used by the ANC was a non-racial concept (Jordan 1988: 115).

7 This section is based on an earlier version published as De Beer (2002).

8 Unpublished remarks made by Mondli Makhanya and Ferial Haffajee during a World Press Freedom Day Conference organized by the Department of Journalism, Stellenbosch University, South Africa, 3 May 2004.

References

Acharya, A. (2003) *The War in Iraq. Morality or National Interest?* Singapore: Institute of Defence and Strategic Studies, Nanyang Technological University. Online. Available HTTP: <http://www.ntu.edu/sg/idss/Perspective/research_050311.htm> (accessed 2 February 2004).

Addison, G. (2003) 'The road to populism', *The Media,* June: 19–24.

Chotia, F. and Jacobs, S. (2002) 'Remaking the presidency', in S. Jacobs and R. Calland (eds) *Thabo Mbeki's World,* Scottsville: University of Natal Press, 145–61.

De Beer, A.S. (ed.) (2000) 'Focus on media and racism', special edition, *Ecquid-Novi* 21(2): 280.

—— (2002) 'The South African press. No strangers to conflict', in E. Gilboa (ed.) *Media and Conflict. Framing Issues, Making Policy, Shaping Opinions,* Ardsley, NY: Transnational Publishers, 263–80.

——(2003) 'A long walk to freedom, and a steep road to nation-building. The role of the media in post-apartheid South Africa', in K. Ross and D. Derman (eds) *Mapping the Margins. Identity Politics and Media,* Cresskill, NJ: Hampton Press, 97–111.

——(2004) 'South Africa', in B.-E. Lange and D. Ward (eds) *The Media and Elections. A Handbook and Comparative Study,* Mahwah, NJ: Lawrence Erlbaum, 77–99.

De Beer, A.S. and Steyn, E. (2002) 'Sanef's 2002 national journalism skills audit', *Ecquid Novi* 23(1): 11–86. Online. Available HTTP: <http://www.inasp.info/ajol/journals/en/vol23no1abs.html#1> (accessed 4 September 2002).

Distiller, N. and Steyn, M. (eds) (2004) *Performances of Race,* Cape Town: Heinemann.

Duncan, J. (2003) *Another Journalism is Possible. Critical Challenges for the Media in South Africa* (Centre for Civil Society Research Report no. 10), Durban: Centre for Civil Society.

Fourie, P.J. (2002) 'Rethinking the role of the media in South Africa', *Communicare,* 21(1, July): 17–40.

Froneman, J.D. (1994) 'Redes vir die gebruik aan 'n ingeligte, lewendige debat oor media-etiek' [Reasons for the lack of an intelligent, lively debate about media ethics], *Ecquid Novi,* 15(1): 123–8.

Giffard, C.A., De Beer, A.S. and Steyn, E. (1997) 'New media for the New South

Africa', in F. Eribo and W. Jong-Ebot (eds) *Press Freedom and Communication in Africa*, Trenton, NJ: Africa World Press, 75–99.

Gouws, A. (2003) 'The importance of political tolerance for fostering social cohesion', in D. Chidester, P. Dexter and W. James (eds) *What Holds us Together. Social Cohesion in South Africa*, Cape Town: Human Science Research Council Publishers, 42–66.

Habib, A. (2004) Public Lecture at the South African National Editors' Forum Media Seminar Series 'A Review of the Media in the First Decade of Democracy', Cape Town, 2 July 2004.

Hachten, W.A. and Giffard, C.A. (1984) *Total Onslaught. The South African Press Under Attack*, Johannesburg: Macmillan.

Haffajee, F. (2004) Public Lecture at the South African National Editors' Forum Media Seminar Series 'A Review of the Media in the First Decade of Democracy', Cape Town, 2 July 2004.

Harber, A. (2002) 'Journalism in the age of the market', Harold Wolpe Memorial Lecture, Centre for Civil Society, University of Natal, Durban, September. Online. Available HTTP: <http://www.nu.ac.za/ccs/default.asp?3,28,10,452> (accessed 13 March 2003).

Jackson, G. (1993) *Breaking Story. The South African Story*, Oxford: Westview Press.

Jacobs, S. (2004) *Public Sphere, Power and Democratic Politics. Media and Policy Debates in Post-apartheid South Africa*, Ph.D. Dissertation, University of London, Birkbeck College.

Johnson, K. and Jacobs, S. (2004) 'Democratization and the rhetoric of rights. Contradictions and debate in post-apartheid South Africa', in F. Nyamnjoh and H. Englund (eds) *Rights and Politics of Recognition in Africa*, London: Zed Books.

Jordan, P. (1988) 'The South African liberation movement and the making of a new nation', in M. Van Diepen (ed.) *The National Question in South Africa*, London: Zed Books, 110–24.

——(2004) 'Uncovering two nations', *The Media Online*. Online. Available HTTP: <http://www.themedia.co.za> (accessed 3 March 2004).

Krabill, R. (2001) 'Symbiosis. Mass media and the Truth and Reconciliation Commission of South Africa', *Media, Culture and Society*, 23(5): 585–603.

McQuail, D. (1983) *Mass Communication Theory. An Introduction*, London: Sage.

Mandela, N. (1994) Address to the International Press Institute, Cape Town, 14 February. Online. Available HTTP: <http://www.anc.org.za/ancdocs/history/mandela/1994/sp940214.html> (accessed 17 March 2004).

Maré, G. (2003) 'The state of the state. Contestation and re-assertion in a neo-liberal terrain', in J. Daniel, A. Habib and R. Southall (eds) *State of the Nation. South Africa 2003–2004*, Cape Town: Human Science Research Council Publishers, 25–52.

Mbeki, T. (2003) 'Our country needs facts, not groundless allegations' [Letter from the President], *ANC Today*, 3(21), 30 May. Online. Available HTTP: <http://www.anc.org.za/ancdocs/anctoday/2003/text/at21.txt> (accessed 16 June 2003).

Media Institute of Southern Africa (2004) *So This is Democracy? State of the Media in Southern Africa*, Windhoek: Misa.

Netshitenzhe, J. (2002) 'Should the media serve the public or national interest?'. Presentation to the Goedgedacht Forum for Social Reflection, Cape Town, 19 October. Online. Available HTTP: <http://www.gcis.gov.za/media/ceo/021019.htm> (accessed 19 February 2004).

Oosthuizen, L.M. (2002) *Media Ethics in the South African Context*, Lansdowne, Cape Town: Juta.

Retief, J. (2002) *Media Ethics. An Introduction to Responsible Journalism*, Cape Town: Oxford University Press.

Rhodes Journalism Review (1997) 'Special edition. The media and the TRC', 14 (May), Grahamstown, South Africa: Department of Journalism and Media Studies, Rhodes University.

Robins, S. (2003) 'Grounding "globalisation from below". "Global citizens" in local spaces', in D. Chidester, P. Dexter and W. James (eds) *What Holds us Together. Social Cohesion in South Africa*, Cape Town: Human Science Research Council Publishers, 23–41.

Satgar, V. (2002) 'Thabo Mbeki and the South African Communist Party', in S. Jacobs and R. Calland (eds) *Thabo Mbeki's World*, Scottsville, Natal: University of Natal Press, 163–77.

Shepperson, A. and Tomaselli, K. (2002) 'Ethics. A radical justice approach', *Ecquid Novi*, 23(2): 278–89.

Switzer, L. (ed.) (1997) *South Africa's Alternative Press. Voices of Protest and Resistance, 1880s–1960s*, Cambridge, UK: Cambridge University Press.

Switzer, L. and Adhikari, M. (eds) (2000) *South Africa's Resistance Press. Alternative Voices in the Last Generation Under Apartheid*, Athens, OH: Ohio University Press.

Tomaselli, K. (2000) 'South African media, 1994–7. Globalizing via political economy', in J. Curran and M. Park (eds) *De-Westernizing Media Studies*, London: Routledge, 279–92.

Tomaselli, K. and Dunn, H. (eds) (2001) *Media, Democracy, and Renewal in Southern Africa*, Colorado Springs, CO: International Academic Publishers.

Tomaselli, K. and Louw, P.E. (eds) (1991) *The Alternative Press in South Africa*, Bellville: Anthropos.

Tomaselli, K., Tomaselli, R. and Muller, J. (eds) (1989) *Currents of Power. State Broadcasting in South Africa*, Bellville: Anthropos.

Vale, P. (2003) 'Sovereignty, identity, and the prospects for southern Africa's people', in D. Chidester, P. Dexter and W. James (eds) *What Holds us Together. Social Cohesion in South Africa*, Cape Town: Human Science Research Council Publishers, 23–41.

Van Diepen, M. (1988) 'Introduction', in M. Van Diepen (ed.) *The National Question in South Africa*, London: Zed Books, 4–11.

Wasserman, H. (2002) 'Between the local and the global. South African languages and the Internet', *African and Asian Studies*, 1(4): 303–21.

Wasserman, H. and Boloka, M. (2004) 'Privacy, the press and the public interest in post-apartheid South Africa', *Parliamentary Affairs*, 57(1): 185–95.

Wasserman, H. and De Beer, A.S. (2004) 'E-governance and e-publicanism. Preliminary perspectives on the role of the Internet in South African democratic processes', *Communicatio*, 20(1): 64–89.

Wasserman, H. and Jacobs, S. (eds) (2003) *Shifting Selves. Postapartheid Essays on Mass Media, Culture and Identity*, Cape Town: Kwela.

Wasserman, H. and Van Zyl, L. (2003) 'Independent or embedded? An exploration of views of the Presidential Press Corps', *Communicare*, 22(1): 117–30.

Wilson, C.C. and Gutiérrez, F. (1995) *Race, Multiculturalism, and the Press. From Mass to Class Communication*, Thousand Oaks: Sage.

5 In journalism we trust?

Credibility and fragmented journalism in Latin America

Silvio Waisbord

After the return of democratic rule in the 1980s and 1990s, opinion polls reported that journalism in Latin America had achieved unusual levels of trust, both in terms of historical standards and in comparison with other institutions.[1] Since then, credibility seems to have been slipping. Whilst trust ranged between 80 and 90 per cent in the mid-1990s, in recent polls the regional average has hovered around 50 per cent.

This change has prompted speculation about the reasons for such ups and downs (Zeta de Pozo 2001). Journalists and press scholars generally explain changes in public trust as the product of press performance. High levels of trust during the early and mid-1990s were interpreted mainly in terms of the impact of watchdog journalism in the region. Amid an unusual climate of freedom of expression in the post-authoritarian period, various news organizations produced a number of exposés of government wrongdoing and other cases of malfeasance (Hernandez 2003; Waisbord 2000). In a region with a long history of authoritarianism and cosy relationships between governments and big media, journalistic exposés had been rare. Ferocious battles inside administrations, publishers' politics and the tenacity and courage of reporters resulted in a series of denunciations that, in many cases, contributed to the resignation of powerful officials – including the presidents of Brazil and Ecuador.

However, the role of watchdog reporting in raising press credibility may not be as straightforward as some have argued. It is not obvious that the investigations conducted by a handful of news organizations benefited the reputation of the press as a whole. Without exception, it was not the press *in toto*, but rather a few news organizations that published hard-hitting stories in each country. We lack evidence to conclude categorically that publishing exposés helped the press or some specific news outlets to become trustworthy in the public mind. Also, variations in public trust in the press do not exactly correspond to the evolution of watchdog journalism. Even when the press began to lose credibility in some countries towards the late 1990s, news organizations continued to publish investigative stories. If watchdog reporting contributed positively to public trust in the press in the first years of democratic rule, why did it not continue to have similar effects?

A similar reasoning is used to explain decreasing levels of credibility in recent years. If 'good' performance accounts for high credibility, then 'poor' performance apparently explains why trust has declined. Current trends in the contemporary press – such as dumbed-down news, unfettered commercialism, the overabundance of celebrity news, blatant partisanism and ethical transgressions – are blamed for decreasing trust (Castro Caycedo 1999; Gargurevich 2000; Torrico 1999). However, such explanations fail to establish an unequivocal causal relation between the quality of press performance and trust. They simply assume that those trends negatively affect public trust. Also, they fail to recognize that those characteristics have been ubiquitous in the region's press for quite some time. Why did they affect public perception negatively only in recent years?

Perhaps press performance affects credibility, but the relationship between them seems more complex than that suggested by conventional arguments. Explanations that single out press performance as the independent variable affecting public credibility *assume* rather than demonstrate the impact of specific forms of news coverage on trust. The assumption is premised on a specific model of what constitutes 'the good journalism' in democratic life. Fluctuations in trust are believed to reflect whether actual news coverage meets the ideal of a journalism that holds government accountable and pursues the truth. So if trust is high, journalism appears to effectively fulfil its democratic mission. In contrast, if trust declines, it is because journalism falls short of serving democratic goals. This line of argument is problematic because its fails to understand trust as the product of a pact between journalism and audiences. A particular social exchange underlies trust in journalism, or for that matter in any other institution (Cook 2001). Trust is contingent on social expectations about performance (Luhmann 1980); it is not determined by performance standards unilaterally determined by journalists or press analysts. Trust in the press rests on specific expectations and whether those expectations are met. Consequently, for the press (or a specific news organization) to be trusted, it does not necessarily have to perform according to prescriptions of what 'the good journalism' should be. Rather, it needs to meet citizens' expectations, which may or may not resemble any of the requirements established in press models.

Yet expectations vary among audiences. Someone's credible, quality reporting may be someone else's unreliable, sloppy journalism. Bonds of confidence between audiences and the press, and between audiences and specific news organizations and journalists run the whole gamut. From highbrow broadsheets to tabloids, all news outlets expect to gain audience confidence. Trust is segmented, however, because audiences and the press are not homogeneous. Matters of cultural distinction (in Pierre Bourdieu's sense) inform not only the audience's taste and preferences but also their expectations about trustworthiness.

Also, the heterogeneity of the press determines how different news organizations build trust and aim to meet audience expectations. In Latin America, the press is a highly diverse institution, integrated by a myriad of organizations that, besides producing and disseminating information about current affairs, share little in common. Various interests and criteria inform news judgments, reporting styles and bonds of trust with audiences. Consequently, when discussing how the press should build and maintain public confidence, we need to define what press we are talking about. The broadsheet that wears its politics on its sleeves? The headline-screaming, blood-drenched tabloid? The television talk-show host who exploits human frailties? The cable news anchor who reads wires? The celebrity pundit who hawks partisan views? The blogger who dispenses first-hand, unchecked accounts? The non-governmental organization that promotes specific policies on its website? Of course, these different forms of journalism are not unique to the region. What is important to underline is that, in addition to the long existence of a variety of journalistic forms and styles, recent developments have further deepened the fragmentation of journalism and the consolidation of different trust-building strategies. More than the 'end of journalism' (Bromley 1997), we are witnessing major transformations in journalistic practices that throw into question the notion of journalism as a unified institution.

This chapter examines the reasons for the dispersion of journalistic practices and the ways in which news organizations aim to gain trust from audiences in Latin America. It suggests that the analysis of trust in the press needs to avoid the assumptions of the professional model of journalism, according to which a trustworthy press needs to be fair, objective and bound to predetermined ethics. The shortcoming of this position is not its promotion of a specific journalistic model, but rather its incapacity to understand that trust is a relational process between journalists and audiences. It is not a question of what journalistic practices are desirable, no matter what practices are prescribed, but rather, the result of a contract between news producers and consumers. Trust is vastly more complicated than whether journalists observe any given set of 'professional' norms. It is an issue of whether journalism actually meets social expectations, expectations that do not neatly fit a conventional model of journalism that fundamentally assigns to the press the role of providing factual information that citizens need to live in a democracy.

Fragmented journalism

Until a few decades ago, it seemed somewhat straightforward what and who the press was: newspapers and newsweeklies, news wire services, and television and radio newscasts. Journalistic practices evolved in a context of relative stability, generally with limited access to technological resources for the production and distribution of news. Today, journalism has become fragmented, with a proliferation of news produced by organizations that follow multiple criteria and interests. The unlimited universe of print and broadcast news that blends information and entertainment, and the wealth of information on the Web, are evidence of fragmented journalism. The production and distribution of news is no longer the monopoly of what had been conventionally understood as journalism. There has been a diversification of the journalistic rules according to which daily events are processed into news.

Fragmented journalism has not resulted in the levelling of opportunities for news production or the democratization of access, as techno-enthusiasts have suggested. The growing power of a handful of companies that reap the lion's share in advertising and audience markets has deepened inequalities in Latin American countries (Belinche 2001; Cajías de la Vega and López 1999; Fox and Waisbord 2002; Rockwell and Janus 2003; Sunkel 2001). However, the fragmentation of journalism and media concentration are not antithetical. The implications of business mergers for journalistic practices and reporting styles are more varied than political economists usually recognize. Multimedia business interests affect news content and reduce diversity, but do not necessarily turn news into a homogeneous, uniform product. The impact of ownership concentration on content cannot simply be predicted (Waisbord 2002). Even within the same media company, different practices and norms are used to produce news for reasons that range from audience segmentation strategies to conflicts among owners.

Nor is it clear that the recent wave of media concentration has affected news content in ways that differ from those seen in the past, when giant companies were quasi-monopolies (the cases of Globo in Brazil and Televisa in Mexico are the most obvious examples) or authoritarian governments held a tight grip on news content through physical repression, formal censorship and subtle intimidation. True, many media markets are becoming imperfect duopolies as two conglomerates control the leading newspapers, magazines, and television and radio stations, and expand into the telecommunications business. However, this process is only one dimension of recent developments in the region. Today, a vast and chaotic volume of news that reaches audiences at local and national levels does not pass through the same newsroom filters. In the multi-level world of journalism, some news organizations still tower above the rest in terms of their power to set the news agenda and reach influential and large audiences. Their brand of journalism, however, is neither homogeneous nor sets common principles for news reporting that are followed across the board. This is why generalizations about 'the press' and 'journalism' need to be taken cautiously in an increasingly diversified news landscape.

What drives the fragmentation of journalism? First, a structure of multiple entry-point and relatively low-cost access promotes the dispersion of news through the Internet. The observation that any person with Internet access could potentially become a journalist exaggerates the point. However, the multiplication of information-producing sites operated by a variety of organizations and individuals that ignore conventional journalistic rules does put in place new conditions that contribute to the dispersion of journalism – if not, as some have rushed to conclude, the complete demassification of the news media and the twilight of large media companies. The latter still have tremendous advantages in terms of political influence and economic power. The proliferation of cyberspace news does, however, usher in new conditions as it bypasses established news organizations and offers information sources that are increasingly used and consulted by established newsrooms.

Second, changes in media content have also resulted in the proliferation of news. Profit goals, particularly when advertising expenditures decrease amid recurrent economic crises, have driven media executives to favour low-budget genres to fill weekly schedules of radio and television stations. What cheaper way to complete the increasing number of programming grids than with newscasts, talk shows and other shows that turn headline news into comedy and commentary? Radio airwaves, particularly during the popular morning slots, are filled with programmes in which DJs and hosts lead chatter about news, and liberally mix facts with opinions, official with unknown sources and information with entertainment. Television offers plenty of talk shows that indiscriminately blend news and entertainment, and 'hard' and 'soft' news. Although these programmes hardly report news according to standard newsroom conventions, their immense popularity makes them part of the daily news flow. Like traditional journalism, they are about 'reality' rather than fiction. Some use typical journalistic resources to present news: talk-show hosts discuss 'the news of the day' with guests and audiences, political satires feature faux anchors reading headlines, and conventional newsmakers (for example public officials, experts, celebrities) are regularly invited to offer opinions on a variety of topics.

Politics and the absence of a journalistic canon

The fragmentation of journalism takes place in a socio-political context already conducive to the dispersion of journalistic practices. Journalistic practices and standards vary widely throughout the region. Some news organizations expect reporters to sell advertising to complement low salaries and bring additional business; others condemn such practices and punish reporters who trade favours. Some encourage reporters to selectively criticize specific actors based on editorial calculations; others avoid hard-hitting news altogether. Some carefully expunge personal views from reporting; others constantly mix facts and opinions. Some are suspected of selling headlines and blackmailing business and newsmakers; others practice honest journalism. Some offer reporters a certain degree of autonomy in selecting news content and frames; others tightly control their newsrooms. Some are mouthpieces for influential politicians and business; others try to maintain some powerful interests at arm's length.

Historically, there has not been a consensus among either the leading news organizations or journalists about news gathering and reporting practices (Fernández Christlieb 2002; Ossandón and Santa Cruz 2001; Peñaranda Undurruga 1999; Zeta de Pozo *et al.* 2004). There has not been a canon that dictates practices across the board. Neither the model of partisan journalism nor the model of 'objective' reporting – the theoretical bookends of modern journalism – became hegemonic. Whilst some have championed the liberal model of a journalism that even-handedly chronicles daily events by reporting facts and observing ethical principles, others have defended a journalism of ideas and opinions. Whilst some believe that journalism's democratic mission is to actively engage citizens in public dialogue, others think that the reporting of government abuses is its main contribution to democratic governance. Constant debates within mainstream journalism about whether journalism is a profession or an art, whether it should be limited to narrate 'real' stories or promote specific world views, or whether it should openly propagandize political and ideological positions, have reflected the lack of a common ground on which to define daily practices.

A journalistic consensus was unthinkable given the absence of a broader political and economic consensus. If we take the US experience in the post-war period, for example, a consensus about fundamental journalistic principles was possible only when a wider consensus existed on key political (liberal democracy, individualism, global supremacy) and economic (free-market capitalism) issues. In Latin America, in contrast, persistent political instability reflected the lack of consensus among key social forces upon which a common set of norms could have existed. Nor were news organizations removed from political divisions. In fact, because they have been typically aligned with specific interests, the press actively promoted divisions, fuelling recurrent political crisis. When news organizations neither pretend to promote distinctive political positions nor attempt to be above the political fray, there is no room for journalism to follow a set of coherent norms.

Despite the consolidation of liberal democracy in the region, such dynamics have not disappeared. Divisions inside the press, subtly expressed when politics runs a normal course, become wide open when political confrontations peak such as, to name a few, during the administrations of Chavez in Venezuela, Fujimori in Peru and Mahuad in Ecuador in the past years (Cordova de Alcazar 2003; Diaz Rangel 2002; Fowks 2000; Macassi Lavander 2001; Sant Roz 2003). In these cases, news organizations relegated any pretence of impartiality, championed partisan positions and actively promoted the political crisis. The press was not simply the stage for political conflicts, but rather it became a main protagonist. Rather than attempting to build a common journalistic ground, news organizations openly confronted and accused each other.

The political fault lines dividing news organizations are not the same as they were in the past. Recent transformations in political and economic structures have altered the articulation between socio-political groups and the press that existed for much of the past century. Recent neoliberal policies coupled with technological transformations have profoundly changed the socio-economic and political map. Groups that historically patronized specific news organizations – such as the 'national' bourgeoisie, industrial workers, and peasants' and miners' unions – have lost much of their power. In Bolivia, for example, union newspapers and miners' radio stations closed down as their social basis became politically weakened and membership reduced.

The weakening of partisan identities and the emergence of new forms of political participation have also changed the linkages between society and the press. The brutal reversal of the electoral fortunes of traditional parties in the 1980s and 1990s in Bolivia, Peru and Venezuela affected the press environment as sympathetic news organizations were forced either to shut down or search for new financial supporters. In countries such as Colombia, the historical linkages between parties and news organizations have become weaker due to the fact that, amidst unprecedented changes in press economies, party leaders sold press organizations to giant business corporations.

In this context, old-fashioned partisan journalism is impossible, mainly because there are virtually no political parties that could serve as long-lasting political and economic anchors. Apart from the news organizations that act as partisan megaphones due to circumstantial interests of their owners or because they are political projects funded by government officials, business pragmatism dictates that the economic interest of leading news organizations are better served by cultivating contacts with a variety of politicians and parties instead of tying their fortunes to one party. In today's Latin America, the big media have a longer lifespan than political parties and electoral coalitions. Under these conditions, news organizations may reap temporary benefits from supporting individual politicians, but tying their long-term future to the uncertain fate of political parties is not a sound business decision. Also, the population is less attached to partisan identities and more prone to offer brief support to individual politicians than to political parties. Selling partisan news makes little commercial sense at a time when traditional partisan identities are weaker.

Simultaneously, changes in media economies affected the position of news organizations vis-à-vis political and market interests, particularly in wealthier countries. The bigger the market, the more news organizations and parent companies will take a commercialized approach, mainly because there are more potential sources of advertising. In some cases, the privatization of state-owned companies and the concomitant reduction of government advertising opened new business opportunities during the 1990s. Such changes make leading news companies more sensitive to the interests of large advertisers than to government officials, particularly if the latter do not control a substantial amount of economic and political resources that affect their corporate strategies.

These changes, however, hardly leave administrations empty-handed in dealing with the media. They are still able to pull levers that can make or break, advance or undermine, the finances of companies (Fernandez Bogado 2002). For example, the break-up of one-party rule in Mexico after the electoral defeat of the Partido Revolucionario Institucional in 2000 caused financial difficulties and the eventual closure of *Excelsior* and other dailies that had been identified with the party. In Peru, the tabloids that acted as the attack dogs of the Fujimori administration during the 1990s had to close after the sudden collapse of the government when extensive cash-for-coverage dealings involving owners and prominent officials were made public (Conaghan 2002). Likewise, news organizations that lived exclusively off the largess of the juntas had to close after their patrons were put out of power in the 1980s. Close ties between governments and the press continue, particularly in economically depressed regions where the former are the leading advertisers and control other resources such as media legislation, import permits, tax audits and credits on state-owned banks. Consequently, national and state administrations continue to play a key role in press economies that underlie *quid pro quo* dynamics between governments and the press.

Against the backdrop of political and economic differences among news organizations, a unified canon of professional norms has also been impossible because journalists themselves have not been particularly interested in developing and consolidating a set of common ideals. The emergence of professional norms requires journalists consciously to pursue internal group solidarity to gain social legitimacy and control reporting practices and education (Schudson 2001). Such efforts have been largely absent in Latin America. In fact, journalists have repeatedly remarked upon the lack of group solidarity, with journalists accusing each other or, more tragically, assisting authoritarian regimes in the persecution of other journalists and publishers (Rey 2003).

Journalists have not put to rest the old debates about whether journalism is a profession or a social practice closer to art or to political militancy, or whether the social legitimacy of journalism should derive from observing 'professional' norms. In some countries, the efforts of journalists' unions to promote the mandatory certification of reporters (including holding a professional degree) neither fostered group solidarity nor contributed to controlling newsroom practices. Even in countries where it was introduced (such as Brazil), certification did not homogenize newsroom practices. Unions generally approached certification as a way of reducing owners' access to the labour market and thus protecting salaries rather than as a way of promoting common reporting norms or activating a professional consciousness.

Nor have university journalism programmes been the catalyst for the development of a common set of professional norms. Although some of the most prestigious programmes have existed since the 1920s, it does not seem that tertiary education is a sufficient requirement to harmonize practices and inculcate similar ideals. In fact, debates about whether college education necessarily qualifies reporters still continue, and the figure of the self-made reporter who learned the craft in the newsroom is still held aloft.

Some forms of collective action do suggest a nascent solidarity among journalists. Since the return of democratic rule in the 1980s and 1990s, groups of journalists have come together to defend constitutional rights, denounce anti-press violence, support the passing and observance of information-access legislation, and oppose government initiatives to pass 'gag' laws in Argentina, Brazil, Chile and Mexico (Canton and Loreti 2000). In Colombia, journalists from different news organizations have agreed common guidelines on covering political violence to prevent the press being manipulated by the drug traffickers, death squads and guerrillas who have been responsible for the deaths of thousands of citizens, including scores of reporters, in the past decades. Such actions of solidarity have had civic rather than professional goals. They aimed to raise attention to political issues and protect rights that affect the work of journalists. They acted as civic movements that exemplified 'social accountability' (Peruzzotti and Smulovitz 2002) in action – that is, citizens' efforts to hold powerful actors accountable for their actions – rather than movements primarily interested in affecting newsroom practices. Also, they were not the catalyst for a consensus on professional practices because labour conditions remain heterogeneous, so reporters need to adjust their skills and practices to different expectations inside news organizations.

Trust-building strategies and models of journalism

Given the fragmentation of journalism and the persistent absence of a consensus on journalistic norms and practices, journalists use different strategies to build trust among audiences. Trust-building strategies are based on two sets of expectations: professional and ideological. Whilst one is premised on the idea that journalism is technically competent to deliver news, the second aims to build credibility on the notion that journalism defends particular interests. Whilst one says 'trust me, I'm an expert', the other says 'trust me, I'm one of us'. Whilst one corresponds to the model of 'journalism of information', the other one embraces the model of 'journalism of ideas'.

I will now analyse the differences between these trust-building strategies.

Journalism of information

Journalism of information aims to build trust based on the premise that journalists are technically competent, that is, they have a unique set of skills that makes them professional experts in news reporting. As Anthony Giddens (1991) has argued, citizens defer to experts with specialized knowledge in complex and differentiated societies. In this sense, journalists are presented as experts whose credentials and reliability are grounded in observing specific professional rules and methods.

The model of journalism of information looks to the scientific model to define its epistemological approach and claim to be a credible form of knowledge. It defines the mission of journalism as the presentation of facts collected through objective methods. Facts are presented as incontestable evidence of objective events that exist independently from ideological views. The methodological objectivity of the scientific discourse offers a way, if not to eliminate, at least to bracket off, subjectivity. Facticity and objectivity are required as guiding principles and legitimizing ideals of the 'journalism of information' because it is assumed that politics are inevitable. Journalism is not agnostic about the existence of politics; rather, it needs to find a way to keep politics at a distance. When politics is rejected as the source of inspiration of journalism's goals and methods, science is the alternative legitimizing discourse.

From this perspective, trust is defined as an issue of professional competency. A trustworthy journalist is the one who follows 'professional' conventions in news selection, gathering and reporting. As members of a community of practitioners, journalists define and accept those conventions as standard practices, taught in journalism schools and observed in newsrooms.

If journalism is expected to be a technical knowledge, trust is based on the idea that 'news experts' effectively follow a set of principles and methodologies to deliver facts. Because journalism reports on an incommensurable reality, the public rarely has the chance to compare whether journalistic accounts effectively render comprehensive, faithful accounts of 'reality'. It trusts journalism to do so. If journalism fails to fulfil its part of the transaction, repairing trust is seemingly difficult. Trust is difficult to build yet relatively easily damaged (O'Neill 2002). From this perspective, falsifying facts or presenting incomplete pictures of events violates trust agreements between reporters and audiences. This is why the invention of facts in news stories or the failure to provide a comprehensive view of events are considered to damage the trust in journalists and the press. Such conclusions are premised on the idea that audiences are expected to judge the performance of the press based on technical criteria rather than ideological sympathy.

This pact of credibility draws inspiration from the Enlightenment model that prescribes the need for an informed citizenship that makes decisions based on facts rather than ideology. One of journalism's main contribution to democratic life is to provide factual information that helps audiences make informed decisions and contributes to enlightened public debates. Journalism is assigned the role of fact-finding and reporting. Facticity is one of journalism's 'God-terms' (Zelizer 2004). Conventional news facts include verbal testimonies from eyewitnesses and experts, written documents, photographs, audio and film. The hegemony of facticity in contemporary journalism is demonstrated in several ways. Press exposés put together facts to demonstrate wrongdoing (Waisbord 2000). Partisan news organizations typically rely on facts to report events. Publications that put out fantastic, weird tales feel compelled to use facticity to support claims to be an authoritative source (think of photographic evidence of two-headed babies and first-hand quotes from Martians and UFO experts). Similarly, 'witness news', a popular feature of television newscasts, implicitly assumes that providing unmediated facts to audiences helps to build trust, such as when reporters are sent out to brave snowstorms, hurricanes and other 'good television moments' or are assigned to cover wars and sporting events *in situ.*

Journalism of opinion

Journalism of opinion uses different trust-building strategies because its pact of credibility with audiences is based on different premises. Whether journalists use 'professional' standards is less important than whether their reporting resonates ideologically with audiences. Emotional and ideological bonds are at the core of the relationship between journalists and audiences. Trust is contingent on whether news organizations and journalists are politically loyal to audiences.

Any journalism that deliberately defends specific views exemplifies this pact of credibility. Although the partisan press is emblematic of this tradition, it's not the only one or, for that matter, the dominant expression in contemporary Latin American journalism. A journalism of opinion is also practiced by news organizations that openly announce their positions on a set of issues or make no attempt to hide their alignments with governments and interest groups. It was journalism of opinion that inspired watchdog journalism as reporters and news organizations showed interest in fighting wrongdoing out of personal, political convictions or with the aim of damaging the reputation of specific officials and institutions.

When journalists are expected to perform as members of 'communities of ideas', typical professional considerations (fairness, ethical behaviour, public interest) are less important in building trust. In fact, the notion of 'professional journalism' is unclear because journalists ambiguously define themselves as members of a 'community of practice' and a 'community of ideas'. Journalism is not conceived as a separate institution with its own set of rules and procedures, but as a field of practice strad-dling politics and business. Ideological bonds rather than technical rules underlie the pact of trust between journalism and audiences. Journalists ask audiences to believe in them not because of their technical expertise, but because they are 'one of them'. What matters, above all, is whether journalists meet ideological expectations more than 'professional' consid-erations. Reporting 'just the facts', observing universal ethics or producing balanced stories are not unanimously accepted as measures of trustworthy journalism (Herrán and Restrepo 1995). Politics trumps professionalism. Greater commitment to certain ideals than to professional rules underlies the trust agreement between journalism and audiences.

Trust-building strategies in Latin America

In Latin America, both trust-building strategies have coexisted because both models of journalism have inspired news organizations and journal-ists. Building trust based on the professional competence of journalists has been difficult given the blurring of the boundaries between newsrooms and business interests, revolving-door dynamics between press and poli-tics, and the absence of efforts by journalists to build and maintain a common professional identity. Institutional expectations determine how trust is built. Political journalists may be asked to report even-handedly on major political parties, but be encouraged to take a defined position in favour of specific policies (as in the recent cases of newspapers that openly supported investigations of human rights abuses or rejected the extradi-tion of drug traffickers). Financial reporters may be expected to produce stock market information and avoid favouring particular business, but sports journalists are encouraged to root for the home team (or, as happens in many cases, the publisher's team). Showbusiness reviewers are kept on a short leash out of fear of favouring interests behind movies or television shows, but may be expected to be good patriots who rave about domestic productions. Health reporters may be expected to write about issues of interest to specific audiences, but travel journalists are expected to warn about potential risks.

Political polarization and fragmented journalism make trust selective and divided. News organizations and journalists that share similar world-views with their audiences are more trustworthy than others, regardless of whether their practices fit professional criteria. In fact, the notion of pro-fessional journalism is questionable. What matters is whether journalism truly represents sectorial interests and viewpoints. 'The good journalism' is the one aligned with one's particular views. Trust is based on moral bonds rather than on technical expertise. Echoing Diego Gambetta's (1988) definition of trust, here trust is the belief that journalists will act in defence of one's interest. Identification with the editorial positions of news organizations shapes trust.

Trust-building and social expectations

The absence of common practices and institutional expectations across news organizations is only one aspect of how journalism builds credibility. Even in the hypothetical case that journalists were trained in a common set of professional principles and leading news organizations enforced the canon of professional journalism, those requirements would be insufficient to build public confidence. Just because journalism aims to present fair-minded, expert accounts of reality, it will not necessarily generate professional-based trust. Whether journalists comply with 'professional' standards in gathering and presenting information is only one condition for the generation of bonds of confidence between experts and the public. Such bonds also require audiences to have a similar expectation about journalism – an assumption that needs to be taken critically.

Standard analyses fail to integrate audience expectations into how journalism builds trust. Premised on a rational model of democracy, they assume that news audiences behave as non-partisan citizens interested in factual information, and approach the press mainly as political actor. If both the press and news audiences are assumed to be active members of a democracy driven by rationality and truth, the trust relationship between them seems pretty straightforward: the press is trustworthy as long as it fulfils its civic role and meets audience needs.

However, neither the press nor news audiences conform to this ideal. The ubiquitousness of sensational news, the widespread tabloidization of political news and the proliferation and popularity of non-political news genres (science, health, sports, travel, food) in contemporary journalism suggest that the press hardly meets rational–informational expectations. Nor are audiences mainly interested in political news, or in consuming news to act as politically engaged citizens. Finding out sports scores, scanning real estate markets, knowing cinema schedules and checking the weather forecast are some examples of what audiences want. Besides its citizenship functions, journalism helps audiences to make sense of the world, anchors a sense of time and reality, connects individuals and communities, and provides cues for affirming cultural identities (Schudson 2003). It is necessary neither to subscribe to the market paean that the press offers audiences exactly what they want nor to see contemporary trends as a fall from journalism's alleged better days to recognize that the rational–informational model of journalism and audiences offers a limited perspective to understand how trust in the press functions.

Regardless of whether one laments or celebrates news trends and audience preferences, it is important to recognize that multiple public expectations underlie trust relationships. If audiences use news for various reasons, perhaps they do not use identical yardsticks to measure the trust of news organizations. What happens when news organizations fail to meet audiences' expectations? Whose reputation is affected? Are pacts of trust renewed? News audiences may still trust reporters even after they have regularly erred on weather forecasts, but withdraw all credibility from financial reporters who give false information or are suspected of favouring specific stocks. If a journalist reports that the initial number of reported deaths in a fire is 200 instead of 300, based on official figures, their credibility may not suffer. But if they wrongly report a kidnapping or produce fake news, it may.

Defenders of the objective, professional model of journalism, who scold reporters who fake news or let politics determine news coverage, assume not only that citizens' expectations are uniform but also that they match their model. The contract of trust between journalism and audiences may vary according to political sympathies and interests. One person's trusted source of news is another's propagandist. Whilst some audiences may expect all media to 'tell the truth', others apply that standard only to specific news organizations. Whilst some watch political news to confirm their views, others have a different disposition. Some trust (or distrust) news organizations because they have ideological empathy (or animosity); others trust them because they dutifully follow technical criteria of professional competence.

The main problem is that conventional recommendations about how journalism should build trust are premised on a model of journalism that is only possible when journalists and society at large share a wide political consensus, along the lines of the one imagined and cherished in the canon of US journalism (Gans 2003). If distrust of the press is mounting, it is assumed that it is because the press has jettisoned its principles of fairness and neutrality. The idea of trust-building on the basis of allegiance to non-partisan, universal ideals (fairness, responsibility, public interest), as recommended by advocates of objective reporting, sounds hollow in contexts dominated by particularistic and polarizing politics. It is not just an issue of reporters not trying hard enough to observe professional ideals. In Latin America, what do professional ideals mean when sectorial interests dictate the goals of news organizations, the workings of newsrooms and the expectations of news audiences? There is neither a historical tradition establishing 'what journalism is trustworthy' nor a wide consensus on expectations about press credibility.

Consequently, trust in journalism is inevitably fractured. When the public does not expect the press to be staffed by virtuous professionals, but instead looks for ideological community with news organizations, trust is fractured. When journalists are not part of a well-defined 'community of practice' defined by common principles, but pursue different credibility-building strategies, trust is fractured. When audiences do not see the press as a democratic-spirited institution situated above political conflicts, but believe it is immersed in commerce and partisan politics, trust is fragmented.

The analysis of how trust functions needs to be placed in contexts characterized by partisanism and political intransigency. Under these conditions, the model of journalistic trust based on apolitical and fact-based arguments is impossible. Moreover, it offers poor analytical guidance to any attempt to comprehend why, for example, audiences lend credibility to news organizations that ostensibly refuse to follow 'professional' principles, and scorn fair and factual reporting. Those arguments may represent well-intentioned efforts to promote a professional identity and a particular model of 'the good journalism'. However, they offer few insights into what audiences expect from the press, particularly in politically divided societies. In democracies where neither press organizations are bound to truth-telling and objectivity, nor audiences expect journalists to be neutral observers, what journalism is trusted is not simply a matter of observing conventional professional norms, but rather, of meeting social expectations and confirming political views.

Note

1 See the results of the annual regional poll conducted by Latinobarometro (www.latinobarometro.org).

References

Belinche, M. (ed.) (2001) *Medios, Política y Poder La conformación de los multimedios en la Argentina de los 90*, La Plata: Facultad de Periodismo y Comunicación Social, Universidad Nacional de la Plata.

Bromley, M. (1997) 'The end of journalism? Changes in workplace practices in the press and broadcasting in the 1990s', in M. Bromley and T. O'Malley (eds), *A Journalism Reader*, London: Routledge, 330–50.

Cajías de la Vega, L. and López, G. (1999) *¿Amenaza o Fortaleza? Concentración de medios de comunicación en América Latina*, La Paz: Friedrich Ebert Stiftung–ILDIS.

Canton, S. and Loreti, D. (2000) *Libertad de Expresión en América Latina*, La Plata: Facultad de Periodismo y Comunicación Social, Universidad Nacional de la Plata.

Castro Caycedo, G. (1999) *'La Televisión nos Mató el Alma'. El periodismo amarillo*, Bogota G. Castro Caycedo.

Conaghan, C. (2002) 'Cashing in on authoritarianism. Media collusion in Fujimori's Peru', *Harvard International Journal of Press/Politics*, 7(1): 115–25.

Cook, K.S. (ed.) (2001). *Trust in Society*, New York: Russell Sage Foundation.

Cordova de Alcazar, G. (2003) *Anatomia de los Golpes de Estado. La prensa en la caida de Mahuad y Bucaram*, Quito: Abya-Yala.

Diaz Rangel, E. (2002) *Chavez y los medios de comunicación social*, Caracas: Alfadil.

Fernandez Bogado, B. (2002) 'Limitaciones internas y baja calidad de la democracia', *Sala de Prensa*, November: 49.

Fernández Christlieb, F. (2002) *Responsabilidad de los Medios de Comunicación*, Mexico City: Paidos.

Fowks, J. (2000) *Suma y Resta de la Realidad. Medios de comunicación y elecciones generales 2000 en el Perú*, Lima: Friedrich Ebert Stiftung.

Fox, E and Waisbord, S. (2002) *Latin Politics, Global Media*, Austin, TX: University of Texas Press.

Gambetta, D. (ed.) (1988) *Trust. Making and Breaking Cooperative Relations*, Oxford: Basil Blackwell.

Gans, H. (2003) *Democracy and the News*, New York: Oxford University Press.

Gargurevich, J. (2000) *La Prensa Sensacionalista en el Perú*, Lima: Pontificia Universidad Católica del Perú, Fondo Editorial.

Giddens, A. (1991) *Modernity and Self-Identity*, Stanford, CA: Stanford University Press.

Hernandez, W. (2003) *Periodismo de Investigación en República Dominicana*, Santo Domingo: Editorial Letra Gráfica.

Herrán, M.T. and Restrepo, J.D. (1995) *Ética para Periodistas*, Bogota: Ediciones Tercer Mundo.

Luhmann, N. (1980) *Trust and Power*, New York: Wiley.

Macassi Lavander, S. (2001) *Prensa Amarilla y Cultura Política en el Proceso Electoral*, Lima: Calandria.

O'Neill, O. (2002) *A Question of Trust*, Cambridge: Cambridge University Press.

Ossandón, C. and Santa Cruz, E. (2001) *Entre las Alas y el Plomo. La gestación de la prensa moderna en Chile*, Santiago de Chile: LOM Ediciones.

Peñaranda Undurruga, R. (1999) *Retrato del Periodista Boliviano*, La Paz: Centro de Estudios Multidisciplinarios Bolivianos.

Peruzzotti, E. and Smulovitz, C. (eds) (2002) *Controlando la Política. Ciudadanos y medios en las nuevas democracias latinoamericanas*, Buenos Aires: Temas.

Rey, G. (2003) 'El defensor del lector: un oficio en construcción', *Sala de Prensa*, March: 53.

Rockwell, R. and Janus, N. (2003) *Media Power in Central America*, Champaign, IL: University of Illinois Press.

Sant Roz, J. (2003) *Las Pautas de los Medios*, Merida: Universidad de los Andes.

Schudson, M. (2001) 'The objectivity norm in American journalism', *Journalism*, 2(2): 149–70.

——(2003) *The Sociology of News*, New York: W.W. Norton.

Sunkel, G. (2001) *Concentración Económica de los Medios de Comunicación*, Santiago de Chile: LOM Ediciones.

Torrico, E. (1999) 'El negocio sensacionalista en Bolivia', *Diálogos de la Comunicación*, 55: 76–84.

Waisbord, S. (2000) *Watchdog Journalism in South America*, New York: Columbia University Press.

——(2002) 'Grandes gigantes: media concentration in Latin America', *Open Democracy*, 27 February Online. Available HTTP: http://www.opendemocracy.net/debates/article.jsp?id=8&debateId=24&articleId=64 (accessed 20 September 2004).

Zelizer, B. (2004) 'When facts, truth and reality are God-terms. On journalism's uneasy place in cultural studies', *Communication and Critical/Cultural Studies*, 1(1): 100–19.

Zeta de Pozo, R. (2001) 'Los medios peruanos en busca de la credibilidad perdida', *Revista Probidad*, October–November. Online. Available HTTP: <http://www.revistaprobidad.info/016/026.html> (accessed 20 September 2004).

Zeta de Pozo, R., Ruiz, F. and Waisbord, S. (2004) 'Los medios de comunicación en América Latina', in C. Barrera (ed.), *Historia del Periodismo Universal*, Madrid: Ariel.

6 Old and new media, old and new politics?

On- and offline reporting in the 2002 Ukrainian election campaign

Natalya Krasnoboka and Kees Brants

These are uneasy times for Eastern European societies, most of which are still in an ambiguous transition from totalitarianism to democracy. Although after the overthrow of the non-democratic regimes they proclaimed a course towards the latter, their political future is still rather unclear as many of their political, economic and social practices contradict the notion and basic principles of democracy. The role of the media, notably press freedom and the many ways in which this is violated, is at the heart of the controversy. On the one hand, most Eastern European countries have adopted progressive media legislation and seem to have welcomed independent and private media outlets. On the other, researchers and international observers report examples of media bias, political pressure on the media and self-censorship of journalists.

While focusing on Ukraine, this paper will look at the logic that drives post-Soviet media developments. Many former republics of the Soviet Union seem to be caught between a logic that is defined by the liberal ideology of the free marketplace of ideas and one that is driven by the traditions of the state/party deciding the political and the public's agenda. In the old days, communist media were an essential part of the socialization, education and cultural integration of the socialist citizen. The post-Soviet situation gives a new importance to the media: for the citizen as a reliable source of political information and education, for the political authorities as a new aid to their informational activities and a means of maintaining power, and for democracy as a watchdog safeguarding its well-being. These are conflicting roles, at least in terms of what the different actors expect from them.

In such a situation of uncertainty and ambivalence for the traditional mass media, the role of the Internet – as a new and difficult-to-control medium and as a platform for dialogue – could be paramount. The arrival of the Internet coincided with the transformation to democracy in Eastern Europe, which helped it to be branded as a medium of and for democracy. Combining the characteristics of an advanced technology and an extended mass medium, the Internet was expected from the start – maybe even more here than in Western Europe and North America – to enhance democratic practices in society. By comparing online and traditional media at election time in Ukraine, we will analyse whether the application of the Internet lives up to this expectation and whether it helps to overcome the problematic relationship between the 'old' media and the state.

Media logic and democracy

It is an open door in liberal democratic theory to say that the media play an important role in making democracy tick. Independent from state and economic powers, they are able (i) to provide the plurality of information and opinions necessary for people to make sense of society's goings on and to perform their participatory rights as citizens; (ii) to probe and enlighten the transparency of the decision-making sphere; (iii) to give a platform for the expression of both society's wants and grievances and decision-makers' responses to these, thus providing the means of dialogue that is necessary for the cohesion of society; and, (iv) to watch over the exercise and possible misuse of power and hold chosen representatives to account.

For analytical purposes, the way the media actually perform in liberal democracies and their uneasy relationship with politics can be located within a three-dimensional space, the corners of which are formed by the different logics that drive the political communication process. First there is a 'partisan logic', characteristic of most West European mass media in the nineteenth and a substantial part of the twentieth century. Here, the media have close links with political parties, acting more as a mouthpiece of the political elite than from an independent point of view. The metaphor best describing the journalists' role is that of a lap dog. Second, there is a 'public logic' in which the media still greatly respect the political parties and the decision-makers as the actors setting the political agenda, but from a more critical distance and without closely identifying with them. Here, the media perform in the public interest and from a sense of responsibility for the well-being of the political system and the democratic process (Brants and Van Praag 2000; Mazzoleni 1987). The well-known metaphor is that of the watchdog.

As a consequence of the growing competition between television channels in a dual broadcasting system and the commercial orientation of the (tabloid) press, we have seen the emergence of a more market-driven 'media logic' (Altheide and Snow 1979). According to this logic, the media content is decided by the frame of reference in which the media make sense of and socially construct what happens. They now identify with the public, that is to say, with what they assume the public is interested in and enjoys. Politics becomes dependent on the functioning, the production routines and the news values of the media. In practice, this results in a journalistic attitude that is not only distanced, but even cynical, often in search of the scandalous and the entertaining.

The question is whether any of these ideal models fit, and thus help to explain, the developments of the media–politics relationship in Ukraine and other Eastern European transitional societies. A superficial look at media developments in these countries reveals the rise of independent and often commercially driven outlets. There is more genre diversity and a level of commercial as well as political advertising that was unknown before. Also apparent is the establishment of partisan media supporting new and different political forces. However, these overt changes could be misleading, as media transformations do not take place unchallenged. The long period of state control and censorship cannot be expected to disappear overnight without a trace. It has left its marks on the development of media policy and practice, and often determines the more recent picture.

So, how can the current performance of the ex-Soviet media be explained and what are the major patterns of state–media–society relations? The evolution of the media of the former republics of the Soviet Union cannot be understood without exploring the way media functioned during Soviet times.

The media before and after independence

Table 6.1 summarizes the logics of media performance in Ukraine during the transition to democracy. The emergence and evolution of modern Ukrainian media began during the years of Soviet rule, under the strict guidance of the Communist Party. In those days, citizens were able to receive at least one national (all-Union) television channel, two republican channels and very often one local (provincial) television channel.

Table 6.1 Logics of media performance in Ukraine

| | *Logic* | | | |
	State	*Fuzzy public*	*(Embryonic) media*	*New state and partisan*
Journalistic role	Propaganda	Criticism of the centre	Nationalism	Kompromat/ loyalty
Identification	Party/state	Nation	Nation	Party/ financial group/state
Agenda-setting	Party	National elite	National elite	Party/state
State interference	Strong	Strong	Moderate	Strong
Censorship	Party	Moderate party	Moderate self	Strong state, strong self
Ownership	State	State	Independent	Private/state
Media law	Formal	Formal	New law	Lawsuits, licensing, tax penalty
Period	Before 1986	1986–91	1991–98	Since 1998

Radio sets were available in all Soviet households, even in the most remote villages. Newspapers, newsletters, bulletins and magazines were published in almost unlimited quantities and editions. Television was particularly important – both as a provider of information and propaganda and as a tool in creating cohesion and order, and preserving a connection between the regions and the centre.

Together with self-censorship, a very high level of party censorship characterized the editorial policy of the media. Oppositional voices were virtually unknown. Ukrainian media in particular were severely censored because of the Communist Party's concerns about potential nationalistic and libertarian ideas among the national cultural elite. At the same time, the Soviet media themselves were elitist (Mickiewicz 1997; Splichal 1994) – as revealed in the personalization of politics and news, the selective nature of the journalists' caste and the direction of the media performance: the leaders of the Soviet Union, especially the General Secretary, dominated media coverage with their presence, references and quotations; journalists represented a highly educated and well-paid group of the Soviet intelligentsia; and any media coverage was directed towards the state and party officials who were considered the major audience of any media outlet. On the basis of a particular two-step-flow model of communication, media events were organized with state officials in mind. The population were considered either indirectly or not at all.

In terms of a defining logic, the Soviet period has traces of partisan characteristics, but it could probably best be described as a 'state logic', which, as we have said elsewhere, is symbolized by 'the undemocratic traditions in which the state apparatus or the [general secretary] hold control over the media and define what is and particularly what is not said' (Brants & Krasnoboka 2001: 301). Truth and truth finding are – potentially at least, practically most often – violated, suppressed and censored. Content is one-sided and is often propagandistic.

Perestroika created a golden age of public journalism in the country. It had all the characteristics of a public logic - journalists as independent, critical watchdogs, driven more by a sense of what was in the public interest than what the public was interested in. It was 'the "honeymoon" between 1989 and 1991, when journalists experienced unprecedented opportunities for reporting' (Voltmer 2000: 472). Neither before nor after perestroika were journalists so independent and so highly respected. Television programmes on the central national channel *Ostankino*, and *Studio-GART* on the first republican channel, became the forerunners and guardians of democratization. Public discussions of these programmes and the leading national newspapers became commonplace.

As agenda-setters, journalists were the real opinion-makers and political leaders of the Soviet people. Their role changed from a propaganda function to information dissemination, political education of citizens and, particularly, analytical opinionating. Not surprisingly, leading journalists were elected to the Soviet parliament during the first independent elections in the Soviet Union in 1989 and later to the national parliaments. But in all their seeming independence, the media had no legal autonomy as they were still state-owned and could be punished if they crossed boundaries. These boundaries, however, were uncertain, as media policy and practice were not yet regulated by a progressive media law. The existing one was burdened with formalistic jargon, rather outdated and distanced from the actual media practice. Moreover, the orientation of the media towards society remained rather selective. It was still very elitist – aimed at and recruiting from 'oppositional intellectuals' (Splichal 1994) who, to a large extent, defined both the media and the political agenda during perestroika. The logic of the media during perestroika would thus be better defined as a 'fuzzy public' logic, with progressive intellectuals transforming political and media systems as well as forming the basis of civil society.

The collapse of the Soviet Union and the introduction of a new media law stimulated an explosion of independent media: many of them were ephemerons, others managed to survive for some time, but few became established. The ownership structure was, however, unclear, with television remaining practically state-owned, bringing with it uncertainty and potential controversy. At the same time, with both a change from authoritarian to democratic rule and national independence, the journalistic attitude changed from propagandistic and educational to strongly patriotic. As in other Eastern European countries, nationalism became the dominant feature of the independent Ukrainian media, with the aim of creating a national identity and defending national sovereignty. This nationalism, however, led the Ukrainian media to overlook the establishment of domestic oligarchs and the conversion of the former local communist leaders into national political figures. Blaming the communists and Russia for all evil, the Ukrainian media closed their eyes to the emergence of domestic 'oppressors'. As Wei Wu and colleagues (1996: 544) have noted in their research on Russia, journalists started to 'believe more in such active roles as setting the political agenda and developing the interests of the public, but not in investigating government claims'. In spite of this, the presidential campaign of 1994 was an example of open political communication: the victory of 'new man' Kuchma over the acting president Kravchyuk was legitimized by the open competition, transparency and by fair and critical political reporting and criticism during the campaign. Taken together, these different elements indicate the hesitant and embryonic birth of a media logic in Ukraine during the first years of independence.

The emergence of a new class of media owners has occurred in a slightly different way in Ukraine than in neighbouring Russia. Starting their media activities a few years later, Ukrainian oligarchs had a clear vision of their media projects: these were used to obtain political power and a position in either the legislative or executive bodies. The oligarchs established their media empires side by side with their political parties. At the same time, loyalty to President Kuchma was a distinguishing feature of Ukrainian private and 'state' journalism. Leading Ukrainian oligarchs, their parties and their media have always been competing for the favour of the president.

Patriotism, amateurism and presidential loyalty characterized the behaviour of the media during election campaigns, showing 'a biased media performance in which personalities and their families, scandal and gossip, horse race and conflict dominated over content' (Brants and Krasnoboka 2001: 298). As we said in that report: 'the different party programmes and policy views, which were characterized by a strong similarity, hardly gave rise to a pluralist portrayal. There were also no television debates, as fear more than democratic accountability ruled these campaigns' (2001: 298). The portrayal of the 1999 election campaign became an ode to the president. Next to issues of the oligarchs' partisanship and the president's loyalty, the Ukrainian media experienced new methods of state pressure that killed (sometimes literally) what critical and unbiased reporting did exist. Media organizations underwent regular and special fire, health, anti-epidemic and tax inspections each time they tried to be independent. Their dependence on licensing and state-owned printing facilities made them wary, while media and journalists had little practical protection from the lawsuits of powerful authorities and local bureaucrats. Overtly or covertly, Ukrainian state authorities returned to the old practice of censorship, expanding it with a new form: 'censorship by killing' (Organisation for Security and Cooperation in Europe 2001).

All this points not to a media logic, but more to a newly emerging state logic 'diluted' by an oligarch-inspired partisan logic. Ukrainian media have not made use of the chance they got with perestroika and independence. From being the main mouthpiece of state and communist party propaganda, the national media managed to establish and quickly abolish the skills of objective reporting and high-quality analysis. Many media outlets often returned to the 'zero-sum' reporting often connected with deep national or nationalistic feelings.

Online media in Ukraine

Early theories of the democratic potential of the Internet suggested that this medium could well become a powerful alternative source of information and a place for marginal and oppositional voices. However, more recent empirical analysis rather suggests that the Internet is becoming just another medium that reinforces the existing division of power in the world (for example G. Davis 1997; R. Davis 1999; Gibson and Ward 1998; Margolis *et al.* 1997, 1999; Resnick 1998; Selnow 1998), as well as providing a new tool for division in society, by contributing to a digital divide (for example Bimber 1999; Davis 1999; Norris 2000). Analysis of the Internet, and particularly online media, in totalitarian regimes also reveals the success of the state apparatus in controlling its use and content (Kalathil and Boas 2001).

Evolution of the Internet as a democratic tool and oppositional voice in Ukraine has two faces. With the possible exception of the authorities, the Internet has rarely been labelled with negative connotations. Although later than McDonald's, the Internet arrived in the post-Soviet societies at almost the same time as independence and became one more sign of a long-awaited freedom. Moreover, the educational and technical skills of the population allowed people to adjust to the Internet quickly and easily.[1] On the other hand, Internet connection and use are relatively low compared with the majority of countries of Western and Central Europe.[2] With around 50 per cent telephone penetration, in 2004 only 8 per cent of the national population (3.2 million people) had access to the Internet, while the number of regular users was even lower. The most active are young, well-educated, urban men, and the majority of users have Internet access from their work or study place rather than home. Moreover, minimum wages and pensions in the country lie between €30 and €50 per month. All this confirms both the backwardness of the country in terms of Internet accessibility and the division between the groups with higher potential for Internet connection and those lacking this possibility.

Until the turn of the century, the impact of the Internet on political information in Ukraine was practically undetectable. In April 2000, the Internet, as a reliable, critical and independent source of information, was born. That month, the first online newspaper was launched in Kyiv. A young, critical television and radio journalist Georgy Gongadze gave up trying to express his views in traditional media and started a new project of online information. Several new online papers followed in its wake; some of them immediately opened discussion forums.

In contrast to the situation in established democracies, online papers in the former republics of the Soviet Union rarely have an offline version and their content is predominantly original. They are flexible and mobile, and run by small groups of professional journalists and/or sufficiently educated enthusiasts. The majority of online journalists started their professional activities after independence or at least during perestroika. The papers are not usually affiliated to political or business groups and they pay for their activities with personal money or grants from international non-governmental organizations. And they are popular: monthly ratings of many online papers easily compete with circulations of traditional newspapers (Krasnoboka 2002). At the moment, there are approximately 1,000 news websites on the Ukrainian Internet. This number includes online papers and information portals as well as online versions of offline media.[3] Although it would be rather difficult to identify the exact number of online papers, one of us has estimated that in 2001–2 around 40 online papers had websites (Krasnoboka 2002).

In December 2000 Gongadze's *Ukrainska Pravda* had registered its first million readers (while official statistics showed an Internet penetration of around 400,000 at that time). The political authorities were clearly unhappy with the development of a new independent platform for political communication. In the middle of this, Gongadze – who had become the forerunner of autonomous online journalism in which information by the political elite was not taken for granted any longer – disappeared and was later found beheaded. When opposition leader Olexander Moroz accused President Kuchma of direct involvement in Gongadze's disappearance, not only did it result in a political crisis, but it also showed the dramatic split between online papers and traditional media as reliable sources of information (see also Krasnoboka and Semetko 2003). In its editorial, *Ukrainska Pravda* observed: 'It is terrible to say that only by learning about the Gongadze-case have millions of citizens of our country heard for the first time the word "Internet"' (December 2000).

It can be assumed that online media constitute a unique, albeit contested, means of communication in Ukraine. But do they indeed – and in contrast to the 'old' media – function as an independent platform for gaining knowledge, creating dialogue and enhancing democracy? This question will be answered on the basis of a content analysis of old and new media coverage of the country's latest parliamentary elections.

The media and the 2002 election campaign: a case study

During the previous election campaign in Ukraine (1998–99), numerous international monitoring groups registered biased behaviour of the national newspapers and television channels. Unequal distribution of media coverage between pro-presidential and oppositional candidates was observed by the Organisation for Security and Cooperation in Europe, the Council of Europe, Freedom House, the Committee to Protect Journalists, Reporters Without Frontiers and the National Democratic Institute.[4]

Our study focuses on a comparative analysis of several traditional and new media outlets during the election campaign in early 2002, the third parliamentary elections since independence. The campaign was characterized by a strong division between pro-presidential and opposition political actors, replacing the division between Communists and anti-Communists and between pro-Russian and pro-Western actors, which dominated previous election campaigns. The new split led to mergers and coalitions within pro-presidential and opposition groups. Several 'parties of power' united in a strong pro-presidential election block, *Za Edynu Ukrainu* (For United Ukraine), which mainly represented powerful civil servants (top government and local officials), guaranteeing for itself total financial and infrastructural support throughout the country.

Similar developments occurred among anti-presidential forces. Consolidated during previous mass protests, the main anti-presidential parties tried to continue that line of cooperation throughout the election campaign. Several prominent right-wing liberal parties united in an election block - *Nasha Ukraina* (Our Ukraine) – headed by Victor Yushchenko, the former prime minister and at the time the most popular politician in the country. A few other right-wing (predominantly republican) parties united in yet another election block, headed by the former vice prime minister in the Yushchenko government and at the time one of the most prominent leaders of the national opposition, Yuliya Tymoshenko. The left-wing opposition was represented by the Communist and Socialist parties which ran independently and did not form election blocks (see Semetko and Krasnoboka 2003). In the end, six parties/blocks entered parliament, only two of these pro-presidential – *Za Edynu Ukrainu* and the Social Democratic Party of Ukraine (united). The four others were opposition parties – *Nasha Ukraina*, Tymoshenko's Block, the Socialist Party and the Communist Party.

Concerns about unbalanced media reporting appeared long before the campaign actually began. Although few journalists admitted biased reporting, opposition parties had limited access to the major national media. Apart from the legally required time schedule for candidates' programmes and debates on television and in the press, they had to rely on their party's newspapers, a number of independent but loyal or partisan newspapers and the Internet.

Expectations and method[5]

From the moment the first online paper was launched in the country, this new medium of political communication gained popularity as a reliable source of alternative and oppositional information. The political crisis at the end of 2000 only reinforced the status of online papers as the main voice of civil and political opposition and established online papers as the major counterbalance to traditional media outlets in their coverage of protest actions (Krasnoboka and Semetko 2003).

The parliamentary elections of 2002 were the first since the beginning of the political crisis, and also the first in which online papers could confirm their status as independent informational media.[6] Taking into account all previous media and political developments in the country, we would expect to see considerable differences between traditional media and online papers in the election coverage, and notably that:

- the president and pro-presidential groups dominate election news in traditional media;
- opposition parties will be ignored by traditional media or receive exclusively negative coverage;
- online papers provide consistent and detailed coverage of the election campaign of the opposition;
- online papers are predominantly negative about pro-presidential groups.

Establishing these differences between traditional media and online papers will help us to answer the main questions about the role of online papers in the democratic transition in Ukraine and whether online papers present us with a different logic of media performance than that dominant in traditional media.

For our analysis we have chosen two leading outlets in each media category. We have selected the state-owned national television channel UT-1 and the privately owned national channel *Inter*,[7] the two largest national daily newspapers, *Den'* and *Facty*, and the two online papers with the highest readership, *Korespondent* and *Ukrainska Pravda*. We analysed coverage one week prior to the election day (31 March 2002). This period covers five days (Monday–Friday) because, according to the law, no political agitation is allowed on the day prior to the elections. (For both newspapers this period covers only four editions, because they are not published on Monday.) The unit of analysis is a news item, defined as a text between two subsequent headlines; for the television channels, each separate news story presented in the major block of the evening's news programme (prior to weather and sport reports) was counted as a news item.

We looked at the following characteristics of news stories:

- topics covered – due to the large amount and diversity of these topics we developed combining categories (for example election campaign, political system, economy, foreign affairs, welfare system). The first main topic was coded per news item;
- news frames – the 'central organizing idea or story line that provides meaning to an unfolding strip of events' (Gamson and Modigliani 1987: 143);
- balance – whenever candidates were quoted in the media, we checked whether their statements were balanced by opposing views in the same news item;
- the overall tone – coded as positive, mixed, negative or neutral;
- main actors – in the order of their appearance in the story. Up to three main actors could be coded per item. We were particularly interested in the saliency of appearances of the pro-presidential and the opposition groups;
- tone of a news item vis-à-vis the main actors – coded as positive, mixed, negative or neutral. This enabled us to show a ratio of balance in the tone of coverage, defined as the difference between the percentage of positive and negative news items in which an actor was mentioned.

Results

In total, 722 'articles' appeared in the different outlets during that week: 203 on television (113 on UT-1 and 90 on *Inter*), 302 in the press (116 in

Den' and 186 in *Facty*) and 217 on the Internet (169 on *Korespondent* and 48 on *Ukrainska Pravda*). We selected and analysed all articles that mentioned national politicians (politically related articles), resulting in 98 news items for UT-1, 75 for *Inter*, 49 for *Den'*, 37 for *Facty*, 150 for *Korespondent* and 40 for *Ukrainska Pravda* (449 news items in total). Election news turned out to be the major political topic covered by the media outlets (appearing on average in 46 per cent of articles).

As Table 6.2 shows, within the election news, both television channels and the newspaper *Den'* tended to present a general overview of the campaign. With the exception of *Korespondent*, all outlets reported extensively on the parties' campaigns, including campaign advertisements/propaganda and meetings and trips of party leaders. Court issues and election scandals were the most important focus of online paper *Korespondent*. It also reported on election fraud, violation of the election law and on crime connected with the elections. Similar topics were of great concern for the *Inter* television channel as well. *Facty* and *Ukrainska Pravda* looked at negative campaigning and sleaze and at misuse of political positions.

Looking at the media frames (Table 6.3), television channels and newspapers framed their stories in terms of the achievements, hard work and devotion of politicians and parties. UT-1 in particular stressed support for and care between politicians and their voters. *Korespondent* was also inclined to see the positive side and to highlight co-operation in political affairs. Both television channels and *Korespondent* discussed challenges that faced the election campaign. Newspapers were keen to see the current political developments in geopolitical terms: the international image of Ukraine and its relations with neighbours. While television channels framed political and election processes predominantly in a positive way, both of the online papers and, to a lesser extent, both of the newspapers focused on the negative sides. One-third of all online articles were organized around the idea of election fraud, illegalities and conspiracies during the campaign. Additionally, newspaper *Den'* and online paper *Ukrainska Pravda* framed political achievements in terms of false and unrealistic expectations.

With regard to the balance of politicians' statements reported by the different media (Table 6.4), television stands out, but in a negative way. Both UT-1 and *Inter* had a dramatic imbalance in their reporting and rarely or never made reference to opposing views. On- and offline papers stood out in a more positive way, both in being balanced and in referring to opposing views. If we look at the 'tone' of these articles, we see a dramatic difference between the television channels and *Ukrainska Pravda*: television gave a more positive or neutral image of the campaign as a whole, while *Ukrainska Pravda* was negative. The tone of the newspaper reports was practically equally distributed along all tone options.

Moving to the political actors, we see that, with the exception of

Table 6.2 Main topics in media coverage the week before the Ukrainian parliamentary elections of 2002

% of items covering topic

	Television			Press			Online papers		
	UT-1 (N = 38)	Inter (N = 37)	Total (N = 75)	Den' (N = 21)	Facty (N = 17)	Total (N = 38)	Kor[a] (N = 87)	UP[b] (N = 18)	Total (N = 105)
Elections: general	21.1	24.3	22.7	42.9	11.8	28.9	12.6	16.7	13.3
Parties' election campaigns	36.8	24.3	30.7	28.6	35.3	31.6	5.7	27.8	9.5
Electoral violations and court issues	13.2	27.0	20.0	4.8	17.6	10.5	48.3	11.1	41.9
Negative campaign, sleaze, abuse of position	5.3	2.7	4.0	4.8	29.4	15.8	14.9	22.2	16.2
Polls and ratings	15.8	10.8	13.3	14.3	5.9	10.5	12.6	11.1	12.4
Protests	5.3	10.8	8.0	4.8	0.0	2.6	1.1	0.0	1.0
Gongadze case	2.6	0.0	1.3	0.0	0.0	0.0	4.6	11.1	5.7
Total	100	100	100	100	100	100	100	100	100

Notes
a *Kor = Korespondent*
b *UP = Ukrainska Pravda*

Table 6.3 Main news frames in media coverage the week before the Ukrainian parliamentary elections of 2002

% of items using frame

	Television			Press			Online papers		
	UT-1 (N = 98)	Inter (N = 75)	Total (N = 173)	Den' (N = 49)	Facty (N = 37)	Total (N = 86)	Kor[a] (N = 150)	UP[b] (N = 40)	Total (N = 190)
Positive achievements, co-operation	46.9	34.7	41.6	24.5	32.4	27.9	24.0	2.5	19.5
Challenges of election campaign	18.4	32.0	24.3	12.2	10.8	11.6	23.3	10.0	20.5
Election fraud, conspiracy	11.2	10.7	11.0	12.2	16.2	14.0	36.0	30.0	34.7
Geopolitics of Ukraine	6.1	1.3	4.0	14.3	16.2	15.1	7.3	10.0	7.9
Opposition, resistance	1.0	4.0	2.3	2.0	0.0	1.2	1.3	2.5	1.6
Media biases	0.0	0.0	0.0	4.1	0.0	2.3	0.0	15.0	3.2
False (political) expectations	1.0	1.3	1.2	20.4	8.1	15.1	1.3	22.5	5.8
Others	0.0	0.0	0.0	0.0	5.4	2.3	0.0	2.5	0.5
No frame/difficult to define	15.3	16.0	15.6	10.2	10.8	10.5	6.7	5.0	6.3
Total	100	100	100	100	100	100	100	100	100

Notes
a Kor = Korespondent
b UP = Ukrainska Pravda

Table 6.4 Balance of statements and overall tone of news stories in media coverage the week before the Ukrainian parliamentary elections of 2002

| | % of items | | | | | | | | |
| | Television | | | Press | | | Online papers | | |
	UT-1 (N = 98)	Inter (N = 75)	Total (N = 173)	Den' (N = 49)	Facty (N = 37)	Total (N = 86)	Kor[a] (N = 150)	UP[b] (N = 40)	Total (N = 190)
Statement									
None made	57.1	29.3	45.1	26.5	35.1	30.2	31.3	52.5	35.8
Not balanced	37.8	48.0	42.2	30.6	24.3	27.9	33.3	20.0	30.5
Not controversial	3.1	9.3	5.8	16.3	8.1	12.8	8.7	0.0	6.8
Balanced	2.0	13.3	6.9	26.5	32.4	29.1	26.7	27.5	26.8
Overall tone									
Positive	42.9	34.7	39.3	14.3	27.0	19.8	14.7	0.0	11.6
Negative	6.1	18.7	11.6	28.6	24.3	26.7	27.3	60.0	34.2
Mixed	13.3	16.0	14.5	30.6	21.6	26.7	15.3	30.0	18.4
Neutral	37.8	30.7	34.7	26.5	27.0	26.7	42.7	10.0	35.8

Notes
a *Kor* = *Korespondent*
b *UP* = *Ukrainska Pravda*

Korespondent, all outlets gave the president a central role (Table 6.5). His presence far exceeded that of any other politician. For *Korespondent* the president was the third most prominent actor after the two right-wing oppositional blocks *Nasha Ukraina* and Tymoshenko's Block. *Korespondent* was the only outlet where the total presence of opposition groups exceeded the presence of pro-presidential groups. All others, including the critical *Ukrainska Pravda,* provided more prominent coverage of pro-presidential actors. On television, pro-presidential groups were 2.5 times as visible as the opposition. The left-wing opposition was the least visible actor in all but *Korespondent,* where it received slightly more prominence than the president.

Whereas the tone of the campaign reporting as a whole was rather mixed, that towards the president was generally positive – at least in the traditional media. As Figure 6.1 shows, television channels and newspapers had no negative or mixed tone towards him. *Ukrainska Pravda,* on the contrary, had not a positive word about the president, and *Korespondent* also introduced a negative tone. A similar pattern was seen for coverage of pro-presidential groups, although in this case the online media were more neutral. The tone of the traditional outlets changed dramatically when applied to the right-wing opposition; the descriptions become highly negative. The left-wing opposition was mentioned so rarely that no clear pattern is apparent.

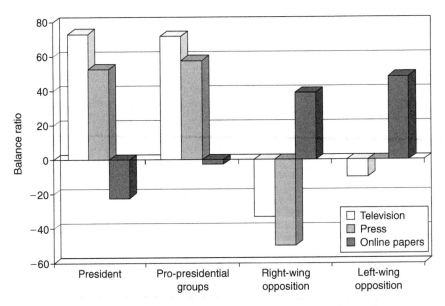

Figure 6.1 Balance ratio of tone coverage towards main actors in media coverage the week before the Ukrainian parliamentary elections of 2002 (the difference between the percenage of positive and negative news items).

Table 6.5 Main actors in media coverage the week before the Ukrainian parliamentary elections of 2002

	Television			Press			Online papers		
	UT-1 (N = 123)	Inter (N = 90)	Total (N = 213)	Den' (N = 66)	Facty (N = 48)	Total (N = 114)	Kor[a] (N = 217)	UP[2] (N = 71)	Total (N = 288)
President/pro-presidential groups									
President	20.3	13.3	17.4	13.6	20.8	16.7	9.7	19.7	12.2
Pro-presidential groups	51.2	68.9	58.7	47.0	47.9	47.4	35.9	36.6	36.1
Total	71.5	82.2	76.1	60.6	68.7	64.1	45.6	56.3	48.3
Opposition									
Right-wing	16.3	17.8	16.9	31.8	22.9	28.1	41.9	32.4	39.6
Left-wing	12.2	0.0	7.0	7.6	8.3	7.9	12.4	11.3	12.2
Total	28.5	17.8	23.9	39.4	31.2	36.0	54.3	43.7	51.8

Notes
a *Kor* = *Korespondent*
b *UP* = *Ukrainska Pravda*

The picture that emerges of the other candidates makes the sympathies and antipathies, and the direct links between certain politicians both clearer and more confusing. While on the whole the traditional outlets demonstrate a similar positive tone towards the other pro-presidential actors, at the same time a certain coldness can be observed in *Inter* and *Den'* with regard to *Za Edynu Ukrainu*. This seems a one-off case, because it coincides with a positive tone towards the second pro-presidential player, Viktor Medvedchyuk, who happens to own both media, and towards his Social Democratic Party (united). State-owned (and thus pro-presidential) UT-1, and *Facty*, which is owned by the president's son-in-law, showed the opposite picture: they were extremely positive about *Za Edynu Ukrainu*. Where coverage of Yushchenko was never positive and coverage of Tymoshenko's block rarely so, *Nasha Ukraina*, as the most popular opposition force, was fairly well represented in the traditional media.

Of the online papers, *Ukrainska Pravda* gave the greatest attention to the opposition and notably Yushchenko and his *Nasha Ukraina* block; the tone of coverage was predominantly positive. Coverage of Tymoshenko and Socialist Party leader Moroz was even more positive, but their coverage was minimal. *Nasha Ukraina* and Tymoshenko's block were the most visible actors in *Korespondent*, followed by the president and *Za Edynu Ukrainu*. With a predominantly positive, but also a critical tone, *Korespondent* again stood out from *Ukrainska Pravda* and the other, traditional media.

Conclusions

So, how far is Ukraine on its way to joining the political communication family of liberal democracies? The answer is ambivalently sombre, with a glimmer of hope. The first prerequisite for fair political communication is to present a balanced picture of existing political actors and opinions in a given society. Political journalism during the 2002 election campaign in Ukraine, notably the visibility of the main political actors and the tone of coverage, hardly fulfils this obligation. The visibility was remarkably unbalanced, with the president – whose position was not at stake in these elections – being the most prominent figure in the news. Of the six most popular parties, only two were constantly present in the media. The tone of the overall coverage and the tone towards particular political actors were often neither impartial nor neutral. Such coverage revealed strong partisan preferences and could qualify as a state-partisan logic.[8]

With relatively little bias towards specific actors and topics, and a balanced tone, the online paper *Korespondent* came closest to the Western democratic ideal. It generally took a neutral, distant position, constantly referring to its sources and providing background information and context for reported events. Its popularity among Internet users confirms their appreciation of such an approach. Although in foreign hands and commercially driven – which neo-liberal position indicates more the ingredients of a media logic – the performance of *Korespondent* points to a public logic. The question remains whether, in a further imbalanced political communication environment, there is much need for this form and style of neutrality.

The second prerequisite for political communication's contribution to electoral democracy is being informative on the policies, plans and qualities of the different parties and politicians. Here again, with the exception of *Korespondent,* the picture of the different media researched was ambiguous. The majority of news stories focused more on the specificities of the campaign – the ads, the campaign train, propaganda – than on what the campaign was about. Neither party programmes, policy achievements, stands and suggestions nor the qualities of the candidates were covered to any great extent. Other topics were often layered with sensationalism, focusing on election scandals, court issues, fraud, violation of the law, sleaze and misuse of positions. The impression was one of a dirty campaign for power, and the negativity was reinforced – particularly in on- and offline papers – by the use of such frames as challenges of election campaign, conspiracy, geopolitics of Ukraine, illegal actions and negative achievements.

Through Western eyes, such a negative and cynical approach, along with limited information on what the competing parties stand for, points to a general media logic. However, in the Ukrainian (historical) context it could also be interpreted as that on- and offline newspapers have and take relatively more freedom than television, and that they use that professional autonomy to perform as the watchdogs in a public logic, however biased they may have been. No wonder that television frames were more positive: focusing on hard work done by and support of or care from a party. One should not forget, however, that fraud has often been a characteristic of elections in the past and that television enjoys a symbiotic relationship with the president, which makes it close its eyes to 'other' information.

Such results invite the logical question: how does the difference between the outlets in terms of actors and tone coincide with the similarities in topic and structure of a message? The answer is that they cover and blame different actors for practically the same deeds. If *Ukrainska Pravda,* for example, accuses the president of illegal weapons trading, money laundering and political murders, television channels and newspapers will accuse Yushchenko and Tymoshenko of financial sleaze and position misuse during their time in government. *Ukrainska Pravda* will complain about pro-Russian tendencies in pro-presidential parties, and the traditional media will accuse the right-wing opposition of nationalism. Television channels will broadcast trips of pro-presidential candidates around the country and their warm welcome by enthusiastic citizens, while *Ukrainska Pravda* will present examples of the opposition being banned from such visits.

These observations allow us to conclude that traditional media and online papers provide a mirror reflection of each other in their reporting; but at the same time this is a distorted reflection because different media highlight and ignore different parts of reality. In the most radical cases and situations such differences between old and new media can result in the presentation of different political realities. Traditional media employ a state-partisan logic, while *Korespondent* follows more a public logic. Due to the inequality of access and presentation, the pro-presidential forces have a practically unlimited space to create their own political reality where the opposition is moved to the very margins or excluded from this reality altogether.

It is in this periphery that *Ukrainska Pravda* seems to operate, and in a way that does not fit well into the typology of logics. On the one hand, its performance shows elements of a public logic, in its critical and independent stance. On the other hand, its *samizdat*-like operations also give an impression of an anti-statist partisan logic. And to top it all, its cynical approach and independent agenda setting resonate elements of a media logic. However, as the opposition parties remain a marginalized political force in society, the Internet also risks remaining a marginalized medium. Where these two margins meet, they are able to present their vision of reality, but only to those groups in society that have access to the Internet.

As the traditional media can be understood only through their relationship with the Soviet past, online media should be understood in terms of their relation to the traditional media. In their current shape, they can exist only in a bipolar world with traditional media. There, they invigorate and support democratization of the country, continuing the tradition of the samizdat that opposed the same traditional media in the Soviet equivalent of the bipolar world. At the same time, many elements of media coverage employed by such online papers as *Korespondent* show more objective and impartial reporting. In many respects they are similar to traditional media. However, the evolution and popularity of online papers has forced more traditional outlets to provide more varied information for their audiences. In order not to be seen as totally biased and undemocratic, traditional media, including television, will have to react to news posted online. The only thing they can do to bring together their loyalty to the president and a minimum of objectivity and pluriformity is to provide both similar and different interpretations of the same events highlighted online.

This research raises at least one final question. We have attempted to apply concepts of media logic developed in Western media studies and based exclusively on Western case studies to a society in transition. In other words, we have looked at current trends in political communication in Ukraine through the eyes of Western theory. The results are not too promising. But does it tell us something about the current inability of democratization, about the specific features of an 'eastern' type of democracy or about the necessity of applying a more in-depth historical context, systematically integrating the previous Soviet experience of transitional media and linking it to the historical development of Western media at earlier stages of their evolution? We leave the answer to the reader.

Notes

1 Even today, despite all difficulties of economic and political development, more than 97 per cent of the Ukrainian population is fully and sufficiently literate (data consulted on the websites of the World Bank and Organisation for Security and Cooperation in Europe).
2 Data on Internet access and use were consulted at: http://www.nua.ie, http://www.pravda.com.ua, http://www.korespondent.net, http://ain.com.ua, http://www.worldbank.org, http://www.osce.org.
3 Consulted on http://www.topping.com.ua.
4 Most of the election and media reports written by international observers are accessible on the websites of the corresponding organizations.
5 Our coding scheme is partly based on the code books developed by Hallin (1986), Semetko *et al.* (1991) and Voltmer (2000).
6 However, the status of online papers is not yet legally defined, meaning that they are not officially recognized as mass media.
7 There is one more nationwide privately owned television channel, UT-2. It competes in popularity with *Inter* while UT-1 lags far behind these two in terms of popularity.
8 This conclusion is in line with Katrin Voltmer's (2000) research into the logic of the nationwide Russian newspaper *Izvestiya.*

References

Altheide, D. and Snow, R. (1979) *Media Logic,* London: Sage.
Bimber, B. (1999) 'The Internet and citizen communication with government. Does the medium matter?' *Political Communication,* 16(4): 409–28.
Brants, K. and Krasnoboka, N. (2001) 'Between soundbites and bullets. The challenges and frustrations of comparing old and new democracies', in Y. Zassoursky and E. Vartanova (eds) *Media for the Open Society. West–East and North–South Interface,* Moscow: Faculty of Journalism/IKAR, 281–305.
Brants, K. and van Praag, P. (2000) 'Politieke strijd: in of met de media?' [Political struggle: in or with the media?] in P. van Praag and K. Brants (eds) *Tussen Beeld en Inhoud. Politiek en media in de verkiezingen van 1998* [Between Image and Content: politics and media in the 1998 elections], Amsterdam: Het Spinhuis, 1–16.
Davis, G. (1997) 'Tocqueville revisited. Alexis de Tocqueville and the Internet', *Harvard International Journal of Press/Politics,* 2(2): 120–26.
Davis, R. (1999) *The Web of Politics. The Internet's Impact on the American Political System,* New York: Oxford University Press.
Gamson, W. and Modigliani, A. (1987) 'The changing culture of affirmative action', in R. Braungart (ed.) *Research in Political Sociology,* volume 3, Greenwich, CT: JAI Press, 137–77.
Gibson, R. and Ward, S. (1998) 'UK political parties and the Internet', *Harvard International Journal of Press/Politics,* 3(3): 14–38.
Hallin, D. (1986) *The 'Uncensored War'. The Media and Vietnam,* New York: Oxford University Press.
Kalathil, S. and Boas, T. (2001) 'The Internet and state control in authoritarian regimes: China, Cuba, and the counterrevolution', *First Monday,* 6(8). Online. Available HTTP: <http://www.firstmonday.org/issues/issue6_8/kalathil/index.html> (accessed 16 August 2005).

Krasnoboka, N. (2002) ' "Real journalism goes underground. The Internet underground". The phenomenon of online media in the Former Soviet Union Republics', *Gazette*, 64(5): 479–500.

Krasnoboka, N. and Semetko, H. (2003) ' "Electronic revolution". The role of the Internet in the ongoing protest actions in Ukraine'. Paper presented at the European Consortium of Political Research Joint Workshop Sessions, 28 March–2 April, Edinburgh, UK.

Margolis, M., Resnick D. and Chin-Chang, T. (1997) 'Campaigning on the Internet. Parties and candidates on the World Wide Web in the 1996 Primary Season', *Harvard International Journal of Press/Politics*, 2(1): 59–78.

Margolis, M., Resnick, D. and Wolfe, J. (1999) 'Party competition on the Internet in the United States and Britain', *Harvard International Journal of Press/Politics*, 4(4): 24–47.

Mazzoleni, G. (1987) 'Media logic and party logic in campaign coverage. The Italian General Election of 1983', *European Journal of Communication*, 2: 81–103.

Mickiewicz, E. (1997) *Changing Channels. Television and the Struggle for Power in Russia*, New York: Oxford University Press.

Norris, P. (2000) 'The global divide. Information poverty and Internet access worldwide'. Paper presented at the Internet Conference at the International Political Science World Congress in Quebec City, 1–6 August.

Organisation for Security and Cooperation in Europe (2001) OSCE Special Meeting in Vienna, 12–13 March 2001. Promoting Freedom of Expression. Online. Available HTTP: <http://www.vir.nl/publications/freedom-of-expression.html> (accessed 16 August 2005).

Resnick, D. (1998) 'Politics on the internet. The normalization of cyberspace', in C. Toulouse and T. Luke (eds) *The Politics of Cyberspace. A New Political Science Reader*, New York: Routledge, 48–68.

Selnow, G. (1998) *Electronic Whistle-Stops. The Impact of the Internet on American Politics*, Westport, CT: Praeger.

Semetko, H. and Krasnoboka, N. (2003) 'Political Biases in the Soviet Style? Television in Ukraine's 2002 Parliamentary Election'. Paper presented at the panel 'Political Stability and Change: Do the Media Matter?' Paper presented at the International Communication Association Conference, San Diego, CA. May.

Semetko, H., Blumler, J., Gurevitch, M. and Weaver, D. (1991) *The Formation of Campaign Agendas. A Comparative Analysis of Party and Media Roles in recent American and British Elections*, Hillsdale, NJ: Lawrence Erlbaum.

Splichal, S. (1994) *Media Beyond Socialism. Theory and Practice in East-Central Europe*, Boulder, CO: Westview Press.

Voltmer, K. (2000) 'Constructing political reality in Russia. *Izvestiya* – between old and new journalistic practices', *European Journal of Communication*, 15(4): 469–500.

Wu, W., Weaver, D. and Johnson, O. (1996) 'Professional roles of Russian and US journalists. A comparative study', *Journalism and Mass Communication Quarterly*, 73(3): 534–48.

Part II

Political parties, governments and elections

Communication strategies and the mediatization of politics

7 Electoral campaigning in Latin America's new democracies

The Southern Cone

Roberto Espíndola

Electoral campaigning is an essential part of political communication, going well beyond the development and implementation of media strategies at election time. It is a complex process of political socialization that ranges from interpersonal exchanges and advocacy (Worcester & Mortimore 2001: 137) to the role played by political parties and the media as sources of political culture. This chapter focuses on political campaigning as part of the consolidation of Latin American new democracies, specifically comparing recent campaigns in Argentina, Chile and Uruguay.[1]

For the first time in the history of Latin America, practically all societies in the region are ruled by democratically elected governments as a result of democratization processes that, since the late 1980s, have given an increased salience to party politics and electoral processes in Latin America. In some cases that salience has been enhanced by highly contested electoral campaigns and by unexpected results, but it has mainly resulted from the central role played by political parties in providing continuity and change – stability coupled with elements of democratic contestation. In other cases, periodical elections do not seem to suffice to provide stability and democratic governance; a key difference in these cases is the absence of political parties with a well-defined and relatively strong organization that allows institutionalized interaction. A major cause of the difference between stable and unstable political systems in Latin America relates to the effect the modernization and professionalization of politics – and particularly that of electoral campaigns – has had on political party structures.

Although the role played by elections is often emphasized by the now-massive literature dealing with democratization, the latter rarely goes beyond that, and does not seek to establish the effect of electoral processes on democratization's main protagonists, political parties. This chapter aims to discuss the professionalization of campaigning and its effects, and to do so with specific reference to three 'new' democracies of the Southern Cone of Latin America: Argentina, Chile and Uruguay, characterized (until December 2001 in the case of Argentina) by relative political stability and by the presence of institutionalized parties, within a context of regular elections. It argues that at least some of these parties have used and adapted marketing techniques, without that significantly affecting their institutional structure or the role of the party as a source of political culture. That is, though, a limited hypothesis, and not one seeking at this stage to develop comparisons with other cases in Latin America.

Comparative work on electoral campaigning makes only passing reference to Latin America, concluding that there has been an 'Americanization' of campaigns in the new democracies south of the Río Bravo (Angell *et al.* 1992: 43; Farrell 1996: 175). When seeking to ascertain what is meant by this Americanization, the most comprehensive definition is the one offered by Swanson and Mancini, who use the term 'to refer descriptively to particular types and elements of election campaigns and professional activities connected with them that were first developed in the United States and are now being applied and adapted in various ways in other countries' (1996: 5–6). They present this Americanization as a working hypothesis, but also as part of a wider process whereby electoral campaigns would become Americanized as part of a modernization that 'fragments social organisation, interests and identity, creating a complicated landscape of competing structures and conflicting symbolic realities which citizens must navigate' (1996: 9).

As argued elsewhere (Espíndola 2002), this labelling focuses attention on important aspects of campaigning, but also carries obvious risks as it could lead to a confusion between the use of techniques and information derived from scientific processes and the idea that decisions might be made by those who control those processes and techniques. Party and campaign organizational instances may receive information derived from opinion polls, focus groups, etc., just as they receive advice from political marketing experts. It is quite a different thing for the experts, pollsters and marketers to make campaign decisions, or decide about programmes and policies, based upon their professional criteria and experiences. A mass bureaucratic party may use political marketing techniques without necessarily adopting the specific organizational patterns that characterize an electoral-professional party. A campaign may use those techniques without taking decision-making away from regular party structures; however, the campaign becomes professionalized to the extent that decision-making is handed over to professionals and experts.

Campaigning and external shocks

If that distinction between technology and techniques is made, it could then be argued that the tools now used in Latin American campaigns include those characteristic of professionalized campaigning, but within organizational contexts different from that associated with the professionalized stage in Western Europe, the United States or Canada. Parties have reacted differently to changes in their opponents' campaigning and to the availability of new political marketing techniques. The Southern Cone experience indicates that different reactions have to a certain degree been related to internal factors, such as a party's history and ideology, but that a deciding element has been external events or shocks that have affected the party or the whole political system. Several shocks can be identified in these cases: (i) proscription during military dictatorships; (ii) economic crises; (iii) external support for democratization; and (iv) electoral defeat and loss of office.

Proscription during military dictatorships

The military dictatorships that plagued Latin America during the 1970s and 1980s meant proscription or at least a severe restriction in the activities of political parties, and in any case long periods without elections. In all Southern Cone cases, this was accompanied by extreme repression, including the imprisonment and execution of activists, appropriation of party property, and the dismantling of party networks and institutional life. Whilst parties managed to survive either by going underground or by going into various forms of hibernation, long periods of socialization by the military authorities – coupled, in the case of Argentina, with war and military defeat – had a profound intergenerational effect. The generations that grew up under military rule had no experience of elections and party activities and were socialized not to trust politicians; whilst the same generation was frequently active in seeking the overthrow of military dictatorships, recent surveys show that those aged between 25 and 40 are more likely not to trust political parties than older generations that had experienced politics in the 1960s and 1970s, or the younger generation that grew up under democratic rule.

When parties emerged from those periods of dictatorship and hibernation, they had to re-adjust to new circumstances. In most cases, and particularly in the left and centre-left, this led to an abandonment of the claims to represent particular sectors of society that characterize the mass party model. Instead, catch-all organizational patterns were adopted, parties becoming inclusive and addressing broader sectors of the electorate. They also had to adjust to the generational gap, as their leadership often still reflected the one they had prior to the period of military rule: as Hite (2000) has shown, the leaders of centre-left parties in the 1990s were already leading figures in the early 1970s. Military regimes did not only affect the left and centre-left, they also did away with the traditional parties of the right, unable to survive the clash between their parliamentary traditions and brutal regimes installed to defend the values and class interests the right claimed to represent. Particularly in the case of Chile, that led to the development of new parties and organizations, initially seeking to channel civilian support for the military regime, and subsequently to defend its economic policies.

Economic crises

In Argentina, the first civilian administration elected after the military regime, the government led by *Unión Cívica Radical* (UCR) President Raúl Alfonsín, collapsed ignominiously in 1989, unable to control a massive economic crisis and rampant hyperinflation, having to hand the presidency over to the newly elected Carlos Menem earlier than constitutionally anticipated. Although the causes for the crisis were largely outside Alfonsín's control and had more to do with the global economy and with the policies of the military regime (including their costly attempt to capture and retain the Falklands/Malvinas), this failure of the civilian administration to handle an economic crisis made a substantial impact on voters' perceptions. As Table 7.1 shows, whilst a sector of the Southern Cone and Latin American electorates does not trust political parties, such lack of trust has been particularly marked in Argentina. This led to the emergence of new groups, both from the left and the centre-right. But it also led to major changes within the UCR that, added to their electoral defeat in 1995, contributed to their successful adoption of professionalized campaigning in 1999.

External support for democratization

By the early 1980s, West European and North American governments, government agencies and foundations began actively to promote a return to democracy in Latin America. In the US, the government launched the Democracy Program in 1982 that then became the National Endowment for Democracy as an independent organization funded by the government. That, coupled to other political development programmes, meant annual budgets focusing on Latin America of some US$25 million during 1983–88 (Carothers 1996: 126–7). By comparison, by 1989 just one West German foundation, the Konrad Adenauer Foundation, was spending US$23 million in its Latin American and Caribbean programmes (Pinto-Duschinsky 1996: 250).

In a few cases, external actors went as far as to provide financial support to political parties and their leaders, but those were the exceptions rather

Table 7.1 Trust in political parties in 1998 and 2004

	% of respondents with 'a lot of' or 'some' confidence	
	1998	*2004*
Argentina	17	12
Chile	24	20
Uruguay	34	30
Latin America	21	19

Source: *Latinobarómetro*, 1998 and 2004.

than the rule. Some of the financial support, mainly from foundations, went to fund research programmes and centres, providing employment for academics and political cadres cut off from their normal jobs by the military authorities.

However, a good deal of the external assistance was provided as training for party activists and campaign organizers, and in the form of political consultants and electoral experts sent as campaign advisers. These were obvious forms of technology transfer, as the training and advice reflected the organizational and technical levels prevailing in the donor country. Thus, the professional campaigning techniques that prevailed in the US and Western Europe in the 1980s were transferred to political parties emerging from periods of authoritarian repression, as these underwent their re-organization as catch-all parties. Nor surprisingly, the result was a combination of the traditional campaigning parties had used in the 1960s, prior to their forced hibernation, and the professionalized techniques favoured in the donor countries.

Electoral defeat and loss of office

As Panebianco has already noted whilst discussing the German Christian Democratic Union of the early 1970s, 'expulsion from central power was the chief catalyst of change' (1988: 258).[2] Undoubtedly that was a main cause for the professionalization of campaigning in the Southern Cone parties, as demonstrated by the UCR in Argentina and the parties of the right in Chile, just as prolonged incumbency has been a cause for the retention of traditional forms of campaigning in the parties of the Chilean coalition *Concertación* (in government since 1990) and in the Argentine *Partido Justicialista* (1989–99).

For the parties of the Chilean right, the *Unión Democrática Independiente* (UDI) and *Renovación Nacional*, the adoption of professionalized campaigning came as a natural development. Most of their leaders had emerged during the Pinochet dictatorship, as part of the neo-liberal civilian technocrats who supported the regime and occupied government posts; a few exceptions hailed from the pre-1973 political parties. Important priming variables were their professional training (mainly in economics, business studies or engineering) and business experience that led them to rely on marketing. Their electoral experience up until 1989 consisted of applying marketing principles when putting forward the dictatorship's case at the 1980 and 1988 plebiscites.

The parties themselves developed during the 1980s and, having not had to campaign for office during those years, when they did face elections from 1989 onwards naturally exhibited electoral-professional characteristics. Their leadership has been highly personalized, consisting of well-known figures who communicated through the media with the party's membership and with the sector of the electorate whose opinion they claim to represent. The parties have a weak vertical structure, relying locally on notables and political bosses rather than on a grassroots membership; funding comes from interest groups, firms and wealthy supporters in a country where there is no limit to political donations.

Another case where electoral defeat and loss of office led to an adoption of professionalized campaigning, but without that having such a major effect on party organization, was that of the Argentine UCR. After having failed to control hyperinflation in 1989, and having been soundly defeated by the Peronists at that year's elections, the UCR went on to lose badly at the 1995 presidential elections, with 17 per cent of the vote compared with the 49.9 per cent received by Menem, the *Partido Justicialista*'s candidate.[3] After 1995, several modernizers elected to the UCR's leadership efficiently adopted elements of professionalized campaigning. By the 1999 elections, the professionalization of the UCR campaign was evident. However, that was mainly reflected in the presidential campaign, not in local campaigns for provincial governors and parliamentarians where many of the traditional techniques continued to be used effectively.

The Southern Cone campaigns

Let us examine the extent to which the 1999 and 2001 electoral campaigns in Argentina and Chile, as well as Uruguay's 1999 campaign, were professionalized.

Nominations and the perverse effect of primaries

In the case of Chile, the electoral confrontation occurred mainly between two large coalitions. One was the centre-left coalition *Concertación de Partidos por la Democracia* (normally referred to as *Concertación*), in office since 1990 and bringing together the Christian Democratic Party, Radical Social Democratic Party, Party for Democracy, Socialist Party and the small Liberal Party. The other, *Alianza por Chile* (Alliance for Chile), was formed by the extreme right-wing UDI and the more moderate *Renovación Nacional*. There were also four minor forces presenting candidates, ranging from Pinochet loyalists to environmentalists and the Communist Party.

The two main coalitions chose radically different methods to nominate their candidates and to face the preliminary stage of the campaign (May–October 1999). *Concertación* had a difficult task in getting its four main partners to agree on a nomination, particularly since the two previous presidential elections (in 1989 and 1993) had been won with Christian Democratic candidates and now the Socialists and the Party for Democracy claimed their rights. Following the precedent set in 1993, the *Concertación* held a primary open to all voters, not only to their party members,[4] hoping to whip up support for their nominee.

The May 1999 primary had a Christian Democratic nominee, Andrés Zaldívar, against one jointly proposed by the Socialist Party and Party for Democracy, Ricardo Lagos. After a bitter campaign that succeed in getting almost 1.4 million people to vote, Lagos won the nomination by a very large margin: 71.3 to 28.7 per cent.

However, the primary had a perverse effect, not anticipated by the *Concertación* leadership. The bitterly fought campaign and Zaldívar's massive defeat left a deep resentment amongst Christian Democrats. This shows the difficulties posed by primaries, in which party structures are by-passed and voters are left with the media as both their main intermediary and the main arena for public debate (Patterson 1994: 182–91).

A similar situation took place in Uruguay, where the centre-left coalition *Encuentro Progresista–Frente Amplio* (EP-FA) was deeply divided at the primaries between its leader and major of Montevideo, Tabaré Vázquez, and the centre Senator Danilo Astori. After a massive triumph for Vázquez, the hostility generated by the campaign led the victor to refuse the vice-presidential slot to the loser, preferring instead to have Christian Democratic leader Rodolfo Nin as running mate. On the other side of the political scale, the right-wing National party and *Partido Colorado* parties, traditionally divided into dozens of factions, a division formally recognized and promoted by the electoral system, had no difficulty in using primary elections to arrive at their presidential nominations. At the ruling *Partido Colorado*, the primaries were won by the *Lista 15* faction, Jorge Batlle, with all other factions uniting under him.

The cases of Chile and Uruguay show the differences between primaries taking place within a party, where factions find it possible after the primaries to coalesce behind the party's nominated candidate, and the same process taking place within a coalition of established parties – such as Chile's *Concertación* and Uruguay's EP-FA – with ideological and historical rivalries.

There is, however, a tendency within the region increasingly to use open primary elections as a means to nominate candidates. One of the influences – negative, in my opinion – received as part of US agencies' support for democracy has been the belief that it is 'more democratic' for candidates to be nominated in open primary elections, rejecting what they caricaturized as selection by 'party bosses' in 'smoke-filled rooms'. As Patterson has argued, the result is a weakening of party structures and a strengthening of the role played by the media.

Campaign tactics

The 1999 campaign in Chile could hardly have been called 'Americanized', since both coalitions fought hard for the traditional ground where campaigning success has been demonstrated in the country since the 1950s: the streets. The techniques that characterize professionalized campaigning in the US and Western Europe were there (even the consultants were the same), but the key asset remained the ability to field party activists or 'volunteers', to hold mass rallies and to cover every wall, lamppost and public space with posters, or just to paint them with the candidates' names. The 'grassroots gladiators' that Putnam misses in US campaigns (2000: 37) remain central to campaigns in the Southern Cone.

Candidates may engage in media-staged debates, but nothing has replaced the attraction of the mass rally or the razzmatazz of the candidates' visits to villages and populous neighbourhoods. The campaign becomes the only game in town in a very literal sense, with even the marketing of supermarket products adopting electoral themes, showing their centrality to social life.

This is particularly the case in Chile, the only Latin American country without a carnival, where campaign activities are the closest thing most people experience to a street party. At the 1999 campaign, Lavín – the centre-right *Alianza por Chile* candidate – avoided public debates, conceding only one television confrontation with *Concertación* candidate Lagos. Instead, from June 1999 onwards, he constantly toured the provinces. Each visit to a village was preceded by massive preparatory work by an advance group of activists and music bands, enabling the candidate's arrival to become a carnival, all of it professionally video-recorded and photographed to be then provided free of charge to the media.

However, if we distinguish between professionalized and traditional, labour-intensive campaigns, there is no doubt that *Alianza*'s was the former. It was highly personalized, run by political consultants, making extensive use of telemarketing, websites, opinion polls and focus groups, and successfully seeking to control media coverage. But to see that campaign as purely capital-intensive would be a mistake. *Alianza* had learnt from previous experiences, when *Concertación* activists had controlled the streets. This time *Alianza* fought also on that ground but, unable to mobilize party activists, it relied on large numbers of paid young 'volunteers' who accompanied the candidate on his constant tours, and stood at street junctions in city centres waving *Alianza*'s blue flags and leafleting drivers and pedestrians, whilst paid bouncers kept an eye on propaganda painted on walls or placed by the side of busy roads. The door-to-door canvassing traditional of *Concertación* campaigns was also emulated by paid 'volunteers'[5] who canvassed low-income neighbourhoods.

On the other hand, *Concertación*'s campaign style stressed door-to-door canvassing, motorcades and neighbourhood meetings that combined carnival-style bands, performances by local artistes, games for children, chess competitions and free services provided by supporters, from legal, medical and social work advice, to hairdressing and fortune-telling. In other words, *Concertación* unleashed its infantry. Whilst the Lavín campaign was by the far the most professionalized and the one making most effective use of political marketing, both main candidates made full use of experts, advisors, television spots, focus groups and every political marketing tool.

In Chile, legislation limits television electoral advertising to two daily free spots simultaneously broadcast by all stations. No such restraint existed in Argentina, where marketing techniques were also much used at the 1999 presidential and parliamentary campaigns.

In the Argentine case, the two main contenders for the presidency were the incumbent *Partido Justicialista* (or Peronists), represented by Eduardo Duhalde, and the *Alianza por la Justicia, el Trabajo y la Educación* (Alliance for Justice, Work and Education, *Alianza* for short – but poles apart from its Chilean namesake), a centre-left alliance of the traditional UCR and the leftist coalition *Frepaso*, putting forward Fernando De la Rúa as their candidate.

Both candidates had highly professionalized campaigns. As in the Chilean case, this emphasis on political marketing went hand-in-hand with a retention of the mass rally and the candidates' touring of provincial villages. Personnel-intensive campaigning, however, was better undertaken by the parties with a territorial network across the country, namely the Peronists and UCR, rather than *Frepaso*, whose main strength was amongst intellectuals, students and the professional middle class.

Political consultants and pollsters

The return to democracy in the Southern Cone brought along with it the emergence of pollsters and political consultants. In some cases marketing experts moved onto the field of politics and began to advise the parties of the right, in others a by-product of the transition to democracy was the emergence of pollsters and consultants, as in the case of Graciela Romner in Argentina, Mori and CERC in Chile and Equipos-Mori in Uruguay.

In Argentina's 1999 presidential campaign top international political consultants were engaged by De la Rúa and Duhalde, the former hiring Dick Morris and the latter being advised first by James Carville and then by the Brazilian Duda Mendonça. However, both campaigns also made use of local political marketers, image specialists and pollsters.

Foreign political consultants and local marketers were similarly observed in the Chilean campaigns. Lavín, the centre-right candidate, was advised by Puerto Rico-based consultant Bruno Haring, and his campaign staff included top local pollsters. The centre-left *Concertación* had access to several foreign political consultants, including Jacques Séguéla, Éric Flimon and German advisors linked to the Christian Democratic Union/Christian Social Union; that was of limited value, since the advice from the French consultants hardly ever coincided with that from their German colleagues.

Foreign consultants did not play a significant role in Uruguay's 1999 elections, where the campaigns were led directly by the candidates themselves. Any advice from local consultants and pollsters was given directly to the candidates, who would make campaign decisions: anyone appointed as campaign manager was more an assistant to the candidate that a decision-maker.[6] During the 1990s, several local pollsters became established in Uruguay: Equipos-Mori, Cifra, Interconsult, Factum and Radar. Whilst some prefer to remain out of politics, the two largest ones have extended their activities to cover political marketing, and at the 1999 elections Cifra provided polls and advice for the candidate of the right, Jorge Batlle, whilst Equipos-Mori advised the centre-left candidate, Tabaré Vázquez.

In Chile, there is also a wide variety of pollsters and consultants, but they are seen – rightly or wrongly – as more closely aligned with the main political coalitions. By the 1999 presidential campaign, several firms appeared to be aligned with the right, or even owned or managed by known right-wing politicians, as in the cases of Larraín y Asociados, Benchmark, Atel and Productora 2000. A smaller number of firms appeared aligned to *Concertación*, or even having emerged from its previous campaigns, such as ADE, Caditel, Visión Comunicaciones and TVCorp. Others are academic research centres such as CERC (*Centro de Estudios de la Realidad Contemporánea*) led by Carlos Huneuus, whose membership of the Christian Democratic Party means CERC is seen as at least close to *Concertación*. The same applies to the local branch of Mori, led by Marta Lagos, despite the fact that they are the main base for the highly professional *Latinobarómetro* surveys.

It was not surprising, then, that for the 1999 presidential campaign, pollsters such as Benchmark played a key role in providing survey and focus group results for the campaign of the right. *Concertación*, on the other hand, relied exclusively on polls and focus groups privately conducted by their in-house pollsters; their results were not – and have never – been revealed, but seemed to have seriously misled presidential candidate Ricardo Lagos into thinking that he would win the first round on 12 December by a substantial ten-point margin when most pollsters were suggesting a very close result, as indeed it was, making it necessary to go to a second round one month later.

The media

The evidence from Latin America's new democracies would allow a refutal of any normative contentions allocating a 'democratic function' to the media, or claiming that the qualities of independence *and* pluralism would both necessarily apply to the media in liberal democracies. By definition, independent media have the freedom not to be pluralistic, and attempts to force a search for pluralism may, in some cases, hinder the media's independence.

In most of Latin America's deeply unequal societies, the ownership and control of newspapers and other media reflects the high level of wealth concentration: powerful economic groups include amongst their assets the main newspapers, television and radio stations. During periods of authoritarian rule, those media invariably supported the rulers and benefited in terms of advertising and even state subsidies.[7] The only breach in their power took place during transitional periods when external support for democratic forces assisted and funded alternative media but, when the democratic process was deemed to have been consolidated, the external funding disappeared and so did those alternative media.

Chile has been a clear case of the contradiction between media independence and pluralism. Two large economic groups, El Mercurio and Copesa, control the main newspapers, dividing a segmented audience amongst their publications, with *El Mercurio* addressing upper to middle strata and Copesa's *La Tercera* going for middle to lower socio-economic groups. Since both groups supported the military regime, in 1987 several Christian Democrats – with West European support – founded an alternative daily, *La Epoca*. However, they never managed to get the circulation of 70,000 copies a day required to make it economically viable. *La Epoca* played an important role during the transitional period, but once President Patricio Aylwin was elected and took office in 1990 the situation worsened for the newspaper. The democratic government had a commitment to pluralism that prevented it from favouring *La Epoca*, as the dictatorship had favoured *El Mercurio*. In fact, *El Mercurio* and *La Tercera* did well once democracy became firmly established. By 1996 *El Mercurio* controlled 61.6 per cent of all newspaper advertising and *La Tercera* had 14.4 per cent, whilst *La Epoca* received only 1.4 per cent. As external support for *La Epoca* dried up, part of its shares were sold to Copesa and the paper closed down in 1996.

Table 7.2 Favourability of campaign coverage of Lagos and Lavín in *El Mercurio* and *La Tercera* in the four-week period from 12 November to 9 December 1999

| | *Favourabilty of coverage* | | | |
	Week 1	*Week 2*	*Week 3*	*Week 4*
El Mercurio				
Lagos	–7	–11	–13	–7
Lavín	–3	+5	+3	–1
La Tercera				
Lagos	–5	+1	–3	–8
Lavín	–7	–5	–2	+5

Note
The orientation of every campaign item is classified as in Patterson (1994: 116–7); discarding neutral items, the table presents the balance of negative and positive items.

The 1999 presidential campaign showed how Chile's two main newspapers were aligned. Table 7.2 presents the results of a content analysis of coverage of the two main candidates in *El Mercurio* and *La Tercera* in the four weeks before polling day. The broadsheet *El Mercurio* maintained consistently negative coverage of the *Concertación*'s candidate Lagos, with a far more favourable coverage of the right's candidate Lavín. The tabloid *La Tercera* adopted a different line, starting with a coverage comparatively less negative for Lagos in week 1, arrived at a balanced view on week 3 and concluded firmly for Lavín and against Lagos the week before polling day. This is significant since local polls indicated that 20 per cent of voters made their minds up during the week prior to the election and that most of them were in the middle to lower strata addressed by *La Tercera*.

Although Chile is a society with a relatively high circulation of newspapers (see Table 7.3), newspapers do not play a crucial role in influencing the population; Tables 7.4 and 7.5 show that, at the time of the 1999 elections, most Chileans trusted television and radio more than newspapers and relied almost twice as much on the former for access to news. That situation has recently changed, with a significant drop in confidence on television, a tendency observed throughout the region. This could be largely explained as consequence of the diversification and commercialization of television broadcasting that has resulted from greater deregulation and the rapid expansion of cable. Conversely, newspapers play an important role where a pluralistic press has been achieved thanks to rivalries between economic groups: for example in Argentina and Brazil, where *Latinobarómetro* has consistently shown greater trust in newspapers than in television.

Recent electoral campaigns have shown the effects of those differences. In Argentina, support for the two main candidates at the 1999 presidential election was divided between the two main newspapers, with *Clarín* supporting De la Rúa and *La Nación* backing Duhalde, whilst television was open for each candidate to buy advertising.

At Chile's presidential election that year, the field was anything but level. The candidate of the right, Lavín, was firmly supported by both main newspaper groups, but under Chilean electoral legislation no television advertising was allowed; instead, television stations were required to provide two daily, free 15-minute spots, shared between all candidates and

Table 7.3 Daily newspaper circulations and ownership of television sets in Argentina, Brazil, Colombia, Chile, Mexico and Spain in 1999

| | *No. per 1,000 inhabitants* | | | | | |
	Argentina	*Brazil*	*Colombia*	*Chile*	*Mexico*	*Spain*
Newspapers sold	123	40	46	98	97	99
Television sets	223	223	115	215	272	409

Source: Unesco, *Statistical Yearbook*, 1999

Table 7.4 Trust in Congress and in the media in Latin America, 2001–04

| | % of respondents with 'a lot' or 'some' confidence | | | | | | | |
| | Congress | | Television | | Radio | | Newspapers | |
	2001	2004	2001	2004	2001	2003[a]	2001	2004
Argentina	17	21	40	29	59	45	53	40
Brazil	23	35	39	34	50	50	51	53
Colombia	14	24	51	39	50	41	40	41
Chile	33	30	69	40	69	49	60	40
Mexico	25	23	54	28	50	48	44	42
Peru	23	14	50	33	49	40	39	30
Uruguay	46	30	55	39	66	52	54	39
Venezuela	37	31	53	38	56	33	52	36
Latin America	24	25	49	38	51	41	46	40

Source: *Latinobarómetro*, 2001, 2003 and 2004

Note

a The question was not included in the 2004 survey.

simultaneously broadcast by all stations. This did not prevent the manipulation of television news bulletins covering the campaign. On a daily basis, the Lavín campaign staff provided all television stations with free, expensively produced videos depicting the candidate's activities. At the same time, television journalists and camera crews covering Lavín's campaign were given free transport, meals and accommodation. Even in cases where there was some initial resistance, after a while television journalists and crews became dependent on such generous hospitality and found it easier

Table 7.5 Number of days in the previous week when respondents read/heard/saw the news in daily newspapers, on the radio or on television, (averages) 2001–04

| | Daily newspapers | | Radio | | Television | |
	2001	2004	2001	2004	2001	2004
Argentina	3.83	3.15	5.66	5.63	5.28	5.44
Brazil	3.90	3.45	5.45	4.79	5.66	5.15
Colombia	2.68	2.55	5.01	4.26	5.43	4.63
Chile	3.32	3.52	5.40	4.92	5.60	5.35
Mexico	4.08	3.40	4.32	4.58	5.00	4.91
Peru	4.01	3.55	4.89	4.96	5.30	4.74
Uruguay	3.44	2.96	5.92	6.04	5.37	5.83
Venezuela	4.59	3.66	4.72	4.38	5.31	4.73
Latin America	3.86	3.37	5.04	4.88	5.16	4.89

Source: *Latinobarómetro*, 2001 and 2004.

to focus on the sound bites sketched by the campaign staff and on the 'infotaintment' provided by the candidate wearing colourful local dress and sharing a meal or spending the night with a local family.[8]

The centre-left candidate and eventual winner, Lagos, could not match that generosity. Besides having no access to funding such as Lavín's, Lagos had no support amongst the economic groups owning television stations, nor could he count on the state channel, since the latter was run by a board with equal number of representatives from each side to ensure its neutrality. However, his main disadvantage was not at the level of editorial control, but at the more micro level of managing the news, the camera angles adopted to report a speech at a rally and the reporting of the candidate's sound bite for the day instead of any contradictions over policy or other embarrassment source.

It could be argued that, since Lagos won despite such campaign short-comings, all this does not really matter. But the impressive electoral gains of this media-wise new right, cleansed from its associations with Pinochet, show that it does matter, particularly in countries with a high circulation of newspapers and access to television. Table 7.3 shows that Argentina, Chile and Mexico exhibit newspaper circulation figures comparable to or higher than those of Spain, a country that shares circulation levels with Italy and Australia. The same applies to television, since 97 per cent of Chilean homes have access to television.

In 1999 that seemed reinforced by the trust and reliance on television found in Chile and Uruguay, as shown in Tables 7.4 and 7.5; in both countries, *Latinobarómetro* found at that time higher levels of political trust[9] as well as a trust in television and a reliance on that medium for news significantly higher than the Latin American averages. As the tables also show, trust in television has declined significantly since then.

Campaign funds

Large sums of money were spent in campaigns in Argentina and Chile; at that time and as in most of Latin America, neither country had any legislation regulating electoral expenditure or requiring transparency in campaign funding.[10] There were, however, substantial differences in the resources available to parties and candidates. In Argentina, the state provides funding for parties, based on their prior electoral results: in 1999 the *Alianza* received US$23.3 million from the state and the *Partido Justicialista* got US$18.5 million, but sources at both campaign headquarters agreed that those funds only covered a small proportion of their costs.[11] In Chile, the candidate of the right, Lavín, had access to massive funding and the support of powerful business groups. Weeks before the first electoral round local newspapers claimed that the Lavín campaign had a projected cost of US$52 million and his representatives did not deny the figure; after the second round, analysts estimated the total cost of Lavín's campaign at nearly US$120 million.[12] The cost of the Lagos campaign had been originally expected to reach no higher than a comparatively modest US$9 million, but a leading member of *Concertación* estimated expenditure to have reached US$40 million by the second round.[13]

The situation is somewhat different for parliamentary campaigns, although where the state subsidizes them – as in Argentina – that subsidy, limited as it is, ensures a degree of campaign centralization in the hands of political parties. In Chile, where no such subsidies exist, funding for parliamentary campaigns is not centralized and candidates must find their own funds, making it an expensive activity. At the 2001 parliamentary elections, *Concertación* candidates were advised not to think of standing unless they could count on some US$70,000 in the case of those aspiring to be deputies and US$0.5m in the case of senatorial candidates; opposition sources, on the other hand, claimed that even that was a gross understatement.

Even pre-candidates failing to get nominated at the Christian Democratic Party primaries found it to be an expensive exercise: one pre-candidate said he had to spend £25,000 in his campaign, whilst in the southern city of Concepción, the defeated pre-candidate claimed to have spent twice that sum.

The impact of new campaigning techniques

Recent campaigns in the Southern Cone have demonstrated a growing presence of professionalized techniques and a similar phenomenon was observed in other Latin American cases; such techniques played a key role in the 2000–1 elections in Mexico, Peru and Venezuela. However, in the Southern Cone their presence went alongside a continuous reliance on labour-intensive techniques.

The presence of modern techniques of political marketing does not, by itself, demonstrate a professionalization of campaigning. Although the main Argentine and Chilean coalitions made extensive use of political marketing in 1999, their campaigns were very different in terms of management, decision-making processes and the use of experts and consultants.

In Chile, both main coalitions had their own professional campaign teams and made use of foreign experts, but kept the latter at a distance. Decisions were sometimes made by experts linked to the parties forming each coalition, but frequently decision-makers were even more closely associated with the candidates themselves. Lavín's campaign team consisted of young professionals in their thirties or forties, whose main asset was their closeness to Lavín. They had access to political marketing experts such as Bruno Haring, with extensive experience of US electoral campaigning, but the decisions rested with the campaign staff.

The Chilean centre-left campaign was not too different. Whilst decision-making was in the hands of a group of leaders from the *Concertación* parties, these have been chosen by the closeness to the candidate, who intervened often to arbitrate in disputes or to take initiatives. Campaign staff also had access to sophisticated data and analysis from think-tanks and pollsters, providing daily forecasts of potential conflicts that could affect the government and therefore the campaign, and analyses of rival campaigns, as well as results from surveys and focus groups. Decisions were, however, taken by the campaign team, and expert advice played only a marginal role, particularly in the case of foreign consultants. That is clearly demonstrated in Séguéla's bitter complaints about his advice being ignored by Lagos's campaign team (2000: 56–7).

That was different from the campaign of Argentina's centre-left opposition coalition, *Alianza*. The situation was not the same, since in 1999 Argentine voters were also electing provincial governors and members of the federal Congress, a process in which local parties had a major say. But at the level of the presidential campaign, management was entrusted to a non-party group of young technocrats, advised by Dick Morris and a team of local pollsters and consultants. This was a mechanism used by presidential candidate De la Rúa to distance himself from the parties forming the *Alianza* coalition. Decision-making for the presidential campaign was under the control of a small group of young technocrats led by De la Rúa's son, Antonio, and locally known as the 'sushi group'.[14] Once elected president, De la Rúa remained dependent on the 'sushi group' – now appointed as government officers – as well as on political consultants, rather than on the *Alianza* parties.

The campaign of Argentina's ruling *Partido Justicialista* showed a similar pattern, but there the situation was made worse by the sharp conflict between the candidate and President Menem, who opposed the Duhalde's candidacy and focused on preparing his own return in 2003. The campaign, hence, was not led by one political team, but split between two.[15] Political consultant James Carville did his best to impress on the candidate the need to conduct the campaign with independence from Menem-dominated *Partido Justicialista* structures. After a while, Carville could not take any longer a campaign he had to fight on two fronts and left in August 1999, claiming that the candidate was 'listening to too many bells at the same time'.[16]

Conclusions

Recent electoral campaigns in the Southern Cone show a significant presence of professionalized campaigning, much of it introduced as a consequence of shocks or events that were largely external to political parties. That professionalized campaigning was, however, combined with traditional, labour-intensive techniques.

Campaign professionalization had a substantial effect on some parties that adopted almost archetypal electoral-professional organizations and whose campaigns were fully run by professionals. Others, however, adopted some of the techniques but kept the campaign under political control, retaining their own mass-bureaucratic characteristics. This has had a clear effect on parties themselves and on political stability, as shown by the riots of December 2001 and the subsequent political instability in Argentina.

The Southern Cone campaigns also showed that professionalization is not a unilinear process: just as all parties have adopted it to different degrees and at different levels of proximity to their leadership, some of the most professionalized campaigns had to adopt labour-intensive techniques or seek commercial alternatives.

Notes

1 This chapter is based on fieldwork conducted November 1999–January 2001 thanks to support from the British Academy (SG-33022) and from the Research Committee, University of Bradford.
2 Panebianco's work was originally published in 1982.
3 The UCR's defeatist state of mind at that time was demonstrated by some of their leaders claiming that the party was putting forward 'a candidate for losing'.
4 Membership of the main *Concertación* parties ranged from the Christian Democratic Party with some 120,000 members and the Socialist Party with 85,000, among an electorate that exceeds 8 million voters.
5 These were mainly unemployed young people. Those we interviewed at a Santiago crossroads claimed to receive US$10 a day plus a packed lunch, to wear the *Alianza* blue t-shirts, wave flags, leaflet car drivers and look neat and cheerful. In Concepción, young left-wing students confessed with embarrassment to supplementing their income by guarding *Alianza* publicity by night.
6 Interview with the head of Equipos-Mori, 20 December 2001.
7 The Chilean right-wing newspaper *El Mercurio* was rewarded by the Pinochet dictatorship even in the latter's last days in office, having its debts refinanced and reduced at a cost of US$12m in state funds (Cortés 1998: 563).
8 Interview with one of Lavín's top campaign coordinators, 4 December 2001. For the concept of 'infotaintment', see Norris (2000: 13).
9 The author follows the lead given by Newton (1999) in using trust in the national congress as the best comparative indicator of political trust.
10 Both countries have now enacted legislation seeking to limit campaign expenditure.
11 *La Nación*, 8 September 1999.
12 The figure was implicitly confirmed to the author by one of Lavín's campaign organizers, who qualified it by saying that it was 'twice, but not three times, what [the *Concertación* candidate Ricardo] Lagos spent'.
13 Figure given by the then-leader of the Socialist bench at the Chamber of Deputies, Francisco Encina, at a seminar in Salamanca, June 2000.
14 Allegedly because of their taste for Japanese food.
15 Menem showed his contempt for Duhalde by telling his lieutenants: 'Give him whatever he wants, he is going to lose anyway', *La Nación*, 7 September 1999, (author's translation).
16 See *Clarín*, 17 August 1999.

References

Angell, A., D'Alva, M., Kinzo, G. and Urbaneja, D. (1992) 'Latin America', in D. Butler and A. Ranney (eds) *Electioneering. A Comparative Study of Continuity and Change*, Oxford: Clarendon.

Carothers, T. (1996) 'The resurgence of US political development assistance to Latin America in the 1980s', in L. Whitehead (ed.) *The International Dimensions of Democratization*, Oxford: Oxford University Press, 128–36.

Cortés, F. (1998) 'Modernización y concentración: los medios de comunicación en Chile', in C. Toloza and E. Lahera (eds) *Chile en los noventa*, Santiago, Chile: Dirección de Estudios de la Presidencia de la República, 557–611.

Espíndola, R. (2002) 'Professionalised campaigning and political parties in Latin America', *Journal of Political Marketing*, 1(4): 65–81.

Farrell, D. (1996) 'Campaign strategies and tactics', in L. LeDuc, R. Niemi and P. Norris (eds), *Comparing Democracies*, London: Sage, 160–83.

Hite, K. (2000) *When the Romance Ended. Leaders of the Chilean Left, 1968–1998*, New York: Columbia University Press.

Newton, K. (1999) 'Social and political trust in established democracies', in P. Norris (ed.) *Critical Citizens*, Oxford: Oxford University Press, 169–87.

Norris, P. (2000) *A Virtuous Circle*, New York: Cambridge University Press.

Panebianco, A. (1988) *Political Parties. Organization and Power*, Cambridge: Cambridge University Press.

Patterson, T.E. (1994) *Out of Order*, New York: Vintage.

Pinto-Duschinsky, M. (1996) 'International political finance. The Konrad Adenauer foundation and Latin America', in L. Whitehead (ed.) *The International Dimensions of Democratization*, Oxford: Oxford University Press, 227–55.

Putnam, R.D. (2000) *Bowling Alone. The Collapse and Revival of American Community*, New York: Simon & Schuster.

Séguéla, J. (2000) *Le Vertige des Urnes*, Paris: Flammarion.

Swanson, D.L. and Mancini, P. (eds) (1996) *Politics, Media, and Modern Democracy*, Westport: Praeger.

Worcester, R. and Mortimore, R. (2001) *Explaining Labour's Second Landslide*, London: Politico's.

8 Democratization and election campaigning in Taiwan

Professionalizing the professionals

Gary Rawnsley

This chapter aims to understand how democratization has transformed Taiwan's election culture by analysing trends in election campaigning and communication since the first direct presidential election in 1996.[1] A detailed comparison of the major campaigns offers an opportunity to track the maturation of election communication during a comprehensive regime transition from authoritarianism to democracy, and suggests that meaningful election communication is dependent on social liberalization and political democratization. Constitutional reforms, for example, have allowed for multi-party elections through direct vote at every level of Taiwan's political system, while liberalization of the media has created new public spheres that allow for greater transparency and accountability of politicians, and greater opportunities for them to communicate with their constituencies in ever more creative ways. These developments signify a growing professionalization of election campaigning that is evident in the way candidates communicate with the voters, mobilize their supporters and respond to changes in public opinion.

This chapter proposes that such professionalization represents a process of modernization that operates as a complement to, not a substitute for, traditional methods of voter communication and mobilization. To fully understand election campaigns in democratic Taiwan, we need to acknowledge a distinct hybridization of approaches that allows the existing election culture to absorb new and streamlined campaign organizations, as well as fresh approaches to delivering the desired message. Taiwan's politicians are now accepting that their electoral success can depend on their emulation of the organization strategies, content, delivery mechanisms and feedback processes that structure election campaigns elsewhere.

The political competition associated with democratic Taiwan compels parties not only to devote more time, energy, and resources to designing campaigns that appeal to the largest number of voters, but also to give equal attention to how they intend to manage the campaign. This will involve understanding and tracking changes in public opinion and adjusting the campaign accordingly. It also means fine-tuning the election strategy according to the tone and content of the opposition's campaign. Finally, given the dominant position of the media in Taiwan, and the rise of the 'permanent campaign', parties must seek to control the news agenda at all times during and between elections (Marrek 1995: 2, 28).

The democratization of Taiwan

The coincidence of three processes transformed the campaign culture and sharpened electoral competition in Taiwan. Democratization and constitutional reforms opened the political system to genuine multi-party competition and provided the basis for the transfer of power that occurred in the 2000 presidential election, ending the monopoly on political power that the Kuomintang Nationalist party (KMT) had had for over 50 years. At the same time, the government decided to completely liberalize the media and this, together with developments in communications and computer technology, created new public spheres for political communication, discussion, electoral competition and mobilization (Rawnsley 2004).

In summary:

- In 1986, the Democratic Progressive Party (DPP) was established and, although technically still illegal, contested elections for the National Assembly and the Legislative Yuan (Taiwan's Parliament).
- In 1987, the state of emergency under the National Security Law During the Period of Mobilization for Suppression of the Communist Rebellion was lifted.
- In 1988, restrictions on the print media were lifted (allowing the registration of new newspapers and removing all limitations on the number of pages newspapers could publish).
- Prior to the 1989 elections, legislation allowed new parties to organize and compete with the KMT. All parties that met a minimal requirement were allowed to broadcast television advertisements during the campaign, and candidates were allowed to place advertisements in the print media.
- In 1991, the Judicial Yuan decided that all parliamentarians elected by mainland constituencies had to retire by 31 December 1991.
- In 1993, cable television was legalized.
- In 1994, the National Assembly passed an amendment to the constitution that allows for the direct popular election of the president and vice-president.[2]

The 2000 presidential election marked the beginning of what is referred to in the literature on regime transition as the 'consolidation phase' of democratization, persuading Freedom House to upgrade Taiwan's rating to a status comparable to that of most members of the European Union

(Freedom House 2001). Freedom House even went on to declare Taiwan and Japan the most democratic societies in Asia, characterized by relatively high voter turnout rates (hovering around 70 per cent[3]) that are the envy of other consolidated democracies. Freedom House is convinced that the institutional design of elections in Taiwan allows for genuine multiparty competition that permits free and fair campaigning for votes (including access to the media). Moreover, there is little evidence of the scourge of modern democracies, voter apathy: anyone who has the good fortune to observe an election campaign in Taiwan will be struck by the excitement, the noise and the obvious enthusiasm of the participants. For a clear insight into the energy of election campaigns, consider the following reports in the English-language *Taipei Times*:

> Overzealous flag waving at campaign rallies ... is leading to a high number of shoulder injuries among political enthusiasts, landing them in hospital . . .. [M]any patients ask for a quick treatment so they can 'go back and continue supporting their candidates' at the campaign rallies.
>
> (6 November 2001)

> Fanatical Taiwan voters and campaigners, stricken with election mania disorders, are packing hospital wards with mental illnesses and physical pains brought on by the uncertain outcome of Saturday's presidential election. In the past two weeks, there has been a 10 to 15 per cent increase in the number of patients diagnosed as having psychiatric disorders linked to the election. ... Passionate advocates of the leading ... hopefuls are suffering from mania, depression, anxiety and panic attacks. ... One patient ... talked incessantly about the poll and spent most of his time on campaign activities, surviving on less than two hours of sleep each day. When his family brought him in, the first thing he asked [the doctor] was 'who will you vote for?' before he started handing out campaign literature.
>
> (16 March 2000)

> Citing a rise in the number of psychological disorders in the run-up to tomorrow's election, physicians warned members of the public to be on the lookout for symptoms of 'election syndrome'. Psychiatrist Chen Kuo-hua ... said yesterday that over the past month, his department has treated 20 to 30 percent more patients than average for symptoms such as anxiety and insomnia. Some of the patients ... even continued campaigning for their favourite candidates after arriving at the hospital ... Officials at Taipei Medical College Hospital have publicized a case of physical injury they said had resulted from a scuffle over voting preferences ... [which] continued in the emergency ward.
>
> (17 March 2000)

Compare the drama and exhilaration described in these reports with the following account of the 1991 landmark National Assembly election:[4]

> In November public polls showed that 56 percent of the voting-age population did not view the election as important. Many people did not watch the television campaign, and some of those who did misunderstood which party stood for what. A telephone survey found that only 18 percent of those polled watched the program; of those polled, about two-thirds viewed the political advertising from beginning to end. Half the households reported that they did not believe such political information would influence how they voted. More than half the voters did not know what the election was about. Nearly 60 percent of those polled reported that they did not understand the various categories of electing candidates.
>
> (Chao and Myers 1998: 232–3)

Clearly the intervening years have witnessed a remarkable transformation in Taiwan's election culture that has energized popular participation and reflects the deepening of democracy there.

The parties respond

Inevitably, the KMT was the first to understand the changes that democratization would impose on election campaigning. Declining popular support, the increasing strength of opposition politicians, 'Taiwanization' (the deliberate co-optation and appointment of more Taiwanese to high positions within the party and government that were previously reserved for those of mainland origin) and the growth of an urban, educated, affluent middle class forced the KMT in the early 1980s to question the value of its tried and tested campaign methods. Party strategists began to select more attractive candidates, survey popular preferences, store and analyse election data, and draw on the expertise of marketing specialists (Dickson 1996: 62). As polls indicated a rising proportion of voters could not decide which way to vote, the KMT began to design particular messages for specific geographic and demographic groups. The KMT's new approach to election campaigning is highlighted by Chao and Myers (1998: 164–6) in their discussion of the 1989 regional-city elections: the party divided the island into 'election combat zones' and thus the election 'quickly took on the character of a small war. Party candidates mapped their campaigns like battlefield manoeuvres; they mobilized their forces, devised their tactics, and attacked their enemies to snatch the spoils of war.'

The DPP has also developed a very clear marketing strategy. Before the new legislation, as the *tangwai* (meaning 'outside the party') – a loose coalition of opposition interests that struggled against the KMT – they were unable to launch a credible and effective electoral challenge. Not only did the *tangwai* face the restrictions on political activity imposed by the authoritarian government, but they also struggled to overcome the organizational advantages of the KMT: astonishing financial strength, a strong base for local organization and mobilization, and the benefits associated with incumbency. Moreover, the *tangwai* were denied access to the mass media under the 1980 Election and Recall Law that prohibited candidates from using the regular mass media, while permitting the use of party-owned media. This clearly benefited the KMT which, as the party of government, owned or controlled most of the island's media (including all three terrestrial television stations). The KMT owned four national daily newspapers, the government owned two, and the military five, but in reality there was little separation of ownership due to the overlapping character of party/state/military political authority. Moreover, privately owned newspapers enjoyed close corporate ties with the KMT: the owners of the two newspapers with the highest circulation, *Chung-kuo Shih Pao* (China Times) and *Lien-ho Pao* (United Daily News), were members of the KMT Central Standing Committee. Had it needed to capitalize on its control over the media to reinforce its own local machinery of mobilization, the KMT would have found it incredibly easy to do so.

Once genuine multi-party competition was first tolerated (after 1986) and then made legal (in 1989), the DPP quickly developed a coherent election machinery that could fight the KMT. In the 2000 presidential election, for example, responsibility for the DPP's campaign fell to a generation of young activists who had first gained political experience when they mobilized as students in the 1980s and went on to help secure Chen Shui-bian's victory in the Taipei mayoral election of 1994. These activists were media-literate and, some having studied in the United States, were familiar with the techniques associated with modern election campaigns. In the 2000 presidential election, the Chen campaign team engaged the services of Fantasy Creative Company, a commercial advertising agency, to develop a modern, media-based and image-conscious campaign strategy. (Fantasy has since designed television advertisements for the KMT – further evidence of the professionalization of election campaigning in Taiwan that is motivated by commerce rather than party allegiance.) Moreover, the '*bianmao*'[5] factory produced a very popular line in merchandise for the Chen campaign, including hats, coffee mugs, teapots and key rings, that not only helped to raise funds for his campaign, but also popularized the candidate, and identified and united his supporters behind an instantly recognizable 'brand name'.[6]

The DPP was also the first political party in Taiwan to create a survey centre that polls registered voters for: 'Party support rates and party image. Satisfaction ratings for DPP officials ... [and] Issue preferences', and carries out 'Targeted surveys of social groups' and 'Election-related surveys' (Rigger 1999: 82). This is a significant development in the modernization of party strategy, for it indicates the high value that the DPP attaches to gathering and responding to public opinion in constructing its platform and election campaigns.

Candidates who cannot afford to engage in the *bianmao* style of marketing or wish to take a principled stand against election gimmicks face difficulty in launching a credible bid for office. An independent candidate in the 2000 presidential election, Hsu Hsin-liang, declined to organize a campaign based on the slick marketing and merchandising that was associated with Chen, preferring instead to contest the election on the issues. Such principles may be good for politics, but they can be a disadvantage for candidates seeking office in a modern media-driven election. Hsu's decision meant he was denied the intensive media coverage that seeks out the dramatic and the exciting campaign over the kind of dull electioneering that does not make good television. Thus, it is possible to conclude that the election culture and media coverage of the campaign penalized Hsu for being a serious candidate.

Democratization and liberalization have clearly had far-reaching consequences for the continuous evolution of election campaigning in Taiwan. The third process – the development and application of new media technology, especially computer-based communications – is having an equally revolutionary effect. Taiwan is one of the most computer-literate societies in Asia (Internet usage in Taiwan increased from 600,000 in 1996 to 6 million in 2000), and candidates seem to have embraced the innovative campaign techniques offered by the Internet, allowing for new methods of interaction between politicians and voters (Glass 1996: 140–6). For example, in 2000, Chen invited 'surfers' to 'E-mail me ... and tell me who should be in my Cabinet.' His website included a comprehensive biography, a list of his most notable political achievements, photographs and regular progress reports on the campaign, all in simplified and complex Chinese characters, as well as in English. Supporters could even donate funds to Chen's campaign over the Internet.

Candidate websites in the 2002 mayoral elections had their own chat rooms, together with 'rich visual effects such as flash and phat-animated designs to attract visitor's attention'. The websites also gave details of press releases, the campaign schedules of the candidates, and the platforms they were promoting. That of the KMT mayor of Taipei, Ma Ying-jeou, included downloadable songs and video clips of the candidate jogging, swimming and engaging in other forms of exercise 'to convey to the public an image that's full of energy'. The site of his DPP rival for the Taipei mayoralty, Lee Ying-yuan, included interactive games and live video footage of his campaign rallies ('Mayor's campaign staff launch Ma's new website', *Taipei Times online*, 2 November 2002).

The consequences of computer-based campaigning have been mixed, and the evidence so far does not suggest that the Internet will replace other more accessible forms of electoral communication. While the elections in 1998 (for the mayors of Taiwan's two municipalities, Taipei and Kaohsiung), in 2000 (for president) and in 2002 (again for the mayors of Taipei and Kaohsiung) witnessed a proliferation of campaign Internet sites, these new media were less important in the 2001 election for the Legislative Yuan, when candidates reverted to more traditional forms of campaigning, devoting less time and expense to designing websites. One reason for this may be the level of the election: perhaps websites are less useful to candidates in small constituencies where voting behaviour is determined more by personal connection and patron–client relationships[7] than other forms of campaigning and persuasion. Clearly the Internet is a new public space that both allows for and encourages a more innovative and exciting style of campaigning, but its value is limited by the fact that voters have to actively seek out this information (unlike other media in which campaign news and information are easily available but users relatively passive), and so voters who do visit these websites tend to already support the candidate. In this way, campaign websites often merely preach to the converted, and thus validate the 'reinforcement theory' of election campaigning.

Image *versus* substance

The evidence presented above implies that increasing numbers of election campaigns are organized less on the basis of the party affiliations and platforms of candidates than on their personal attributes. In other words, Taiwan is as susceptible to image-based politics as any other modern democracy. This is understandable, since elections for metropolitan mayors and president necessarily focus on the political skills, qualifications and platforms of individual candidates. Politicians standing for these most senior elected positions in Taiwan tend to be very experienced national celebrities, prominent in the media through their years of political service. These candidates are not under any serious pressure to invest excessive amounts of precious campaign funds or time in ensuring that they are easily identified and associated with a particular platform. However, it is common for such candidates to engage in brutal personalized negative campaigning since their celebrity makes them more vulnerable to exposures of character blemishes and flaws in their political and personal lives.

Consider the way Taiwan's media rounded on the rather staid image of the KMT presidential candidate, Lien Chan, in 2000:

> Unfortunately, Lien . . . does not have the genetic makeup for popular moves. He does not sound humorous when he tells a joke. He does not sound mean when he condemns others. He sounds awkward when he tries to sell himself. He is like a poker player who can screw up a great hand.
>
> (*Taipei Times*, 19 January 2000)

The 'great hand' that Lien threw away included his incumbency as vice-president and the KMT's advantage as one of the most affluent political parties in the world. The report suggests that these are now less important than his image, and that the electorate cannot differentiate between Lien the politician and Lien the product of marketing strategies. And it is here that we identify the fundamental flaw in the argument that image is politically decisive, for not only does it underestimate the political sophistication of voters, but it assumes that anyone can be voted into office regardless of policy, provided the packaging is attractive. Clearly this is not the case. When American political consultants, usually credited as the pioneers of image-based politics, were recently surveyed on this question, while over half believed that it is difficult to sell a 'mediocre candidate', they also admitted it is equally difficult to sell unpopular platforms to the electorate. The consultants themselves insist that substance is still crucial to the success of an election campaign (Thurber *et al.* 2000).

In election campaigns during the late 1990s, Jaw Shaw-kong, Secretary-General of Taiwan's New Party, gathered his party's candidates together to watch video footage of American political advertisements, advising them that the party should model their campaigns on the American experience. The early electoral successes of the New Party seemed to confirm that 'a model of "tripartite politics" had taken root' in Taiwan, especially after its candidate in the 1994 Taipei mayoral election pushed the KMT into third place (*Free China Journal*, 9 December 1994). However, it should be noted that after 1997 the party's influence declined at a dramatic rate, due primarily to the absence of a clear political programme that could mobilize both members and voters. Its support was limited to disenchanted mainlanders, its development of policy was weak and its organization was tarnished by infighting. Evidence of its weakening credibility came when it failed to nominate a candidate for the 2000 election, backing instead the vocal cultural critic Li Ao, who never failed to deliver his criticisms of the party and urged his supporters to vote for the maverick KMT-heavyweight turned independent (James) Soong Chu-yu. The New Party is no longer a significant political actor: its rise and fall demonstrates that the adoption – explicit or tacit – of professional campaign techniques cannot compensate for unpopular or unworkable platforms and an unmanageable party machinery.

It is a fact of political life that parties do lose elections despite their aggressive or creative and well-funded campaign techniques. Consider the following description of the DPP's campaign for the re-election of Chen as mayor of Taipei in 1998:

> The DPP has tapped into all possible resources for promoting its candidates to Taiwan's voters, wherever they may be. The party's campaign advertisements are appearing on the internet, on commercial

television and on TV walls at train stations. They are also being shown during previews at local cinemas.

(*Free China Journal*, 20 November 1998)

But such advertising could not prevent KMT candidate Ma from retaking control of Taipei for his party. Likewise the KMT may be the richest party in the world, but even its resource base could not compensate for the combination of events that propelled Lien Chan into third place in 2000 (in particular, the candidacy of James Soong and Chen's youth and charisma).

Such evidence suggests that image should never be a substitute for strong party organization, grassroots mobilization and a credible policy platform. Campaigns are designed as a more streamlined and effective means of delivering the party message. The image must sell the politics, not the other way round – the tail must never wag the dog.

Moreover, observers have started to question in a systematic fashion the idea that selling a credible candidate is more important to voters than advancing a relevant policy platform. Dafydd Fell (2003) has undertaken exhaustive qualitative and quantitative research on Taiwanese election propaganda between 1991 and 2000, and discovered that 'issues' accounted for almost 70 per cent of advertisements placed in newspapers during election campaigns. Fell concludes that 'although candidates are important in Taiwanese elections, parties do stress issues' (2003: 35, Table 1.2). This is reflected in the content of campaign advertisements. For example, in 2001 the KMT designed negative advertisements to highlight the coincidence of Chen's inauguration as president in May 2001 with the onset of the recession that has swept through Taiwan, suggesting that the DPP had destroyed Taiwan's economy.[8] Incumbents like Chen are particularly vulnerable to negative campaigning. Their high profile in office means they must carry the responsibility for structural or administrative problems and for any failure to deliver their election promises. All things being equal, an incumbent enjoying the authority of position, guaranteed visibility and the opportunity to be seen as a competent and feted leader should secure clear electoral advantages over his or her challengers. These advantages of incumbency are either created or sharpened by a highly mediated political process. Television in particular provides a visual and easily accessible framework of interpretation for audiences who respond to politics as a series of specific crises that must be handled by competent and dependable individuals. Hence, the news media have personified and personalized the political process, so events and crises are associated more with individual actors than with political institutions or broad social movements.

Challengers can therefore compensate by forcing the incumbent to defend his or her record, and thus do not find it necessary to offer any realistic solutions to problems that the electorate may face: their main concern is to identify an association between the incumbents and their failure to manage these problems in any meaningful way, which they do by associating the person (candidate-centred politics) with their record of service (issue-based politics). So, for example, the DPP has attacked Taipei mayor Ma Ying-jeou for failing to tackle the capital's growing drugs problem and its sex industry. In Kaohsiung, voters were told by the KMT that voting for the incumbent, the DPP's Frank Hsieh, 'means that social order will decline, corruption will persist and mosquitoes will continue to plague the city' (*Taipei Times*, 7 December 2002).

Most advertisements that might be branded 'issue-negative' focus on political corruption and the economy. The DPP has used political corruption to attack the KMT in every election since 1992 (except in 1996 – see Rawnsley 1997), acknowledging that the issue is 'the KMT's Achilles Heel' (Fell 2002: 53). Before the 2000 election, the DPP commissioned polls on the issues that most concerned voters, and since corruption topped the list, once again concentrated on attacking the KMT's record of 'black-gold' politics (corruption), producing some of the most memorable and visually engaging advertisements of the campaign. Meanwhile, the KMT accused the independent candidate, James Soong, of having diverted KMT funds to his own and relatives' bank accounts when he was the Secretary-General of the party. These accusations only resulted in short-term gain for the KMT and, despite a slight dip in the polls at the height of the allegations, Soong still finished the election in second place. This is probably because the KMT are not associated with attacking corruption – rather they are usually branded the beneficiaries – so this was unfamiliar issue ownership for both the party and the voters. In addition, voters were convinced that the KMT's attacks against Soong were calculated only to attack a 'maverick' politician who reduced the party's chance of winning the election. The beneficiaries were the DPP who decided to avoid becoming entangled in the KMT–Soong spat altogether.

The campaign agenda that the 'pan-blue'[9] camp followed in both 2001 and 2002 – focusing on the economy and the performance of the Chen administration – appears to have made an impact: in 2002, the DPP lost the support of floating voters who had previously accounted for between 5 and 10 per cent of their vote, and the party now recognizes that the administration must improve its performance in order to recapture the floating vote (*Taipei Times*, 9 December 2002). Hence, the DPP has been forced on to the defensive, designing campaigns that refute criticisms and reminding voters of the many achievements of the recently elected Chen administration (in contrast to the alleged inertia under 50 years of KMT government).

Such offensive/defensive strategies have involved careful demographic segmentation of the electorate, itself a powerful indicator of the professionalization of election campaigns. Market segmentation borrows from the world of commerce the idea that 'producers' must first identify the needs of different 'consumers', then design specially created advertising to appeal to that segment, and finally sell to specific consumers the benefits of the product. Adapted to the political arena, a candidate's marketing team will design campaign themes and images to appeal to a particular segment or group of the voting population. Its use in Taiwan was first noticed in the 1996 presidential election (Rawnsley 1997) and has since become standard practice for those seeking political office. The segmentation may be geographic (there is a clear difference in the attitudes of voters in northern and southern Taiwan), ethnic (politicians readily demonstrate at every opportunity their proficiency in minority languages) or demographic (women, military veterans, fishermen, farmers and disabled people are all presented with a cornucopia of policies to persuade them that the politicians have their best interests at heart).

Traditional methods of mobilization

It is clear, therefore, that Taiwan's political parties have responded to the experiences of democratization and liberalization, and the development of new communications technologies. However, it is essential that we acknowledge how election campaigns continue to use structures of communication, socialization and mobilization based on the strong personal networks and relationships that have defined Taiwan's election process since the 1950s. For example, politicians often attend religious and civil ceremonies, such as weddings and funerals, to strengthen their grassroots relationship with voters. These reinforce the most valuable methods of gathering support at the local level that depend on factions and patron–client networks and emphasize the personal contribution that individuals may make to their constituency. The success of former KMT-heavyweight James Soong in the 2000 presidential election was based on the local support he had cultivated as Taiwan's extremely popular and hard-working last provincial governor. His frequent visits to all townships and villages, especially after the devastating earthquake of September 1999, helped him to strengthen his personal connections with local leaders. This enabled him to finish the election only 3 per cent behind Chen, seizing from the eventual victor many voters who might have been considered core DPP supporters (for example, Hakka minority voters).[10]

Factions have always been important political actors in Taiwan, especially for the KMT. In fact, prior to 1986, an average 60 per cent of candidates with KMT support in elections at provincial and county levels enjoyed close relationships with local factions. It is noticeable that candidates with factional support had higher rates of electoral success than those without (Schafferer 2003: 112). The KMT's position within the political process, together with its close affiliation to powerful factions at every level of political life, has helped the party smooth the election of its preferred candidates. As the ruling party, the KMT made all the administrative and judicial appointments at the level of central government, as well as some important appointments at the municipal level. The DPP argued that this gave the KMT an unfair advantage, as many government officials (tax inspectors, policemen, etc.) used their privileged position to campaign for KMT candidates, and sometimes even harassed voters and opposition candidates.

Integral to this localized mobilization is the *zhuang-jiao*, a kind of vote-broker whose job is to deliver a specific number of votes in return for particular rewards. Although such practices have facilitated vote-buying, the intention is not to get rich. Rather, the act of buying a vote in this way has been used to consolidate a personal relationship – in other words, it is accepted more as an exchange of favours than a method of securing financial gain, and has diminishing effect the more national the election. As the KMT found to its cost in the 2000 presidential election, factions expect little return when the candidate is not a local politician and so have less motivation to support a particular individual,[11] while for the parties the costs of buying votes for such high office can be exorbitant. Factional power is structured around their connections to local politicians: in a national election with just five candidates, the main incentive to engage in local mobilization is lost.

Traditional-style campaigning in Taiwan is vigorously represented by the habitually noisy and vibrant election rallies that continue to be the preferred method of mobilizing supporters and familiarizing the electorate with candidates. Sound-trucks patrol the roads of every major town urging voters to cast their ballot for their favoured candidate, and every street is adorned in campaign leaflets and flags in the colours of the main parties bearing the appropriate candidate's name or number. However, even election rallies have adapted to the media environment, as their timing and staging are as much for media consumption as for the benefit of voters. Coverage of the rallies on television and now the Internet projects a national image of strength and unity, and allows candidates to reach beyond the core supporters who attend such events.[12] Rallies are also useful ways of gathering local and national publicity for less well-known candidates. For example, the *Taipei Times* described one of the campaign rallies of candidate Lee Ying-yuan in the 2002 mayoral election as having 'all the trappings of a rock concert, with air horns blaring and people screaming *dong suan* – meaning "get elected" in Taiwanese'. As Lee's spokesperson, Peng Tien-haw explained: 'In order to boost Lee's candidacy in a given period of time, as his face is relatively new to Taipei residents, we've chosen to stage this kind of campaign rally, which is a great way to centralize support and enhance the candidate's confidence and popularity' (*Taipei Times*, 18 November 2002).

In Taiwan, candidate-centred politics are most influential at the local level (that is, in elections to the Legislative Yuan and the National Assembly[13]), and the reason for this is systemic: candidate-centred politics are encouraged by the electoral system used to select local politicians, rather than by a conscious modernization or professionalization of campaign organization. Because Taiwan still uses the single non-transferable vote in multi-member constituencies formula in local elections, candidates often find they have to fight two campaigns in one constituency, since they must compete with candidates from both the opposition and their own party (Hsieh 1996). This voting system has serious implications for a party's campaign structure and methods, diverting attention from the issues and policies that separate party platforms and compelling party organizations to identify ways of distinguishing between candidates of the same party. Campaign organizations have therefore discovered innovative methods to allocate votes among known supporters to ensure that the ballots are evenly distributed among the party's candidates in any one constituency, thus minimizing the damage from the single non-transferable vote. For example, in the 2001 legislative election, the DPP asked its voters in Taipei to vote for different candidates depending on the supporter's national identity card number. In other elections, dates of birth are the criteria for allocation of votes.[14] None of these processes depend on image.

Negative campaigning

In many respects, there are serious systemic shortcomings to Taiwan's 'consolidating' democracy. In particular, vote buying and 'black gold' politics remain endemic, with the going-rate in the 2002 election allegedly NT$1,000 (US$30) per voter. This is despite a nationwide media campaign since 2000 to discourage the practice as anti-democratic (the 2001 election has the distinction of being the cleanest in Taiwan's history). Moreover, the persistence of vicious and personal negative campaigning is encouraged by both the voting system used in local level elections and the media's thirst for sensationalism. During interviews about the 1998 mayoral election campaigns, one television news organization in Taiwan admitted that they are merely responding to public demand for coverage of negative campaigning.[15] Candidates, often with the complicity of the media, engage in a style and volume of personalized negative campaigning that would not be permitted or tolerated in other consolidated democracies. Rather, it is accepted as a characteristic of democracy: the 'electoralism' that pervades Taiwanese political culture – a national approval of the procedural approach to democracy that uses the frequency of elections as a benchmark of democratic maturity – accepts it as one of the costs of free speech, allegedly the defining feature of any democratic political system.

Democratization and liberalization have nurtured personalized negative campaigning as a routine and acceptable characteristic of political life in Taiwan. In many of the election campaigns between 1996 and 2002, candidates have been accused, often by anonymous sources, of heinous crimes, ranging from rape and association with gangsters, to belonging to the Communist Party and betraying Taiwan (Rawnsley 1997, 2000). For example, President Chen, Vice-President Annette Lu and former KMT president Lee Teng-hui all questioned the loyalty of the incumbent mayor of Taipei, Ma Ying-jeou, during the 2002 mayoral election campaign, suggesting that he was a direct threat to Taiwan's national security. President Chen 'joked' that Ma has *xianggang jiao* (literally 'Hong Kong foot', or 'athlete's foot'), implying that the mayor will sell out Taiwan in the same way the British 'sold out' Hong Kong (Ma visited Hong Kong, his birthplace, prior to the election campaign). Chen had even insinuated that Ma wanted to be 'chief' of a Chinese Special Administrative Region (as per Hong Kong) rather than a mayor in the Republic of China.[16] Electoral politics in Taiwan turns on such subtlety, double meanings and veiled attacks on one's political opponents.

Allusions to Ma's identity and competence by presidents, vice-presidents and former presidents hint that Taiwan's election culture is now entertaining the idea of the 'permanent campaign', meaning that voters are presented with images and issues in and between elections by candidates determined to frame the political process in terms of the next crucial ballot.[17] One cannot help sensing that Chen used the 2002 election to criticise Ma, a potential – and strong – opponent in the 2004 presidential election.[18] Thus, the mayoral election became a vote of national significance and was presented by candidates and the media as a personal duel between Ma and Chen (after Ma had defeated Chen in the Taipei mayoral election of 1998).[19]

There are three important conclusions to draw from these attacks against Ma in the 2002 campaign. First, they demonstrate that national issues (and national politicians) can and do infect what are ostensibly local election campaigns. Second, the examples show how ownership of the national security issue floats between the two main parties. That the KMT should focus on relations with China is hardly surprising: this has been their dominant theme for over 50 years (Fell 2003; Rawnsley 1997, 2000, 2003). What is instructive is that the DPP administration must respond to these challenges from the KMT and defend its record as incumbent government, and has itself decided to attack the KMT on the issue of national security. Third, Ma's victory in the 2002 election (and James Soong's second-place showing in 2000) confirm that negative campaigning does not guarantee results. In fact, the DPP's personal campaign against Ma backfired: in 1998, he won the election in Taipei with only 51 per cent of the vote. In 2002, he actually increased his share of the vote to 64 per cent (a clear indication that voters increasingly feel they can no longer identify with one main party). The floating voters are rapidly becoming the most important constituency for Taiwan's politicians.

Conclusions

This chapter has made a series of interconnected points about election campaigning in Taiwan to demonstrate how the election culture has combined processes of modernization and professionalization with more traditional forms of voter mobilization. It has suggested that Taiwan's democratic transition and social liberalization have imposed far-reaching consequences on politics and the media, as well as on voting behaviour, and that these changes have filtered through the process of the election campaigning. Understanding systemic change is important: without appreciating the process of Taiwan's democratization, the transformation of the election culture appears superficial. A comprehensive analysis of Taiwan's election culture depends on acknowledging that the changes have occurred because institutional frameworks were created to *allow* such changes.

Moreover, the development and application of new media technologies, especially e-mail and the Internet, has opened up new spheres for political communication and mobilization but, as in other political societies, their effect is limited and contested.

The most significant change is the professionalization of campaign organization and delivery. This is a consequence of democratization, for only where genuine contest is allowed do parties have to design their campaigns to sharpen their chances of electoral victory. For the KMT, this professional approach was dictated by two principal events: the emergence of the *tangwai* and the DPP as a legal opposition, and the decision to allow voters to elect the president and vice-president. These political developments have eroded the reliability of factions at the local level. Traditionally the main source of KMT support, factions expect little return when the candidate is not a local politician and so have less motivation to support a particular individual. As the KMT discovered in 2000, affiliations with factions and *zhuang-jiao* do not offer any guarantees in national elections.

Professionalization was equally important for the DPP. Once the party was legalized, the DPP realized that it had to project a more positive image of its candidates to deflect the characterization of the opposition movement as violent, subversive, exclusively Taiwanese and only concerned with securing independence for Taiwan – in other words, to turn the DPP into a modern and political party that might be considered a credible alternative to KMT government. Moreover, the DPP had to challenge the KMT's incumbency and the advantages the party had accumulated over 50 years in office. Now, the DPP administration is facing many of the same challenges as its KMT predecessor and has quickly learned the differences between government and opposition: it is always easier to attack than defend. Hence, in the 2004 presidential election campaign, Chen studiously avoided discussing areas in which he was weakest, such as the economy (for whatever the reasons, the only economic recession that Taiwan has experienced has been during Chen's presidency), and focused instead on cross-Strait relations and identity. This was achieved partly through the controversial referendum that was held on the same day as the presidential elections and dominated discussion in the run-up to voting. It also explains the use made of the incident of 28 February 1947 (when Taiwanese were massacred by KMT military forces). A national chain of hand-holding from north to south Taiwan, designed to encourage national reconciliation, unity and ethnic harmony, was instead hijacked by electoral campaigning and transformed into a pro-Chen mobilization exercise.

Contrary to expectations, however, professionalization has not entirely 'Americanized' election campaigns in Taiwan. Image is important because of the level of office contested – mayoral and presidential elections necessarily focus on individuals – but there is no evidence to suggest that substance is being sacrificed and issues are no longer relevant. In fact, issues have decided the last two presidential elections: relations with the People's Republic of China in 1996 and political corruption in 2000.

The most important conclusion is that the defining features of election campaigns in Taiwan – the colour and noise of election rallies, the dependence on patron–client networks in local elections and even the declining practice of buying votes – continue to energize electoral politics, indicating that democracy has not transformed Taiwan's election culture beyond recognition. Nobody has managed to describe this distinctly hybrid approach to election campaigning more eloquently than Eric Sautedé:

> the electoral campaigns [of 2000] accurately reflected contemporary Taiwanese society: a studied mixture of tradition and modernity, a curious alliance of symbols drawn from the land and icons of American-style showbiz, a subtle cocktail in which expressions of civil allegiance were flavoured by communal loyalties with strong spiritual overturns.
>
> (Sautedé 2000: 52)

Notes

1 This chapter does not survey the 2004 election campaign, already underway when the final version was submitted. The research and publication deadlines precluded detailed discussion of this election.

2 For a critical assessment of some of these constitutional changes, see Myers *et al.* 2002: 73–90.

3 The turnout rates (per cent) for the past three Legislative Yuan elections were 68 (1995), 68 (1998) and 66 (2001). In the presidential elections, the rates were 76 (1996) and 83 (2000).

4 'After more than forty years, a political institution dominated by mainlander politicians became one of representatives from Taiwan and its offshore islands'

(Chao and Myers 1998: 239). Further assessment of this election campaign can be found in Wachman (1994, chapter 7).

5 The *bianmao* is an olive-green hat that displays a tag featuring A-bian, a small, cute character that represents, but in no sense bears any likeness to, Chen Shui-bian. According to Eric Sautedé (2000: 55) this 'became the main external sign of the personalization, not to say fetishization, of politics.' One of Chen's posters even pictured Dr Sun Yat-sen, the father of republican China, wearing a *bianmao*, suggesting that he too would endorse the candidate.

6 Reporting on the 2001 legislative election, Bruce Jacobs noted how 'Strict rules set a limit of NT$30 (US$0.87) for any gift to voters. As a result, the baseball-style caps worn by candidates' supporters were of markedly poorer quality than in the past' (see 'Cementing Democracy', *Taipei Review*, February 2002: 36).

7 Patron–client politics 'refers to a reciprocal exchange between two actors of unequal political power and socioeconomic status. Patrons offer material and nonmaterial goods to supportive clients, who in turn lend political support to their patrons' (Huang 1996: 107).

8 It seems that Taiwan had caught the tail-end of the Asian financial crisis that had started in Thailand in 1997. Recession, including a record unemployment rate of 5.2 per cent, was due to global trends in 2000–02 and because many Taiwanese manufacturers were moving their production to The People's Republic of China to take advantage of lower labour costs and more relaxed environmental laws. There were even reports that the recession had been engineered by the KMT (companies affiliated to the party having withdrawn their capital, thus forcing a sharp decline in the stock-market) to discredit the DPP after the 2000 election.

9 'Pan-blue' refers to parties that are affiliated to the KMT, including parties that have split from it (the People's First Party and the New Party). Parties affiliated to the DPP, including the Taiwan Independence Party and the Taiwan Solidarity Union, are know as 'the green camp'. The names reflect the dominant colours of the flags of the KMT and DPP.

10 The corresponding data can be found in Cheng and Hsu (2002: 168–9).

11 This assessment is based on conversations with KMT sources who wish to remain anonymous, about their election campaigns from 1996 to 2000.

12 Television stations broadcasting campaign activities outside news programmes stand accused by the Central Election Commission of violating the Public Officials' Election and Recall Law, although in the December 2001 election most cable news stations broadcast rallies for parties throughout November. Many cable stations are involved not only in the broadcast of rallies, but also in their production.

13 Executive-level elections for mayoralties and president are conducted under the Single Member District plurality system.

14 This is known as the *pei piao* (forced vote distribution) system. To see how the single non-transferable vote system forced parties to devise ways to divide up constituencies among their competing candidates, see Rigger (1999: chapter 7).

15 Interview with Hsaio Tsui-ying, Formosa Television, Taipei, 2 September 1999.

16 In response, Lien Chan, chairman of the KMT, said such outbursts demonstrated that President Chen realized he was in trouble because he had to resort to using ethnicity as a campaign issue: 'His trick might be useful in some counties and cities,' said Lien, 'but it will not function in Taipei city' ('Opposition says Chen too involved in election', *Taipei Times*, 29 October 2002).

17 Media speculation that Chen Shui-bian would run as the DPP candidate in the 2000 presidential election began on 5 December 1998, the day he lost his position as mayor of Taipei. His successor to that post, Ma Ying-jeou, was immediately

considered a future KMT presidential candidate on the morning after the 2000 election. Throughout the 2002 election, the press published opinion polls that asked the public for their views on the mayoral candidates as possible candidates in the 2004 presidential election.

18 This is reflected in the way the Chen administration has been attacked by the opposition: in the run up to the 2002 election, James Soong, chairman of the People's First Party, said: 'The country is virtually in anarchy. We don't have a president now, but only a presidential candidate. We don't have a government, but only a campaign headquarters' (*Taipei Times*, 15 November 2002). Ma did not contest the 2004 election (Lien Chan and James Soong joined forces to create a 'blue' alliance), but is considered a contender for 2008. In 2004, Ma was the blue camp's national campaign manager.

19 The animosity between Chen and Ma can be traced back to this campaign. Much of Chen's campaign in 1998 revolved around the issue of 'Taiwan's Chen and China's Ma' (see Rawnsley 2000).

References

Chao, L. and Myers, R.H. (1998) *The First Chinese Democracy. Political Life in the Republic of China on Taiwan*, Baltimore, MD: Johns Hopkins University Press.

Cheng, T.J. and Hsu, Y.M. (2002) 'The March 2000 election in historical and comparative perspectives. Strategic voting, the third party, and the non-duvergerian outcome', in B.J. Dickson and C.M. Chao (eds) *Assessing the Lee Teng-hui Legacy in Taiwan's Politics. Democratic Consolidation and External Relations*, Armonk, NY: M.E. Sharpe.

Dickson, B.J. (1996) 'The Kuomintang before democratization. Organizational change and the role of elections', in H.M. Tien (ed.) *Taiwan's Electoral Politics and Democratic Transition. Riding the Third Wave*, Armonk, NY: M.E. Sharpe.

Fell, D. (2002) 'Party platform change in Taiwan's 1990s elections', *Issues & Studies*, 38(2): 31–60.

——(2003) 'Party change and the democratic evolution of Taiwan, 1991–2001', Ph.D. thesis submitted to the University of London.

Freedom House (2001) 'Freedom in the World 2000–2001'; table of countries: comparative measures of freedom. Online. Available HTTP: <http://www.freedom house.org/research/freeworld/2001/table1.htm> (accessed 22 September 2004).

Glass, A.J. (1996) 'On-line elections. The Internet's impact on the political process', *Harvard International Journal of Press/Politics*, 1(4): 140–6.

Hsieh, J.F. (1996) 'The SNTV system and its political implications', in H.M. Tien (ed.) *Taiwan's Electoral Politics and Democratic Transition. Riding the Third Wave*, Armonk, NY: M.E. Sharpe.

Huang, T.F. (1996) 'Elections and the evolution of the Kuomintang', in H.M. Tien (ed.) *Taiwan's Electoral Politics and Democratic Transition. Riding the Third Wave*, Armonk, NY: M.E. Sharpe.

Marrek, P. (1995) *Political Marketing and Communication*, London: John Libbey.

Myers, R.H., Chao, L. and Kuo, T.C. (2002) 'Consolidating democracy in the Republic of China on Taiwan, 1996–2000', in B.J. Dickson and C.M. Chao (eds) *Assessing the Lee Teng-hui Legacy in Taiwan's Politics. Democratic Consolidation and External Relations*, Armonk, NY: M.E. Sharpe.

Rawnsley, G. (1997) 'The 1996 presidential campaign in Taiwan. Packaging politics in a democratizing state', *Harvard International Journal of Press/Politics*, 2(2): 47–61.

——(2000) 'Where's the beef? The 1999 mayoral election campaigns in Taiwan', *American Journal of Chinese Studies*, 7(2): 147–69.

——(2003) 'As edifying as a bout of mud wrestling. The 2000 presidential election campaign in Taiwan', in G. Rawnsley and M.Y.T. Rawnsley (eds) *Political Communications in Greater China*, London: RoutledgeCurzon.

——(2004) 'Treading a fine line. Democracy and the media in Taiwan', *Parliamentary Affairs*, 57(1): 209–22.

Rigger, S. (1999) *Politics in Taiwan. Voting for Democracy*, London: Routledge.

Sautedé, E. (2000) 'Electioneering Taiwan-style', *China Perspectives*, 29: 52–6.

Schafferer, C. (2003) *The Power of the Ballot Box. Political Development and Election Campaigning in Taiwan*, New York: Lexington.

Thurber, J., Nelson, C. and Dulio, D.A. (2000) 'Portrait of campaign consultants', in J. Thurber and C. Nelson (eds) *Campaign Warriors. Political Consultants in Elections*, Washington, DC: Brookings Institute Press.

Wachman, A.M. (1994) *Taiwan. National Identity and Democratization*, Armonk, NY: M.E. Sharpe.

9   Where's the party?

Television and election campaigns in Russia

Sarah Oates

Although political parties were created long before anyone had dreamed of television, it is now difficult to imagine how parties would function without this broadcast medium. Television brings citizens the words and images of their leaders on a daily basis, giving them at least the illusion of contact with their politicians and government. During election campaigns, television typically provides the most important source of information for voters. Yet in Russia, the development between parties and television has been reversed. As a strong and influential television system existed before political parties were founded in the young Russian state, parties have had to learn how to market themselves through television instead of the medium learning how to cover existing political parties. Evidence from 1993 to 2004, including how political parties choose to market themselves and how the evening news covers politicians, shows that the institution of television has come to dominate the institution of political parties.

This chapter will first consider how Russian political parties and presidential candidates market themselves on television, then analyse how major television channels have covered election campaigns and, finally, examine how voters responded to these marketing attempts. It would seem that Russian television has fuelled the creation of media-driven parties: 'broadcast parties' that have no real roots in the electorate, no tangible ideology beyond serving the needs of their political masters and, most ominously, no accountability to the public.

The role of television in politics and elections

Where does the study of Russian media and voting behaviour fit within the broader context of the voting behaviour literature? It is principally valuable for shedding light on existing theories about the nature of the relationship between media and voting, in particular because the Russian political system was formed along a Western model. In addition, Russia has held eight elections for parliament and the presidency between 1993 and 2004 – contests that have failed to meet the democratic expectations of many analysts, scholars and some Russian politicians themselves. In this sense, Russia is the 'big bang' of media and politics: a chance to observe the critical intersection of media, parties and the electorate in a time of rapid change and in an environment relatively free from established democratic institutions. This is particularly useful as the literature on media and politics at times seems mired in arguments about ownership and effects, rather than about the broader questions of long-term or cultural relationships between media and political systems.

The classic model of the relationship between party and voters comes from the Michigan School of voting behaviour (Campbell *et al.* 1960). Building on the findings of Berelson *et al.* (1954) that voting intention was relatively fixed and unaffected by media messages, scholars in the United States developed theories of long-term partisan identification. In Europe, Lipset and Rokkan's work (1967) suggested that party development and success paralleled societal cleavages, such as religion and class. In both of these theoretical approaches, media would play only a marginal role. This is not an uncontroversial point, as some scholars argue that the US voting studies in the 1950s and 1960s were carried out in a different, more stable era. In addition, party strength has eroded, while the power of the media through cable television, digital television and the Internet has grown exponentially. Still, it is clear that party and media formation were much more parallel than in the Russian case.

Where does this leave the study of the Russian media and voting behaviour? It would suggest that the well-rooted media system inherited from the Soviet Union could subsume or even overwhelm a nascent party structure. There is ample evidence to suggest that media matter a great deal in Russian elections, as voters have not had much opportunity to build up loyalties or fixed preferences to particular parties. Rather, public opinion surveys before both parliamentary and presidential elections from 1993 to 2003 have shown large shifts in public opinion and voting intention for parties and candidates within weeks and even days of the polling dates. At the same time, studies of nightly news coverage during Russian elections show a pattern of unfair political coverage, with a biased emphasis on pro-government parties and candidates, as well as some virulent mud-slinging campaigns against government opponents (European Institute for the Media 1996a and b, 2000a and b; Oates 2004; Oates and Roselle 2000). Although these tactics are obvious and are noted by Russian viewers, the question becomes why the media in Russia has managed to distort the political system to the extent that, arguably, Russian television is now the most powerful political institution in the country.[1]

Public opinion data suggest that television remains a central influence in society in Russia. This is due in part to economics, as many consumers can no longer afford newspapers, and television is still distributed without a licensing fee. Personal computers are out of reach of most consumers, not to mention the dearth of broadband access. There are six major nation-wide channels (see Table 9.1). Seventy-seven per cent of the

Table 9.1 Russian television channels: ownership and audience share

	Name	*Ownership*	*Daily viewership (%)*
1	First Channel[a]	51% owned by the state, rest by a mix of public and private corporations, effectively controlled by the Kremlin	83
2	Russian Television and Radio (RTR)	State-owned	71
3	TV-Centre	Funded primarily by City of Moscow administration	16
4	NTV[b]	Commercial; taken over by interests friendly to the Kremlin in 2001	53
5	Culture	State-owned cultural channel created by presidential decree in 1997; only channel that does not carry paid advertising	8
6	TV-6	Currently a commercial sports channel. Was briefly a platform for opposition journalists from NTV	N/A

Source (media use): a survey of 2000 adults conducted by Russian Research in April 2001.

Notes

a Previously known as *Obshchestvennoe Rossiskoye Televidenie* (Russian Public Television) – and before that as *Ostankino.*

b Often referred to as *Nezavisimayoe Televidenie* (Independent Television) but, according to station heads interviewed by the author in 1999, the initials do not actually stand for anything.

respondents in a 2001 survey reported watching television daily. Sixty-five per cent of the respondents felt that state television was the 'most unbiased and reliable' source of information. In fact, more of the respondents (57 per cent) had 'full' or 'considerable' confidence in state television than they had in the armed forces (50 per cent), the government (30 per cent) or the parliament (16 per cent). Conversely, only 11 per cent of the respondents claimed they had 'full' or 'considerable' confidence in political parties, placing them on the bottom of the trustworthiness scale.

Neither trusted nor appreciated, Russian political parties have nonetheless proliferated, but generally failed to consolidate power since the collapse of the Soviet Union in 1991. The electoral system created by the 1993 Russian constitution encouraged political parties in two vital ways. First, 225 of the 450 seats in the lower house of the parliament (the Duma) were elected through a nationwide party-list system. Any party that earned more than 5 per cent of the national vote received a proportional amount of the party-list seats in the Duma. In addition, individuals who ran for the rest of the seats through 225 single-member districts across Russia could affiliate with a political party (as could those running for the 178 seats in the upper house of the parliament).[2] The first Duma elections were held in 1993, with early elections slated for 1995 and then regular elections planned for every four years. The role of political parties was left more nebulous for the presidential elections, also scheduled for every four years. The successful presidential candidates, Boris Yeltsin and Vladimir Putin, have declared themselves 'above parties' and won without party affiliations.

In theory, the party system should have eliminated extremism with the 5 per cent barrier, encouraged party consolidation and served as an impetus for the creation of a relatively stable party system. The practical results have been far different, particularly after the surprising outcome of the first Duma elections in 1993 (for abbreviated results of the Duma elections 1993–2003, see Table 9.2). While the leaders of the pro-government and market-oriented Russia's Choice party expected a strong showing, it was the nationalist, xenophobic Liberal Democratic Party of Russia that dominated in the party-list election. As the Liberal Democrats were just the sort of extremist party that was supposed to be eliminated by the 5 per cent barrier, it was a blow to the Yeltsin administration. Russia's Choice did much better in the single-member constituencies, however, leaving the first Duma with a bare plurality held by pro-government forces. Despite being banned for a time and garnering little media attention, the Communist Party of the Russian Federation (the acknowledged successors to the Communist Party of the Soviet Union) also had a respectable showing, with 12 per cent of the party-list vote in 1993. A total of eight parties won seats in the 1993 party-list race, while other parties were represented by candidates who were successful in single-member district races.

Over the next three Duma contests from 1995 to 2003, the ability of parties to pass the 5 per cent barrier weakened, with only four parties successful in 1995, six in 1999 and four in 2003. There are only two parties that have been successful in the party-list race in all of the Duma elections – the Liberal Democrats and the Communists ('Communist' here refers specifically to the Communist Party of the Russian Federation). Yabloko, a relatively liberal party, won party-list seats in 1993, 1995 and 1999. In all four elections, the other successful party-list contenders were those sponsored – or at least supported – by pro-government forces: Our Home is Russia in 1995; Unity, the Union of Right Forces and Fatherland–All Russia in 1999; and United Russia and *Rodina* (Motherland) in 2003. An average of 26 parties has run in the party-list race in the Duma in each election. While a handful of these parties have been able to propel their leaders into the national limelight and a Duma seat, only those listed above have been able to win party-list seats. Thus, there has been immense labiality on the one hand, with the large number of parties on the ballots, but stability on the other as the same handful of parties and pro-government forces return, under different names, to the Duma on the party-list ballot each election.

Within this pattern are some important trends in Russian political party marketing. The pro-government parties have learned to be both less pro-market and less pro-Western, a lesson they would have learned from

Table 9.2 Russian Duma party-list election results, 1993–2003: parties that crossed the 5 per cent barrier

Year	Party	Political orientation[a]	% of vote
1993	Liberal Democratic Party of Russia	Nationalist	23.0
	Russia's Choice	Broadcast/pro-government	15.5
	Communist Party of the Russian Federation	Communist	12.4
	Women of Russia	Special interest	8.1
	Agrarian Party	Special interest	8.0
	Yabloko	Liberal	7.9
	Party of Russian Unity and Accord	Pro-government/liberal	6.8
	Democratic Party of Russia	Liberal	5.5
1995	Communist Party of the Russian Federation	Communist	22.3
	Liberal Democratic Party of Russia	Nationalist	11.2
	Our Home is Russia	Broadcast/pro-government	10.1
	Yabloko	Liberal	6.9
1999	Communist Party of the Russian Federation	Communist	24.3
	Unity	Broadcast/pro-government/ Kremlin	23.3
	Fatherland–All Russia	Broadcast/pro-government/ Moscow + regions	13.3
	Union of Right Forces	Broadcast/pro-government/ liberal	8.5
	Liberal Democratic Party of Russia	Nationalist	6.0
	Yabloko	Liberal	5.9
2003	United Russia	Broadcast/pro-government	37.6
	Communist Party of the Russian Federation	Communist	12.6
	Liberal Democratic Party of Russia	Nationalist	11.5
	Motherland	Broadcast/nationalist/ pro-government	9.0

Source: Russian Central Electoral Commission bulletins.

Note
a The orientation is the author's own, based on party documents, media coverage, statements by party leaders, and free-time and paid advertising.

watching the populist campaigning of nationalist Vladimir Zhirinovsky and his Liberal Democrats. Zhirinovsky carefully targets his messages at various segments of the population and articulates clear, if sometimes extreme and unworkable, policy suggestions. In addition, he is careful not to associate himself with Western ideas, choosing instead to make xenophobic statements and play on feelings of Russian nationalism. It was clear by the 1995 Duma campaign that parties were turning more to images of Russian/Soviet patriotism than Western ideals. In this sense, parties were aping the ideas of the Liberal Democrats (who saw their party-list vote roughly halved from 1993 to 1995). In addition, a study of the party platforms shows that Russian political parties overall became less pro-Western, more nationalistic and much less in favour of a market economy from 1993 to 1995 (Oates 1998). No other party leader could match Zhirinovsky for outrageous antics or posturing, but other parties did capitalize on his ability to better target the ideological preferences of the Russian voter. By the 1999 Duma elections, the pro-government party Unity was relying on images of the Russian military in Chechnya, law enforcement and even a famous Greco–Roman wrestler throwing opponents to the mat in its free-time and paid advertising. The Communists have led quieter campaigns, particularly in that they do not buy television advertising and have a hard time getting unbiased news coverage.

The 2003 Duma election saw a consolidation of some trends in Russian elections and party building, as traditional parties lost votes and the newer, media-based parties generally gained votes. Two former rivals who started party life as 'broadcast' parties – Unity and Fatherland–All Russia – joined forces in 2003 to create the formidable United Russia party. This party, which enjoyed enormous state resources, the overt blessing of the president and extensive media favouritism, acheived the greatest ever success in a Duma election, garnering almost 38 per cent of the party-list vote. Meanwhile, the fortunes of the Communists, ignored or vilified in the media, dropped to about 13 per cent of the vote. A review of media coverage – as well as of political party platforms, advertising, free-time statements and other material – shows that various parties deliberately pursued the traditional Communist supporter with a double-edged strategy, claiming the Communists had sold out to business interests and that their own party better met the social needs of workers, veterans, retirees, rural people or other groups traditionally considered Communist supporters. This strategy appeared particularly important for the new party, Motherland, which enjoyed some government support and favourable media coverage. The Liberal Democrats also bounced back to a degree, winning almost 12 per cent of the vote.

One of the most worrying trends in Russian party development from 1993 to 2003 has been the tendency to rely increasingly on style over substance. All parties use a certain amount of marketing to 'sell' their ideas to the voters. However, over the course of a decade in Russia, it was sometimes very difficult to tell what, if anything, that really resembled a political party was behind the campaign façade. This led a television analyst to dub some parties no more than 'broadcast parties' (*yefirnie partii*) during the 1999 Duma campaign.[3] It is an evocative term, suggesting that parties are little more than a selection of images and sound bites in the nightly news and their advertising. Another particularly worrying trend is the consolidation of the mass media, particularly powerful national channels, in the hands of pro-Kremlin forces. The regime has used dubious financial tactics to oust outspoken news producers, notably to wrest control of commercial television stations from those unsupportive of the Putin administration both in 2001 and in 2003. Those legal manoeuvres are underlined by the widespread violence against journalists, many of whom have been killed trying to report on stories ranging from corruption to the war in Chechnya.

Only a handful of parties have had sufficient means to virtually create themselves over the airwaves. It has been particularly important for parties to be able to influence news coverage and other programming content on at least one national television channel, preferably the state-run *Pervyi kanal* (First Channel). The party has to be well funded, not only to buy a large amount of airtime, but also to pay bribes for coverage when necessary (although political influence is generally more useful). It is important for the party to be fresh and new, without an unpopular track record. In addition, the party has to be able to call on a large network of resources, most commonly the current government administration. Finally, as the Yeltsin government learned in 1993, it is not enough to press for reforms from the top down. In order to succeed, the parties must appeal to a large segment of voters, which means aiming a message somewhere in the centre of the political spectrum. The success of the Communists and the nationalist Liberal Democrats in 1993 showed pro-government forces that this centre lay farther to the left economically and to the right in nationalist terms than their own party ideology in 1993.

As this set of requirements for a potential 'broadcast' party suggests, very few groups aside from the central government are able to mobilize such resources. In addition, it became much harder after the 1995 elections to find a powerful media source outwith the control of the presidential administration. Nonetheless, a select group of elite power bases have created successful broadcast parties. The Kremlin produced Our Home is Russia in 1995 and Unity in 1999. A regional coalition, with powerful Moscow Mayor Yuri Luzhkov at its centre, created Fatherland–All Russia in 1999, using the Moscow government television channel TV-Centre as its mouthpiece. In 2003, the Kremlin and Moscow forces of Putin and Luzhkov joined to create the formidable United Russia party.

But are these parties merely marketing efforts? There is evidence on both sides of the argument – that they function as little more than vote-seeking vehicles and that they have some elements of traditional political parties. On the side of the ephemeral nature of these parties, the best evidence is their generally short life span. Our Home is Russia, Unity and Fatherland–All Russia were all gone by the next Duma election. They had few concrete policies and many of those who campaigned at the top of the party list did not take up their seats in the Duma. The creation and behaviour of party factions within the Duma bore little relation to the party's statements during the campaign. On the other hand, Our Home is

Russia, Unity, Fatherland–All Russia and United Russia were not unknown entities to the voters. It was clear that these parties supported strong elites within the national or regional government: politicians who were very vocal about their desires for the direction of the country, albeit not particularly clear on individual policies. Although the names changed, the forces behind the parties did not. In addition, although Unity and Fatherland–All Russia did not run again, a merged version of the parties did run very successfully in 2003 as United Russia.

Did the appearance of 'broadcast' parties halt or corrode the development of more traditional political parties in Russia? When results for the Russian Duma party-list contest are viewed through the lens of party type, the impact of the 'broadcast party' appears quite significant (see Figure 9.1). By the 1999 elections, it is clear that 'broadcast' parties were dominating. Other parties did succeed, notably the Communist Party, which has had

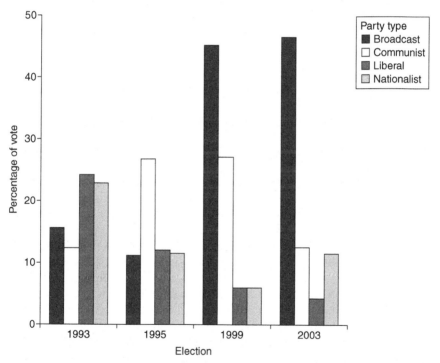

Figure 9.1 Percentage of votes in 1993–2003 Duma elections by party type (according to author's analysis). Broadcast parties: Russia's Choice (1993), Our home is Russia, Ivan Rybkin Bloc (1995), Unity, Fatherland–All Russia, Union of Right Forces (1999), United Russia, Motherland (2003). Communists: Communist Party of the Russian Federation Working Russia for the Soviet Union (1995 and 1999), Stalinist Bloc (1999). Liberals: Yabloko, Party of Russian Unity and Accord, Democratic Party of Russia (1995), Social Democrats (1995 and 1999). Nationalists: Liberal Democatic Party of Russia, for the Motherland (1995).

a coherent set of policies and a platform that was often cited and circulated during campaigns. Although the central ideology of the Communists slid further to the right from 1993 to 2003, it remained relatively coherent and predictable, both during elections and in the Duma itself. It did very well in the 1995 and 1999 elections, winning about one-quarter of the party-list vote, but dropped to about half that amount in other Duma elections.

The situation is complicated because, at times, the line between ideology and image is difficult to define in party politics in Russia. Although Figure 9.1 categorizes the Liberal Democrats as 'nationalist' and Yabloko as 'liberal', their party images are linked closely to those of their charismatic leaders rather than a particular ideology or policy direction. For example, although the Liberal Democrats project a strong ideological element that could best be described as pro-Russian, anti-state and anti-Western during campaigns, the party often supports the government in actual voting in parliament.

Television coverage of election campaigns in Russia

Presidential elections

Russian presidential elections are much more about personality than ideology, policies or party identification. Only one political party has played an important role in all of the elections: the Communists have provided the only remotely viable contender to challenge the incumbent president in 1996, 2000 and 2004. However, the election was far closer in 1996 than in later years, which in turn dictated a different media strategy on the part of the sitting president. However, the co-optation of the media into the Yeltsin campaign in 1996 created long-term problems for the role of the commercial media in Russian elections.

The Kremlin had learned enough about campaign strategy by 1996 to manage the re-election of Yeltsin, whose popularity had sunk into single digits by the start of that year. The victory was not won through television alone; rather, the Kremlin pursued a strategy of appeasing the populace, particularly by taking steps to end the first Chechen war, promising important economic reforms and negotiating with regional governments. Nor was a Communist president palatable to a majority of Russian voters. Yet television had a critical role to play on several fronts. First, it was used to inform the public, primarily via news and current events programs, of Yeltsin's initiatives. The prime commercial station, NTV, modified its critical stance on the government to campaign for Yeltsin, a move channel executives have defended as necessary to stave off a possible victory for Gennady Zyuganov and a return to Communist rule. This support included hiding the information that Yeltsin suffered a heart attack during the campaign. During the campaign itself, Yeltsin's team ran evocative advertisements under the slogan 'I believe, I love, I hope', in which citizens talked about their support for the president. Yeltsin's image as the protector of the Russian nation during the collapse of communism was emphasized, in tandem with dire warnings of the consequences of a communist return.

The Communists have often announced that they eschew television and prefer 'traditional' methods of mobilizing support among Russians, such as mass meetings, party handouts and door-to-door canvassing. However, they did pursue a media strategy in 1996, including making good use of free-time spots to discuss policy and the cultivation of their image as media outsiders. Yeltsin barely beat Zyuganov in the first round, but he did win handily in the second round (54 per cent to 40 per cent). Given Yeltsin's lack of popularity just a few months before the elections, it was an astonishing victory for the incumbent.

In contrast to Yeltsin, Putin has never needed such an extensive marketing strategy as he has maintained a far higher popularity rating. In fact, Putin did not bother to use his free-time allotment in either 2000 or 2004. It would have been largely irrelevant as the nightly news on the state-run First Channel relentlessly framed Putin as a leader, almost to the sycophantic level of former Soviet party chiefs. By 2004, the most routine task undertaken by Putin was shown on television – as well as a reaction from Putin to virtually any news item of note. It is significant to note that neither Yeltsin nor Putin used the resources of a political party to win. However, given their dominance and control over both mass media and the state apparatus, a party organization would have been unnecessary and perhaps even burdensome.

Duma election campaigns

Coverage of the Duma elections on Russian television has become less free and fair since 1993, despite the introduction of NTV as a powerful commercial television station by the time of the 1995 elections. Although by 1995 Russian law promised fair coverage, pro-government parties and incumbents received unjustly large amounts of media attention. Those who are considered the most plausible opponents to the Kremlin have been virtually shut out of the news or, by 1999, become the victims of mud-slinging campaigns on state-run television. Both the Communists and Yabloko have been victims of either a surprising lack of coverage or mud-smearing campaigns (European Institute for the Media 1994, 1996 a and b, 2000 a and b; Oates 2004; Oates and Roselle 2000). The Liberal Democrats, however, have received far less critical coverage. Some Russian journalists attribute this to the ability of Zhirinovsky to make good television, while others claim it is due to his cooperation with the government in parliament.

While some elements of the Russian electoral system could be viewed as attempts to equalize access – particularly in that all parties get free time on television and can buy advertising[4] – the framing of parties and candidates by the main news programmes is more important in the campaign.

Viewership of free-time slots is low, according to Russian television producers, and most free-time political advertising is quite poorly produced. In addition, advertising time (which reached up to $40,000 a minute on the First Channel at prime-time during the December 1999 elections) was far too expensive for most parties.[5] Neither free-time nor paid political advertising carries the weight and authority of news reports, particularly on the First Channel's flagship news programme *Vremya*.

A review of the studies by the European Institute for the Media and others from 1993 to 2004 shows a consistent trend toward unfair coverage and bias (European Institute for the Media 1994, 1996a and b, 2000a and b; Organization for Security and Cooperation in Europe/Office for Democratic Institutions and Human Rights 2004a and b; Oates 2004; Oates and Roselle 2000). This bias is apparent not only on the prime state-run channels, but also on the commercial NTV channel. On the state channels, the pattern over the course of four Duma elections has been clear: support pro-government parties, back the incumbent president and ignore or belittle any serious opposition to the government/president. As a result, the prime state-sponsored 'parties of power' (Russia's Choice in 1993, Our Home is Russia in 1995, Unity in 1999 and United Russia in 2003) received an abnormally large amount of coverage on channels 1 and 2. For example, in 1993, pro-state parties received more than 16 *hours* of coverage, while the Communist Party garnered a mere 13 *minutes* on state television (European Institute for the Media 1994). It is clear, however, that Russian voters did not merely absorb these messages and support only the parties that conducted extensive television campaigns, either paid or through editorial coverage. Despite their dominance of television, pro-government parties received less than one-quarter of the party-list vote in 1993.

In 1995 there was an enormous increase in both the amount of paid advertising and the editorial coverage of the parties in the elections. As in the 1993 campaign, the major parties, particularly pro-government Our Home is Russia, dominated the election news. It is important to note that by 1995 NTV was a well-established commercial television broadcaster. While studies have shown that NTV was more balanced than the state-run First Channel in presenting election news in 1995 (European Institute for the Media 1996a, Oates and Roselle 2000), the commercial channel was focused much more on war coverage than on the election campaign. When there was coverage of the 1995 Duma elections on NTV, it was often filtered through issues surrounding the war (such as whether Chechen citizens wanted to vote, rumours of terrorism for election day and possible violence at the polling stations).

The 1996 presidential elections were one of the clearest examples of how much the nascent Russian media system differed from libertarian systems in the West. As discussed above, NTV was voluntarily co-opted by the Yeltsin administration, with a top executive from the commercial station even joining the campaign team. While NTV had been critical of the government, particularly over the Chechen war, station officials did not want Communist leader Zyuganov to win the presidency. Thus, all major television stations colluded to market Yeltsin as a vigorous, capable president and failed to present Zyuganov as a feasible leader. Viewers were exposed to information about Zyuganov, particularly on NTV, but this was overwhelmed by the positive spin that Yeltsin was receiving.

The same patterns were clear in the 1999 parliamentary elections and the 2000 presidential elections, although there was a rise in mud-slinging and 'black' propaganda aimed at Kremlin opponents. In particular, Mayor Luzhkov and other leaders of the new Fatherland–All Russia party suffered from both negative news coverage and outrageous reporting of *kompromat* ('compromising material'). This meant that news shows, particularly on the First Channel, often reported rumours and innuendoes as facts in order to damage the reputation of Luzhkov and others. This included broadcasting information to suggest that Luzhkov embezzled money or that his 70-year-old running mate was too old and infirm to serve. By the 2000 presidential elections, NTV was trying to keep a distance from the government, but there were no viable opponents to Putin. However, the First Channel took no chances and used news pro-grammes before the election as an 'infomercial' for Putin, providing exces-sive coverage of every detail of Putin's political engagements. The channel also broadcast negative coverage of presidential candidate Grigory Yavlin-sky, with dubious stories about alleged Western funding of his Yabloko party and his possible cosmetic surgery. NTV was more balanced than the First Channel in its coverage in 2000, although some focus-group particip-ants complained that it appeared that Yavlinsky was 'their' candidate.[6]

The 2003 Duma elections saw further distortion of election news cover-age. The coverage was predictably pro-Kremlin, although it was clear that Mayor Luzhkov had moved from enemy to ally in this election. The First Channel provided particularly extensive coverage of Putin – from his most mundane state visit to his response to a terrorist attack on a Russian train that left 40 people dead during the last week of the parliamentary cam-paign, while Luzhkov joined a favoured cast of characters, who were con-sistently framed in a positive and non-questioning manner. However, the channel was clearly more anti-Communist than in previous elections. While before it had mostly ignored the Communists, during the 2003 cam-paign it featured several stories that were blatant *kompromat*, such as extended coverage of a tiny rally in Moscow allowing participants to make strange accusations against the Communists. Most other parties and candidates were ignored.

It was clear that by the 2003 elections NTV had lost its critical edge. Its news coverage, while not as sycophantic as that of the First Channel, was careful not to criticize the president or even bring up sensitive issue.[7] However, it did retain its somewhat more ironic tone and broader interests. Thus, although reports on his fate were guarded, the jailed oil oligarch

Mikhail Khodorkovsky was mentioned nine times on NTV's prime-time news during the election campaign (but just once on the First Channel's *Vremya*).[8] True to the NTV style, the station's main news typically carried a few ironic or unusual news stories, including one on a restaurant which had sculpted the heads of the oligarchs in chocolate: despite the grave issues of personal freedom and the possible economic impact of the oil oligarch's arrest, the chocolate-head report was Khodorkovsky's largest amount of exposure on the main nightly news during the month-long campaign.

Voter response to political marketing strategies in Russia

The evidence presented above suggests that Russian voters have received increasingly less useful information about political parties and candidates in each election. Initially, the liberal laws on party and candidate access to television seemed to allow for a large amount of information to be distributed to the electorate. However, it quickly became clear that money and influence (enormously difficult to separate in Russia) were critical factors in how well parties and candidates could get their ideas across to the public. Few parties and politicians have been able to parlay the free time on national television into a lasting political organization. There are exceptions to this, notably Zhirinovsky's campaigning abilities that touched a chord of Russian nationalism not recognized by other parties at the time. However, in most cases, the relatively large amount of free-time and virtually unlimited access to paid advertising did little more than create a platform on which the parties could fail. Few parties had the resources for political marketing tools such as public opinion surveys, professional filmmakers, image-makers or consultants. As a result, the handful of parties that were able to fund more professional free-time spots and buy advertising had a disproportionate amount of impact on the viewers.

Recent studies have suggested that Russian viewers have a somewhat schizophrenic attitude toward Russian television. In the 2000 focus groups, it was clear that viewers were aware of deep bias on television news. Yet they retained a very high level of trust, particularly in state-run television. Many claimed that expectations of objectivity or even balance would be naive, but at least they understood the particular biases of the state-run media (particularly the First Channel). In fact, some even openly pined for the days of Soviet censorship, in part because the rules were very clear, but primarily because of the way that they remembered television as providing a hopeful, optimistic portrayal of their society. There was much suspicion of commercial television, particularly as the focus groups surmised that the station owners had their own particular agendas, and they found agendas connected to big business even more suspicious than those linked to government control.

How did these attitudes resonate into response to election coverage? The participants in the focus groups, which were held immediately before and after the 2000 presidential elections, were asked to discuss both the recent Duma contest and the presidential elections. Many of the respondents, particularly the older ones, claimed the smear tactics in the Duma campaign disgusted them. However, at the same time, they seemed to follow the mud slinging with great interest and, often despite initial protestations, admitted that some allegations had led them to change their vote. In terms of the presidential elections, the respondents were more resigned to and more approving of the greater decorum of the 2000 presidential contest. They pointed out that there was far too much coverage of Putin and occasionally remarked that they were getting little concrete information on policy plans or even the real personality of the man – but at least the coverage was decorous. The pattern of being presented with a pre-selected leader, being shown the leader engaged in a variety of unexciting activities and then being urged to vote for the leader was at least a familiar one to the respondents who were old enough to have voted in the Soviet era.

The findings of the focus groups suggest that the Western paradigms of the relationship between the media and the voters may have missed an important element of the model. It appeared that viewers in Russia were willing to give up an element of information flow for some degree of authority and order dictated by television, notably by the prime, state-controlled First Channel. This curious duality between knowledge of bias, yet trust in state television, was present throughout the population, according to a survey of 2,000 Russians in 2001. While about 43 per cent of respondents reported either 'complete' or 'almost complete' confidence in the objectivity of news programmes, almost as many (42 per cent) had 'not much confidence' and 8 per cent had very little confidence. Although the First Channel's more obvious bias does not go unnoticed among Russians, it still commands a higher level of trust than other media outlets: one-third of the survey respondents selected it as the 'most trustworthy channel in its news coverage', while one-quarter chose NTV. The division between trust in state and commercial television was even more stark in response to a more abstract question: 65 per cent of the respondents felt that national state television was the 'most unbiased and reliable source of information', while just 13 per cent picked commercial television for the same role.

Since its takeover by pro-government interests in 2001, NTV has lost a degree of openness and combativeness with the Kremlin. It is clear that some subjects are forbidden, especially the sort of open mocking of the president that was present in such satirical shows as *Kukli* (Puppets) in the 2000 campaign. By the summer of 2004, NTV had dropped its most controversial political debate shows and appeared even more ready to toe the governmental line. This is quite a difference for a channel that openly challenged the presidential administration with its coverage of first Chechen war. Yet the new, tamer face of NTV may matter little, as the commercial channel never rivalled the First Channel in its influence on elections. Survey respondents in both 2001 and 2003–04 overwhelmingly nominated state television (43 and

40 per cent respectively) as an 'important' source of information for making a vote choice in Duma elections.[9] Only a handful of respondents claimed national commercial television was important to their vote choice. The same pattern held for the 2000 presidential election.

How do attitudes about media relate to the development of a political system in Russia? This chapter posits that the acceptance of authority over truth in mass media has led to a particular phenomenon in Russia, namely the growing success of the 'broadcast party' or even the 'broadcast candidate'. Political image plays a part in elections in other countries, notably in the US presidential elections, but this is in addition to developed party systems. In Russia, the media have shown an unusually strong ability to not only *promote* parties, but *create* them as well. The dilemma lies in the growing electoral strength of these broadcast parties. If one defines broadcast parties as organizations that are without well-defined ideologies, platforms or even quantifiable policy statements, lacking grass-roots organization, funded by a government entity, and with no history prior to the elections or accountability after the elections, then each subsequent election in Russia has improved their fortunes. It is fair to note that in the 1993 elections virtually all of the parties except the Communists were essentially new and, in a sense, 'created' by mass media since they were heavily reliant on television to put across their ideas and images. Yet, instead of parties developing as well-rooted political institutions, the reliance on mass media to spread political messages seems to have become strengthened at the cost of real party organization.

In Western political systems, mass media are considered the servants of political parties. Politicians and political scientists alike often complain that the media, especially television, distort their messages or, perhaps even worse, ignore them. Nonetheless, political parties still function as a key link between voters and the governmental institutions of power. In Russia, it would appear that the broadcast media have hijacked the role of parties to mobilize the electorate. Unfortunately, the media have no particular responsibility in making sure that the politicians fulfil election promises or even live up to a particular image. When the central media are in turn controlled by the central government, there is little hope for expansion of political freedom and expression of divergent viewpoints.

Notes

1 This evidence comes from 24 focus groups commissioned by the author and carried out in Moscow, Ulyanovsk and Voronezh by Russian Research Ltd in 2000. The focus groups and a survey from April 2001 cited in this chapter were funded by the British Economic and Social Research Council.

2 The Council of the Federation has never been re-elected; representatives are now appointed. In addition, the Duma election law is now amended and all seats will be assigned through the party-list system.

3 Author's interview with Yelena Rukovtseva, Moscow, December 1999.

4 Free-time became much more limited in the 1999 campaign, when the Russian Central Electoral Commission announced that parties that received less than 2 per cent of the vote would have to repay the state for their television time.
5 From the author's interviews with television station directors and advertising executives, December 1999.
6 From the focus groups cited above.
7 Based on the author's analysis of the primetime NTV news show *Sevodnya* during the 2003 campaign.
8 Author's research.
9 The survey was carried out in December 2003 and January 2004 by Russian Research Ltd under the direction of Professor Stephen White (University of Glasgow). The research was funded by the Economic and Social Research Council.

References

Berelson, B., Lazarsfeld, P. and McPhee, W. (1954) *Voting. A Study of Public Opinion Formation in a Presidential Campaign*, Chicago, IL: Chicago University Press.

Campbell, A., Converse, P.E., Miller, W.E. and Stokes, D.E. (1960) *The American Voter*, New York: Wiley.

European Institute for the Media (1994) *The Russian Parliamentary Elections. Monitoring of the Election Coverage in the Russian Mass Media*, Düsseldorf: EIM.

——(1996a) *Monitoring of the Media Coverage of the 1995 Russian Parliamentary Elections*, Düsseldorf: EIM.

——(1996b) *Monitoring of the Media Coverage of the 1996 Russian Presidential Elections*, Düsseldorf: EIM.

——(2000a) *Monitoring of the Media Coverage of the 1999 Russian Parliamentary Elections*, Düsseldorf: EIM.

——(2000b) *Monitoring of the Media Coverage of the 2000 Russian Presidential Elections*, Düsseldorf: EIM.

Lipset, S.M. and Rokkan, S. (eds) (1967) *Party Systems and Voter Alignments. Cross-national Perspectives*, New York: Collier-Macmillan.

Oates, S. (1998) 'Party platforms. Towards a definition of the Russian political spectrum', in J. Lowenhardt (ed.) *Party Politics in Post-Communist Russia*, London: Frank Cass.

—— (2004) 'Post-soviet political style. Parties, television and voters', in G. Flikke (ed.) *The Uncertainties of Putin's Democracy*, Oslo: Norwegian Institute of International Affairs.

Oates, S. and Roselle, L. (2000) 'Russian elections and TV news. Comparison of campaign news on state-controlled and commercial television channels', *Harvard International Journal of Press/Politics*, 5(2): 30–51.

Organization for Security and Cooperation in Europe/Office for Democratic Institutions and Human Rights (2004a) *Russian Federation: Elections to the State Duma, 7 December 2003. OSCE/ODHIR Election Observation Mission Report*, Warsaw: OSCE/ODHIR. Online. Available HTTP in English: <http://www.osce.org/documents/odihr/2004/01/1947_en.pdf> (accessed 1 July 2004).

——(2004b) *Russian Federation. Presidential Election, 14 March 2004. OSCE/ODHIR Election Observation Mission Report*, Warsaw: OSCE/ODHIR. Online. Available HTTP in English: <http://www.osce.org/documents/odihr/2004/06/3033_en.pdf> (accessed 1 July 2004).

10 The Internet in politics

Democracy in e-government in Taiwan

Ming-Ying Lee

With the widespread increase in access to advanced information communication technologies throughout the 1990s, a shift to so-called 'electronic democracy' has occurred, involving citizens and governments. The e-democracy debate is about whether such communication technologies can increase participation and involvement in public life. Thus, 'governments and civic societies are in the process of adapting to information technologies, and the structure of political opportunities' (Norris 2001: 95) – and the Internet will only strengthen democracy if it expands opportunities for political participation (2001: 103). This has become an incentive for many democratic counties to develop e-government as an interface between citizens and the government. What impact does e-government have on the political system and civil life in new democracies, as some of them adopt these initiatives?

In the world map of democracies, Taiwan has drawn the attention of the Western world as a 'young' democratic country. In the last decade, Taiwan took steps toward several different phases of democratization. The first direct presidential election, held in 1996, was 'an important step on the road to democratic consolidation' (Diamond & Plattner 1997: xli). After the presidential election of 2000, which completely reversed over half a century of one-party dominance in Taiwan, many scholars suggested that democracy in Taiwan appeared to be consolidated (Chu 2001; Chu *et al.* 2001; Rawnsley 2004).

The Taiwanese government, like many other governments around the world, has embarked upon developing an 'e-government' initiative since the mid-1990s. Amongst the advanced e-government countries, Taiwan has achieved remarkable scores in many international assessments. The World Markets Research Centre ranked Taiwan as the second best in e-government out of 196 nations in 2001, while the Center for Public Policy at Brown University assessed it as best in 2002 and fifth best in 2003 out of 198 nations (World Markets Research Centre 2001; Center for Public Policy 2002, 2003). The Taiwanese government loudly declared its success in e-government. However, at the present time, many authorities depict the nature of e-government as a set of digital processes for improving governmental effectiveness, 'with its dominant managerial discourse of cost cutting and efficiency' (Chadwick 2003: 444), and pay limited attention to the issue of whether it is fundamentally correct to keep watch on the citizen's relations with government (Morison and Newman 2001: 171). The Taiwanese authority has also been more inclined to use information technology to reorganize itself than to incorporate the public more fully into its operation (Lee 2003).

Therefore, this study focuses on the needs of Taiwanese users, especially citizens at all levels, and examines how they participate in e-government. Does the public show as much enthusiasm for e-government as the authority does? Furthermore, can the use of e-government contribute to democracy? To answer these questions, I take the Taiwanese experience in developing e-government as an example and focus on practical participation in social and political life through the use of e-government. I will first illustrate the democratic values that were applied to e-government and show how e-government can be assessed. Second, I will begin mapping a brief background of the e-government progress in Taiwan. Finally I will draw on some empirical data concerning the use made of e-government in Taiwan and conclude by discussing whether e-government can serve democracy.

Pursuit of democracy via e-government

Effect of governance: efficiency and participation

Democracy, based on the principle of 'government by the people', is essentially an art of governance – governing and being governed. More recently, the concept of governance has shifted attention from the institutions of the state to its political processes. Such changes imply that, in effect, democratic performance in polity can be divided into two key dimensions: efficiency and participation. The former refers to the decision-making capacity of the government and its ability to 'deliver the goods' and services to citizens, while the latter refers to the effective inclusion of citizens in the processes of decision-making with the government.

Efficiency can be judged by the administrative and material performance of a government. The core purpose of government is to govern, to rule, to ensure stability through the exercise of authority. Frederickson (1996) argues that the effectiveness of democratic government and modern governance, not merely for the majority of but for all citizens, depends on the energetic exercise of bureaucratic discretion. It is also argued that the most reliable means of generating wealth and achieving material prosperity can be the precondition, as well as the processes, for democratization. Efficiency has become an impetus for democratic governments to reach stability.

The discussion of efficiency is central in relation to the government, while the discussion of participation emphasizes the way in which citizens may be empowered and increase their personal autonomy in the government's decision-making processes. The government looks much like the sort of political community in which citizens have a capacity to participate, rather than be passively served by the state as agent. Such content can be significantly interpreted from the perspective of citizenship. 'The status of citizen implies a sense of inclusion into the wider community and it is an active rather passive status' (Faulks 2000: 4). Participation reflects much more the adjustment of the relationship from passive customer to active citizen.

Application of e-government to democracy

E-government is an interesting product, which incorporates the elements of efficiency and participation in an Internet-based system. Most definitions of 'e-government' depend on the new communication technologies, not least Internet-based applications. The Organization for Economic Co-operation and Development defines 'e-government' as the use of information and communication technologies, and particularly the Internet, as a tool to achieve better government (2003: 23). The United Nations Online Network in Public Administration and Finance explains e-government as 'utilizing the Internet and the world-wide-web for delivering government information and services to citizens' (2003). Most of the pioneering countries setting up e-government aimed to improve the efficiency of delivery of public services and save some of the cost of administration. As Fountain (2001) argues, e-government brings government 'closer to the people' by meeting the expectations of service users regarding convenience, accessibility and timeliness.

More and more studies have turned to focus upon the incorporation of citizens into the policy-making process. E-government promises to be more open, which in turn improves the quality of democracy. The themes include increasing accountability and transparency, facilitating consultation and civic engagement between governments and citizens (Chadwick 2003; Lenihan 2002; Morison and Newman 2001; Norris 2001). Such perspectives go beyond simple electronic service delivery and move to various types of participation. Online consultation, online voting and online discussion forums create more opportunities for citizens to deliberate and make direct decisions, which are examples of active citizenship. This change is particularly significant for the advocates of direct democracy or 'strong democracy'. Therefore, the main potential of the Internet for the government lies in strengthening public participation and improving administrative effectiveness.

Nevertheless, some scholars tend to suspect that the new technology will have the result of undermining democratic values rather than supporting democracy. New information technology is likely to reinforce pre-existing inequalities both within government and between government and citizens (Danziger *et al.* 1982; Lax 2001) and widen the gap between information 'haves' and 'have-nots' (Rabb *et al.* 1996: 285). Such viewpoints have become the basis of the issue known as the 'Digital Divide'. The social inequities have not diminished with the development of e-government. Moreover, the managerial model has dominated at the expense of 'consultative' and 'participatory' possibilities. This reinforces the existing power structure and falls short of anything approaching 'e-democracy' (Chadwick and May 2003: 293, 296). In other words, if the existing mechanism remains the established norm (for example, the agent-state model), the advocacy of e-government falls again into a spiral of utopias for the privileged section of society.

There is another cause for scepticism concerning the possibility of 'freedom of information' through new communication technology. Information communication technology is likely to intrude upon personal privacy and increase surveillance and control over persons and groups (Rabb 1997: 155–6). Lyon (1994) frankly points out the attendant invasion of privacy and unwarranted surveillance of individuals, which are of course incompatible with liberal democracy. Transactions in e-government involve the integration and sharing of data across bureaucratic domains. This leads to online security becoming one of the most worrying issues. People may fear how their personal information and transaction records can be protected from investigation. Moreover, e-government promises to be open government, yet the degree of transparency is questioned as selected information may be a tactic for the government to intentionally control its people's minds. Therefore, information technology is a double-edged sword. 'Technology may be used for surveillance, monitoring, control, and disinformation as easily as it might be leveraged to promoted transparency, accountability, and access to information that promotes human development' (Fountain 2003).

Evaluation of e-government in practice

The performance of e-government involves many factors within and outside government. For many practitioners, the factors of 'front office' and 'back office' are taken into account. The former means the information and services provided and the interaction between governments and citizens. The feature of government websites is the immediate factor affecting citizen use of e-government. The public perception of and feeling toward e-government can be quickly and rapidly built up through experiencing government websites. As regards the 'back office', this refers to the hidden sides of e-government, such as information infrastructure, the institutional framework and administrative reform. Most efforts are steered by the government itself and the outcomes mainly demonstrate the enhancement of efficiency within the public sector.

Many organizations evaluate e-government on the basis of the presence of a government website. As the Organization for Economic Co-operation and Development has indicated, current studies tend to focus on the breadth of the online service (for example, the number of services provided), online service span (for example, the customer target group to which online service are delivered) and, to a lesser extent, online service quality (for example, the extent to which online services achieve their stated objectives) (Organization for Economic Co-operation and Development 2003: 137). Some studies incorporate elements of democracy into their assessments, but they are still based on the presence of government websites. The Arizona-based research team, Cyberspace Policy Research Group, for example, has developed the 'Website Attribute Evaluation System' to assess the contents and format of national-level e-government websites according to two principal criteria: transparency and interactivity (Cyberspace Policy Research Group 1998).

The Website Attribute Evaluation System, at least, does not simply treat information transparency as a necessity but also exploits the relationship between government departments and citizens through the evaluation of interactivity. Norris employs the same system in a discussion of the democratic functions of government websites and, significantly, incorporates levels of democratization, technological diffusion and socio-economic development into her investigation of government websites worldwide (2001: 125). She concludes that it seems more appropriate to compare government online activity with its role in the real world. Therefore, 'government websites should be evaluated in terms of the quality and effectiveness of their informational and communication functions' (2001: 129).

The World Markets Research Centre (2001) and the Center for Public Policy (2002, 2003) evaluate the presence of government websites according to three dimensions: information availability, service delivery and public access. Six criteria are employed: online service, privacy and security, disability access, foreign language access, advertisements and user fees, and public outreach.

However, these reports overemphasized the content of online service and technical levels, consequently leaving out local e-governments. While the 'one-stop service' has been highlighted as a mainstay of e-government, the reports list it only as a feature of the internal link. Provided that the one-stop service is to be a single window, its content should be evaluated along with that of other central governments websites. Finally, insufficient attention was paid to local users' needs. The reports relied on either a few foreign readers or used a machine translation if the websites did not present in English. Since this approach appears likely to suffer from subjectivity or technological bias, it is necessary to refer to other data concerning the use of e-government and users' satisfaction in each country.

Overview of the e-government infrastructure in Taiwan

Origin and progress

The mid-1990s were a crucial time for the development of the Internet as well as e-government projects in Taiwan. The international trend around that time was to apply the latest developments in communications, particularly the Internet, to public administration. For example, the Clinton–Gore administration of the United States beavered away at the National Information Infrastructure project, which highlighted the idea of e-government. In parallel with the countries of the European Union, the G7 Government Online Project also suggested that the use of computer technologies in public administration could improve governmental effectiveness and productivity.

In Taiwan, the government followed the American example, launching a task force to develop a Taiwanese National Information Infrastructure in 1994. The main mission of the National Information Infrastructure Unit is to promote and to develop the information infrastructure across the whole country. Its priority was to increase the number of the Internet users and it began with the striking slogan, 'Aiming to Reach Three Million Internet Users in Three Years'. The mass media was quickly flooded with this slogan. The campaign was very successful: statistics from the Institute for Information Industry (ACI-FIND) show that the number of Internet users increased from 440,000 to 4.02 million between 1996 and 1999 (ACI-FIND 2002: 4).

As in the US, the Taiwanese National Information Infrastructure aimed to set up e-government to facilitate public service and public administration. Prime Minister Wan-Zhang Xiao highlighted the importance of reinventing government on various public occasions and claimed three reinventing themes: networks, human resources and civil service, and legitimacy. In particular, in the theme of human resources and civil service, e-government would be the leading actor. The government meant to build up a national project centred on the information network in response to the idea of 'rein venting government' in accordance with National Information Infrastructure plans, encompassing all aspects of economy, transportation, education and culture, with the ultimate aim of achieving the 'information society'. As the Taiwanese National Information Infrastructure Unit put it in the Action Plan for the National Information Infrastructure in Taiwan:

> it is necessary for us to establish information networks and electronic systems as well as e-government ... to promote innovative policies based on the information infrastructures. As a result of this, we would reinvent our strength.
>
> (National Information Infrastructure Unit 1997)

The Executive Yuan (often referred to as the Cabinet) officially passed the Medium Term Electronic Government Project in 1997. The project includes five foundational plans: information infrastructure, government service network, electronic gateway system, network security and electronic certification service – each of which includes several sub-plans (e-taxation, e-procurement, e-publication, one-stop service and so on).

One-stop government service

As the number of available areas and aspects of e-government services grows, it becomes possible to offer citizens seamless rather than fragmented access to a set of related services. The impetus driven by 'service integration' results in a holistic government. The channels for delivery of such an integrated service include websites, one-stop shops and call centres, which can deliver services flexibly to target groups (Horrocks and Bellamy 1997). Thus, in the United Kingdom, the Blair government, an advocate of 'joined-up' government, adopted a 'one-stop shop' that would allow citizens to find information and transact their business in one searchable integrated portal, while also strengthening linkages among the public sector.

Similarly, the Taiwanese government passed the plan for the Integrated E-government Entry Point of Taiwan in 2001. This is a unified window for public service, which claims to provide links to all relevant government websites, thousands of downloadable forms and hundreds of online application services. This project conforms to the requirements and the deployment of systems development set out in *The Action Plan of the E-government: 2001–2004* (Research, Development and Evaluation Commission 2001) and the *Action Plan of National Information and Communications Development* that was published later the same year (National Information and Communications Initiative Committee 2001).

The e-government plan principally follows the previous Medium-term Electronic Government Project and includes measures such as 'strengthening infrastructure', 'promotion of widespread computerization, raising of government information application levels', 'enhancement of government information dissemination sharing and integration' and 'implementation of government online service'. The government has committed itself to promoting both government-to-business and government-to-citizen services and to operating procedural reform so as to provide a 'single window' and 'one-stop service' (Research, Development and Evaluation Commission 2001).

It was not until 2002 that a clearer picture was developed of the design of the government's portal site. The portal site was officially introduced to the public in March 2002 and named 'My e-government – the e-government entry point of Taiwan'. The service of this portal site consists of three dimensions: information queries, electronic service delivery and interactive communication between citizens and the government (Research, Development and Evaluation Commission 2002). First, the website provides a powerful Internet search engine, a subject directory service and a real-time (webcam) service. Second, the portal site plans to make 1,500 downloadable forms and documents and 400 online application services available by 2004. Third, it covers many news services, including the daily activities of government agencies, real-time news and an electronic bulletin board. The site also provides an email query system, discussion forum, online public opinion survey and online poll.

It is understandable that the Taiwanese government has been keen to promote e-government infrastructure. The government's aim essentially is to improve the convenience and efficiency of government service. The emergence of the one-stop service further extends its benefits (including exemption from need for physical transcripts, paperless applications, multi-points, multi-channels and at-home service). The one-stop service seems a new concept; however, it is best seen as an instance of joined-up government: 'Joining up is the latest manifestation of one of the oldest preoccupations in the field of politics and public administration – the coordination of policymaking and administration' (Pollitt 2003: 36). Therefore, it is cooperative, not simply addressing from the top down but requiring interaction with customers.

Utilization of e-government in Taiwan

The government reached its target of three million Internet users by 1999 and the Internet penetration in Taiwan has grown incrementally ever since. National statistics show that the Internet penetration of households in Taiwan was 20.1 per cent by January 1999, 37.5 per cent by March 2001 and 48.6 per cent by March 2003. Furthermore, more than 50 per cent (53.5 per cent in 1999, 59.7 per cent in 2001 and 66.8 per cent in 2003) of Taiwanese Internet users have at some time accessed the government websites (Department of Statistics 1999, 2001, 2003).

Activity of users

For the most part, it can be inferred that Taiwanese Internet users who visit e-government do so to browse for information. In 1999 and 2001, the percentage of e-government users who reported this activity reached nearly 90 per cent (see Table 10.1). The rate at which the users participated in other activities was always lower than 20 per cent. The second most popular activity changed from 'academic activities' in 1999 and 'ordering tickets' in 2001 to 'requesting public service' in 2003. However, it must be noted that the study did not specify a particular government website or websites so the results give only a general picture of e-government users.

As for the use of the government portal site, the authority of e-government, the Research, Development and Evaluation Commission

Table 10.1 User activity on Taiwanese government websites

	% of users reporting activity[a]		
	January 1999 (N = 2,129)	*March 2001* (N = 1,894)	*March 2003* (N = 2,060)
Browsing (information/news)	90.0	89.6	81.0
Ordering tickets	–	15.9	2.6
Academic activities	15.8	13.2	10.3
Requesting public services	8.4	8.9	16.8
Job hunting	12.0	7.7	2.4
Voicing opinions	6.9	5.7	2.2
Public bidding	3.4	5.3	6.0
Others	3.7	1.8	0.8

Source: Department of Statistics. *A Survey of Internet Use amongst the Taiwanese Population.* Taipei: Ministry of Transportation, 1999, 2001 and 2003.

Note
a Multiple responses were possible.

conducted surveys of satisfaction in March and September 2003 (2003a and b). From the responses of those who had experience of 'one-stop service' (shown in Table 10.2), it appears that 'browsing for information' is still the most popular online activity, followed by 'searching online application information and downloading forms'. 'Voicing opinions' was the least popular activity.

In addition, according to ACI-FIND (2001), neither government websites nor the government portal site are prominent in terms of the website reach rate. ACI-FIND takes the definition of a website reach rate from iRate, a private sector company that specializes in Internet ratings. A 'website reach rate' is found by dividing the whole Internet population by the number of visitors to one website within a given survey period. The reach rate of the government portal site is 1.68 percent, which ranks only twenty-fourth amongst all government websites (ACI-FIND, 2001: 25). This is unusual that the portal site should have a much higher reach rate than other websites.

The reach rate undoubtedly does not completely reflect the use of e-government. An analysis of the behaviour of e-government users may provide another clue. Research conducted after the Taiwanese government launched the government portal site (My e-government) in March 2002 reveals some interesting points (Chen and Lin 2002). First, from a cross-analysis of the visitors' duration of stay and the number of pages viewed, it emerges that more than 80 per cent of visitors tend to stay briefly and only browse one or two pages. The average duration of stay in the portal site is less than one minute. This may be because visitors do not find the service and information they need there and leave immediately. Thus, there may be a difference between the users' need and the content

Table 10.2 User activity on the Taiwanese government portal site

	% of users reporting activity[a]	
	March 2003 (N = 36)	*September 2003* (N = 46)
Browsing (information/news)	39.1	84.5
Searching online application information and downloading forms	21.2	35.1
Appling for online public services	16.0	32.4
Webcam service	11.9	19.7
Drawing prizes	3.4	0.0
Voicing opinions	3.1	6.7
Others	5.2	6.7
No response	0.0	3.1

Source: Research, Development and Evaluation Commission, Executive Yuan. *A Survey of People's Satisfaction with Public Services.* Taipei: Executive Yuan, 2003.

Note

a Multiple responses were possible. The results exclude users from other government websites (n = 352 in March 2003 and n = 345 in September 2003) and only count the users who have had experience of the government portal site.

provided by the portal site. Second, the users who visit the portal site not only stay briefly but also like browsing the 'shallow', 'short' and 'immediate' images more than using any other services. The popular pages are centred on the real-time photos taken by the webcams set up in a number of tourist attractions – the most popular function of the site (2002: 26–38). Although the real-time images may attract some users to view this portal site, it is doubtful whether they subsequently use other services if their average duration of stay is taken into consideration.

Internet users normally visit different websites to seek what they need. The content and the service showed by different government websites are varied. If all resources can be covered in one website, users can save time and energy. Therefore, the idea of a one-stop service derived from the integration of different online resources indeed makes sense. 'Joined-up government', on the one hand, can improve administrative efficiency for the government. On the other hand, for the public, it can serve as an alternative channel for access to public affairs. However, amongst numerous websites, can the government website be as attractive to Internet users as general websites? Moreover, is the one-stop service attractive enough to Internet users? The government websites thus not only have to compete with those powerful commercial websites in the operational interface, but also, in the effectiveness of their procedures, they must cater to users' requests as much as possible.

Service quality

As the Organization for Economic Co-operation and Development report says, 'the quality of e-government service is often assessed as citizen satisfaction' (2003: 146). This can reflect the fact that customers' expectations and habits are evolving rapidly in a changing service environment. Most of the surveys mentioned above also investigate user satisfaction with government websites.

According to government figures, it seems that the majority of Taiwanese Internet users are reasonably satisfied with their use of e-government. Amongst users, the level of satisfaction was 67.9 per cent in 1999, 78.8 per cent in 2001 and 72.7 per cent in 2003 (Department of Statistics 1999, 2001, 2003). Yet academics present a different picture, indicating some uncertainty over the adequacy of e-government. In a survey of the structure and motivation of Taiwanese Internet users conducted in the late 1990s, Wang (2000) found that only 40.3 per cent of users were satisfied with the performance of e-government. However, 35.9 per cent failed to respond to the question, which may be because they had not heard of e-government before or had little understanding of it (2000: 71). Hu (2001) carried out some complementary research into participation in public affairs amongst Taiwanese Internet users. Interestingly, although more than 70 per cent had heard of e-government, only 20 per cent of the service items had been used (2001: 77). This study's overall assessment of e-government was even less positive: only 9.8 per cent of the Internet users were satisfied with the general performance of e-government. Most of the Internet population either had negative attitudes towards or did not understand e-government. Hu suggests that government should make greater efforts to promote e-government and to stimulate people's motivation to access it. Above all, he recommends the establishment of a portal site as a means of solving these problems (2001: 83).

Significantly, e-government has yet not been proved to work, because the work of e-government will need more time to prove itself. The results of two surveys of Taiwanese people's satisfaction with public services proved very interesting (Research, Development and Evaluation Commission 2003a and b). In the survey of March 2003, while 43.4 per cent said that they were satisfied with the government's efforts in e-government, 37.1 per cent still did not understand its benefits. When the survey was repeated in September 2003, there was no great increase in the level of satisfaction (now 44.6 per cent) or decrease in the proportion who did not understand its benefits (now 35.6 per cent). Although in the September survey, nearly 80 per cent of portal site users said that they were satisfied with the one-stop service, the result needs to read with care as the samples are limited: 80.8 per cent of e-government users said that they had no idea what 'My e-government' (the one-stop service) was and, thus, are unlikely to know where it is to be found (2003b). It seems that, for Taiwanese users, the 'one-stop service' is nothing but one of a number of websites. Lacking appropriate understanding of e-government is the primary barrier for Taiwanese people.

There are many other factors deterring e-government users from going on to use e-government services. Because so many e-government users use government websites mainly for browsing information, it is not surprising that their complaints tend to be based around issues of insufficient information. Among reasons for dissatisfaction with government websites, 'service items and information provided is too limited' always ranks top in the league table, followed by 'information is out of date' and 'information is imperfectly set out' (Department of Statistics 1999, 2001, 2003).

With regard to online application services, the service available online may not accurately meet the users' needs. Many portal site users (65.2 per cent in the March survey and 82.2 per cent in the September survey) said that they did not have any need to use them (Research, Development and Evaluation Commission 2003a and b). Inevitably, dealing with an online application service involves the transmission of personal information. When asked whether they hesitate about or do not intend to use the online application services, more than 40 per cent said that they were reluctant to transmit their personal information through the Internet. E-government users worry a good deal about their personal information being revealed during a transaction.

In the most successful year of Taiwanese e-government, although 96 per cent of Taiwanese government websites contain privacy statements, only 35 per cent offer security statements (Center for Public Policy 2002). The Taiwanese government has been aware that personal details should be protected, but does not appear to have taken effective action to ensure online security. Moreover, with the increasing number of hackers stealing personal information through the Internet, even in 2004 the *United Daily News* reported that 'people still feel more secure to use traditional ways of filing taxation, not the Internet' ('Most people still worry about e-tax reporting', 31 May 2004). It appears that e-government users do not trust online security to be powerful enough, and would rather 'retreat' to an offline submission than risk losing their data through e-government spies.

Bringing democracy closer to the people

From the establishment of an information infrastructure and more recently the 'one-stop service', what the Taiwanese government stresses is the change in the administration and the improvement of efficiency within the public sector. This is closely related to the modernization of government. Such 'back office' factors have paved the way for democratization in Taiwan. However, it seems to have been primarily a managerial approach, since any bureaucracy runs its affairs primarily for its own benefit. If one considers instead the degree of democracy, letting citizens participate is more important than administrative efficiency.

In the Taiwanese case, the data show that general acceptance of and participation in the Internet for citizens has reached a satisfactory level. However, the general use of the Internet in Taiwan remains at the level of 'browsing for information', mainly for entertainment and personal communication. This is a primary level of Internet use. Examination of the use of e-government has reconfirmed such a tendency. For many citizens, e-government simply means the existence of websites where they can potentially find information that they need. Although there is nothing wrong with this level of use, the government's 'one-stop service' initiative was developed to facilitate three distinct activities: supplying answers to queries, delivering services electronically and interactive communication. Even the popular real-time webcam service in the 'one-stop service' can also be considered to be a kind of provision of information – albeit one that is orientated towards entertainment so as to attract users. The real-time photo is essentially a 'short' and 'quick' image. The phenomenon demonstrates that entertainment-orientated information is able to catch the participants' attention, but the information it can show tends to be 'slight' and 'shallow'.

As Delanty indicates, 'in a society dominated by information, access to information and the ability to act upon it is one of the main dimensions to participation' (2000: 130). E-government passes on government regulations, governmental news, government policies and navigational tools. Such an immense quantity of information may help facilitate the development of better-quality citizen participation. In the Taiwanese case, if the 'one-stop service' can successfully integrate discursive governmental information, it is likely to serve as the best single window for citizens to access public information. Yet from the users' perspective, e-government has not fitted the level of transparency required, as most of them still complain that the information it gives them is out of date and inadequate (Department of Statistics 1999, 2001, 2003). Even when people are interested in using online service delivery, they would naturally expect to obtain sufficient and up-to-date information before they used the service. If the first level of information queries fails to meet users' primary needs, it may be difficult to attract them to use the other services of interactive e-government.

The characteristics of information and communication are both important for democracy. One of the ideals of e-government is communication between the government and civil society as well as inviting citizens into the government's decision-making process. The optimists even predict that e-government can be the 'public sphere' or the mediated arena between the state and civil society. The Taiwanese case also fails to meet the interactive indicator. As Tables 10.1 and 10.2 indicate, very few of the interactive functions of e-government (such as online discussion or online voting) have been used to any extent. Similarly, Chen and Lin's investigation into users' behaviour made no mention of 'interaction' in its league table of pages reviewed (Chen and Lin 2002: 26–38). Email is commonly considered to be the easiest method of contact, yet one of the senior officials in the authority of e-government in Taiwan has admitted that the normal procedure for dealing with an email request takes three to five days.[1] If the authority takes so long to answer a citizen's question, does it seem likely that citizens' comments will have any effect? Here, e-government is not serving as a two-way channel of communication in effect but potentially obstructing the citizen's intention to communicate with the government.

From the outset, the Taiwanese government has deliberately planned the e-government service to act as both a mechanism to reduce the cost of red tape and a vehicle for the distribution of information. The presence of e-government provides a primary need for information, but that in itself is not sufficient to justify e-government in the eyes of many users. E-government does little more than satisfy an online need. A working communication in e-government between citizens and the government is further required. There are many 'technical' strategies to improve the presence of e-government. For example, positive publicity can be created through successful public relations strategies; a powerful search engine, updated information and user-friendly online procedures can appeal to users. The difficulty, however, is to maintain citizens' active participation.

Being a citizen, of course, is not merely a matter of being well informed. The main requirement for being an active citizen is a channel and the competence to access public affairs. E-government can offer a channel for citizens, but it cannot determine how they use it. Citizens may be informed, but may not spontaneously become active. Changing the perceptions of the users of e-government is not easy, but in the long run it will be necessary.

Conclusions

The Taiwanese government has quickly embraced the idea of e-government. It declared the aims of the initiative to be a customer-oriented government, and the subsequent 'one-stop service' even committed itself to providing a more open, accessible and communicable forum for its customer–citizen.

However, people tend to see the Internet as a tool to achieve their personal fulfilment by means of the information that it provides. E-government users in Taiwan remain at the 'information' level. They are better informed by the facilities of e-government. They mainly browse for information to satisfy their curiosity, which may be seen as one way of engaging in e-government. Thus, the public shows its enthusiasm for e-government but only within a limited area. Citizens are informed but still far from active. Should e-government merely serve as an 'online library'?

The establishment of a 'one-stop service' is intended to deliver a package of service to citizens. This brings the administration closer to the people. Like most other providers of such services, the Taiwanese government enthusiastically offers online service breadth and online service span. The main impetus for this is increased efficiency, which is to the government's own benefit. However, there is hardly any inter-action and transaction, except browsing for information, to be seen on the government website. If the concept of 'one-stop service' is the coun-terpart of a 'shopping mall', the power to make transactions is a neces-sary utility. Yet the evidence shows that many online application services do not meet users' needs. Do many services mean better ones? Or is it the case that current online application services are not what users need? E-government users can always be content with online 'window-shopping', browsing for information as they do on other websites. They are not concerned by whether there are other online services available. They may not feel that there is any greater efficiency and convenience to be gained from e-government, as the authority optimistically anticipates.

E-government as an information provider or a one-stop mechanism reflects only part of the justified expectations of its users and the author-ity. Rather, e-government should be an arena for two-way communication between governments and citizens. E-government offers the chance for more interactive and effective discussion, consultation and feedback on public policy debates. This is a feature that only e-government can bring – a virtual political system that contributes to democracy. However, this aspect seems to have been neglected by the government, and citizens have not challenged it. Of course, they have their own perceptions of e-government. In effect, for the users, e-government is used mostly for acquiring information; while for the authority, it is used for distributing information and transacting government service. Therefore, the expan-sion of democratic participation has not happened yet. The missing link is interactive communication. E-government in Taiwan has bridged the gap between citizens and the government, to a limited extent.

Although many new democracies have adopted the Internet to communicate with their customer–citizens, this has not guaranteed that democratization accompanies it in the form of virtual polity. Yet the effi-ciency of enhanced government service brings the administration closer to the citizens, while interactive communication in public debate brings citizens closer into the process of democratization. The Internet certainly has an impact on the form of government service offered, but it has not brought about an essential change in the process of decision-making between the government and citizens. The quality and quantity of e-government can easily be improved with the latest development of technology, although the level of use will not change automatically in response to newer 'communication' technologies. E-government has not shown any effect in consolidating democracy. Its potential depends on a change of attitude to its use, by both the government and citizens. Consequently, the challenge of e-government is not into what form participation will change to but rather how democratic values are to be enhanced through new ways of connecting the government to its citizens.

Acknowledgements

I am grateful to Professor Steve Fuller for insightful comments on earlier versions of this paper.

Note

1 Interview with Mr Ming-Chung Lee, Associate Research Fellow, Department of Information Management, Research, Development and Evaluation Commission, Executive Yuan in the Office, 15 December 2002.

References

ACI-FIND, Institute for Information Industry (2001) *The Year Book of the Internet Development and Application at 2001 in Taiwan*, Taipei: ACI-FIND, Ministry of Economy.

——(2002) *The Year Book of the Internet Development and Application at 2002 in Taiwan*, Taipei: ACI-FIND, Ministry of Economy.

Center for Public Policy, Brown University (2002) *Global E-Government Report, 2002*, Providence, RI: Center for Public Policy, Brown University. Online. Available HTTP: <http://www.insidepolitics.org/yegovt02int.html> (accessed 7 February 2003).

——(2003) *Global E-Government Report, 2003*, Providence, RI: Center for Public Policy, Brown University. Online. Available HTTP: <http://www.insidepolitics. org/egovt03int.html> (accessed 14 February 2004).

Chadwick, A. (2003) 'Bringing e-democracy back in. Why it matters for future research on e-governance', *Social Science Computer Review*, 21(4): 443–55.

Chadwick, A. and May, C. (2003) 'Interaction between states and citizens in the age of the Internet. "E-government" in the United States, Britain, and the European Union', *Governance*, 16(2): 271–300.

Chen, H. and Lin, M.-t. (2002) 'The analysis of users' behaviour to e-government entry-point in Taiwan', *Journal of Library and Information Science*, 28(2): 26–38.

Chu, Y.-h. (2001) 'Democratic consolidation in the post-KMT era. The challenge of governance', in M. Alagappa (ed.) *Taiwan's Presidential Politics. Democratization and Cross-strait Relations in the Twenty-First Century*, Aromnk, NY: Sharpe.

Chu, Y.-h., Diamond, L. and Shin, D.C. (2001) 'How people view democracy. Halting progress in Korea and Taiwan', *Journal of Democracy*, 12(1): 122–36.

Cyberspace Policy Research Group (1998) *Website Attribute Evaluation System*. Online. Available HTTP: <http://www.cyprg.arizona.edu/waes.html> (accessed 15 February 2004).

Danziger, J.N., Dutton, W.H., Kling, R. and Kraemer, K.L. (1982) *Computers and Politics. High Technology in American Local Governments*, New York: Columbia University Press.

Delanty, G. (2000) *Citizenship in the Global Age. Society, Culture, Politics*, Buckingham: Open University Press.

Department of Statistics (1999, 2001, 2003) *A Survey of Internet Use amongst the Taiwanese Population*, Taipei: Ministry of Transportation.

Diamond, L. and Plattner, M.F. (1997) 'Introduction', in L. Diamond, M.F. Plattner, Y.-h. Chu and H.-m. Tien (eds) *Consolidating the Third Wave Democracies. Themes and Perspectives*, Baltimore, MD: The John Hopkins University Press.

Faulks, K. (2000) *Citizenship*, London: Routledge.

Fountain, J.E. (2001) *Building the Virtual State. Information Technology and Institutional Change*, Washington, DC: Brookings Institution.

——(2003) 'Electronic government and electronic civics', in B. Wellman (ed.) *Encyclopedia of Community*, Great Barrington, MA: Berkshire.

Frederickson, H.G. (1996) *The Spirit of Public Administration*, San Francisco, CA: Jossey-Bass.

Hu, Y.-z. (2001) *A Study of Participation in Public Affairs amongst Taiwanese Internet Users. Research Report*, Taipei: Research, Development, and Evaluation Commission, Executive Yuan.

Horrocks, I. and Bellamy, C. (1997) 'Telematics and community governance. Issues for policy and practice', *International Journal of Public Sector Management*, 10(5): 377–87.

Lax, S. (2001) 'Information, education and inequality. Is new technology the solution?' in S. Lax, (ed.) *Access Denied in the Information Age*, Basingstoke: Palgrave Macmillan.

Lee, M.-Y. (2003) 'Information age governing in Taiwan. Evaluating the presence of electronic government in Taiwan', Paper presented at the 53rd Annual conference of the Political Studies Association, University of Leicester, UK, 15–17 April 2003.

Lenihan, D.G. (2002) *E-government, Federalism and Democracy. The New Governance*, Ottawa: Centre for Collaborative Government.

Lyon, D. (1994) *Electronic Eye. The Rise of Surveillance Society*, Cambridge: Polity Press.

Morison, J. and Newman, D. (2001) 'Online citizenship. Consultation and participation in New Labour's Britain and beyond', *International Review of Law, Computers and Technology*, 15(2): 171–94.

National Information and Communications Initiative Committee, Executive Yuan (2001) 'The Action Plan of National Information and Communications Development'. Online. Available HTTP: <http://www.nici.nat.gov.tw/content/application/nici/faq/guest-cnt-browse.php?(nt_id= 134> (accessed 16 August 2005).

National Information Infrastructure Unit, Executive Yuan (1997) *The Action Plan of the National Information Infrastructure in Taiwan.* Online. Available HTTP: <http://www.ey.gov.tw/planning-old/pz871022-1.htm> (accessed 15 August 2005).

Norris, P. (2001) *Digital Divide. Civic Engagement, Information Poverty and the Internet Worldwide*, Cambridge: Cambridge University Press.

Organization for Economic Co-operation and Development (2003) *The E-Government Imperative*, Paris: OECD.

Pollitt, C. (2003) 'Joined-up government. A survey', *Political Studies Review*, 1: 34–49.

Rabb, C. (1997) 'Privacy, democracy, information', in B. Loader (ed.) *The Governance of Cyberspace*, London: Routledge.

Rabb, C., Bellamy, C., Taylor, J., Dutton, W.H. and Peltu, M. (1996) 'The information polity. Electronic democracy, privacy, and surveillance', in W.H. Dutton and M. Peltu (eds), *Information and Communication Technologies. Visions and Realities*, Oxford: Oxford University Press.

Rawnsley, G. (2004) 'Treading a fine line. Democratisation and the media in Taiwan', *Parliament Affairs*, 57(1): 209–22.

Research, Development and Evaluation Commission, Executive Yuan (2001) *The Action Plan of the E-government. 2001–2004*, Taipei: Executive Yuan.

——(2002) *My E-government. The Booklet of the E-government Portal in Taiwan*, Taipei: Executive Yuan.

——(2003a) *A Survey of People's Satisfaction with Public Service – March Version*, Taipei: Executive Yuan. Online. Available HTTP: <http://www.rdec.gov.tw/home/survey.htm> (accessed 15 December 2003).

——(2003b) *A Survey of People's Satisfaction with Public Services – September Version*, Taipei: Executive Yuan. Online. Available HTTP: <http://www.rdec.gov.tw/home/survey.htm> (accessed 15 December 2003).

United Nations Online Network in Public Administration and Finance (2003) *Global Survey of E-Government*, New York: UNPAN. Online. Available HTTP: <http://www.unpan.org/egovernment2.asp> (accessed 20 January 2003).

Wang, S.-f. (2000) *An Analysis of Structure amongst Taiwanese Internet Users and Their Motivation. Research Report*, Taipei: Research, Development, and Evaluation Commission, Executive Yuan.

World Markets Research Centre (2001) *Global E-government Survey*, London: WMRC. Online. Available at www.worldmarketsanalysis.com (accessed 10 January 2003).

Part III

Audience responses to political messages

Interpretations and effects

11 Does 'trust' mean attention, comprehension and acceptance?

Paradoxes of Russian viewers' news processing

Ellen Mickiewicz

The shaping of media institutions and the messages they produce – the varying degrees of dependence on political power and commerce – are increasingly understood as critical to the functioning of democratic polities. Even though new technologies have dramatically expanded both information and interactivity, it remains true that most people depend on mediated information: their personal experiences and observations are bounded. However, without probing how messages are *received* – what consumers make of the news and information they get – it is impossible to determine whether or not at least some of the assumptions of those who control the message are being met. It is a matter of framing: are the frames of the broadcaster and the viewer congruent?

This is a matter of enormous importance to a political leadership that deems control of television coterminous with control of the frame the viewer receives. For largely economic reasons, there has been a growing dependence on the medium for news and information among Russians across all the time zones, and that dependence is overwhelmingly on the information broadcast by a few networks based in Moscow. Regional stations are primarily viewed for other reasons. Especially at election times, the fragile structure of the media market has not been able to withstand the zero-sum-game pressure of a political leadership determined to ensure its preferred outcome. Although the research findings that follow focus on 'normal' times (i.e. a period in which there are no national elections), there are obvious implications for thinking about television and elections.

The Moscow leadership derives much of its confidence in the successful transfer of its preferred frame from its reading of large-scale, frequent surveys of viewers' behaviour. That confidence may be found to be misplaced, however, if we choose, instead, to explore the viewer's construction of the state's message through discourse in a social setting, for it is much more likely that news is processed in this way (Graber 2001; Tetlock 2000). The process of constructing meaning is a question partially of message production and partially of reception. The latter is distinctly more variable, derived as it is from as many different experiences, values and mental schemas as there are recipients. The question, then, concerns the best way to access the construction of meaning by television viewers. The mass survey has distinct advantages, most particularly in its representativeness and generalizability. However, as Doris Graber writes of mass surveys:

> In the ordinary interview situation, where closed-ended questions predominate, people's thought processes are guided only in a limited number of directions. The few cues that are provided to assist in memory searches may not resonate at all with the respondents' memory structure. ... More open-ended approaches may be the solution because they encourage respondents to think about issues from multiple perspectives, which may then trigger appropriate memories. ... This dialogue creates alternative keys for each focus group member for tapping into related stored experiences. Stored opinions may then surface, thanks to the additional cues, which are also useful for formulating new opinions on the spot.
>
> (Graber 2001: 50–1)

The rationale for the use of focus groups in cases like these is well described by William Gamson, who concludes by quoting David Morgan's summary that focus groups 'are useful when it comes to investigating *what* participants think, but they excel at uncovering *why* participants think as they do' (Gamson 1992: 192, emphasis in the original).

Some aspects of large surveys are inevitably problematic. For example, self-reporting of exposure tends to be unreliable because of memory erosion or alteration because of subsequent events. For example, recall of exposure to partisan political material tends to be associated with support for the candidate (Bartels 1993). In any case, exposure, even if it could be reliably measured, cannot be equated with reception. Another aspect of surveys – respondents' assessments of what influences them – demands a level of analysis of the conscious and the subconscious which is not fully accessible to most people. Focus groups, the alternative method I use here, are particularly helpful in the analysis of viewers' construction of meaning from political messages. The social setting is closer to the real-life process of discussion than is a session with an interviewer who asks for a top-of-the-head answer.

The study reported here was designed to address the following question: based on the discourse of ordinary Russian viewers as they watch a typical story from what the surveys say is the *most trusted* news programme (the state-controlled *Pervyi kanal*, or First Channel), how is the news processed, what frames emerge from the discourse, and how does this discourse help us to interpret what is meant when news framed as the state prefers is said by survey respondents to be 'trusted'? Clarification of this question would also give us more purchase on the use of 'trust in the First Channel' as an independent variable in a variety of studies, both Western and Russian. The toolbox Russians use to make sense of their news is adapted to particular conditions, it is true; it is certainly an asset where the provenance and reliability of information is obscure and advocacy without trade-off cues is the norm.

Contemporary journalistic practices add to the burden placed on the viewer, using his or her store of heuristics, to navigate the story. Some news stories are the product of commercial or political interests. They are planted or sold outright, either by the station or by the reporter or photographer on the spot: the Russians call such a practice *zakazukha* (ordered or commissioned). Sometimes particular attributes of such stories cue viewers that they have encountered *zakazukha*, as seen below in the discussion of positive stories. However, since the practice is reasonably pervasive, and the country has a long history of the use of the media for propaganda, the post-Soviet viewer is uniquely equipped to evaluate it. Viewers *expect* commercial and governmental involvement in shaping the news. They believe it is the viewer's responsibility to extract significance and correct for bias. Multiple sourcing, comparisons with experience, observations from friends and relatives closer to the scene: the burden is on the viewer to expend time and energy on sifting out the truth among differing accounts (Mickiewicz 1999).

Some truth can be extracted from any story, but it needs to be completed. That is what viewers do when they offer their own examples or experiences to flesh out a story they know to be planted. That is why they repeatedly conclude, as does Andrei, a budding neurosurgeon from Nizhny Novgorod, that 'I think that this story is commissioned. Objective but commissioned'. Similarly, Maxim, a 53-year-old bookkeeper in Moscow, finds a story 'truthful, yes, but commissioned'. With heavy dependence on the limited choices for national television news, viewers extract meaningful information from obviously biased sources. That is what they expect and they have honed tools and developed analytic strategies for it.

The research findings presented below are drawn from a large project with many parts. This chapter addresses what Russian television viewers mean when they say they trust or believe a story on the most watched newscast in the country, and the degree to which viewers' portrayals of trust are congruent with criteria of persuasiveness. The First Channel, formerly *Obshchestvennoe Rossiskoye Televidenie* (ORT, Russian Public Television), has continuously enjoyed the highest news ratings in Russia. In part, this is a benefit of the legacy of *Vremya* (Time), the authoritative Soviet news programme that came on at 9.00 p.m. and pre-empted programming on every other channel. The station also has the advantage of the most favourable technological infrastructure for virtually total penetration. Given the centrality of this station in reach, ratings and research on the influence of its news, this chapter will consider viewers' reactions to a story typical of the pro-governmental success stories it features.

The data are drawn from 16 focus groups – a total of 158 participants –

in four cities (Volgograd, Rostov, Nizhny Novgorod and Moscow) in January 2002. The focus groups were conducted during a period chosen for its relatively normal character, in that national election campaigns were neither ongoing nor about to begin.

The cities were chosen on the basis of variation in political profile and size of media markets, but with enough geographical commonalities to limit extraneous large differences. [Characteristics of the four cities, taken from the Russian Regional Report (*Obshchestvennaya expertiza*) for 2000, are given below.] There is a considerable variety to the areas of inclusion, and a large enough group overall to make for a very rich set of conversations. As Alan Wolfe put it in describing his methods: 'I have not undertaken a representative national sample. But I think it is also important to emphasize that this is not one of those studies that generalizes from only one neighbourhood, firm, or family to the country as a whole' (1998: 34).

It should be noted that, although Moscow-based networks have been called 'national', their respective degrees of penetration are quite varied. Figure 11.1 shows the degree to which signals from the different stations could be received in Russia at the time of this study.

Volgograd Region borders Kazakhstan, is roughly 300 miles from

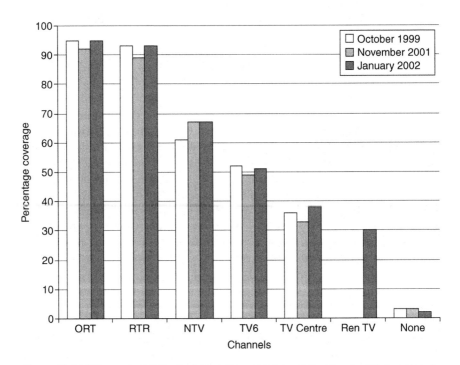

Figure 11.1 The coverage of television channels across the Russian Federation in October 1999, November 2001 and January 2002.

Source: Public Opinion Foundation, Moscow.

Chechnya, and has a stagnating economy with a weak private sector. It has traditionally been part of Russia's 'red belt', strong enough in allegiance to be called its 'buckle'. In media pluralism and editorial autonomy the city ranks lowest among the four, and media density is low.

Rostov, on the river Don, is the capital of the Southern Federal District, one of seven administrative units that President Putin created for the Russian Federation. Long-serving, investor-friendly governor Vladimir Chub, backed by the pro-Putin party, was re-elected in the autumn of 2001 by 78 per cent of the voters; his strongest competitor, a Communist Party leader, had been disqualified on the dubious charge of too many invalid signatures. It has reasonably high media density, especially in radio and television, and efforts of the government to control the media have often met with private-sector resistance.

Nizhny Novgorod (Lower Novgorod), 250 miles east of Moscow, was called Gorky in Soviet times, and it was here that Andrei Sakharov was exiled until Mikhail Gorbachev allowed him to return to Moscow. Until 1991, it was a 'closed city', a defence industry powerhouse; now it is capital of the Volga Federal District. The market reforms of the first governor, Boris Nemtsov, slowed significantly under his successors, and foreign investment dropped sharply. The media market is relatively large, with a strong private sector in electronic media, notwithstanding attempts of the government to interfere.

Moscow is by far the most educated region of the four: as of 1994, it had 299 people with college education for every 1,000 in the population (Rostov region had 161, Volgograd 142 and Nizhny Novgorod 137). Muscovites can access a very large number of television stations over the air and by cable and satellite. In this, it exceeds by an order of magnitude any of the other three cities. At the time of the focus groups, Volgograd had the narrowest range of non-state television choices of the cities outside Moscow (two); Nizhny Novgorod had eight and Rostov seven.[1]

All the cities except Moscow are situated within a large and populous area (home to 37 per cent of Russia's population) of the adjacent Volga and Southern Federal Districts, thus reducing confounding differences that more dissimilar population points would produce. Focus groups were differentiated by college and secondary education – a pattern shown by pilot studies to enhance participation. There are twice as many college-educated groups, reflecting their current and future centrality to the political and economic development of Russia. Before the discussions, participants filled out a short questionnaire covering socio-demographic and media use information, as well as political knowledge and political ideology.

To address the generational question – will Soviet-era information processing patterns be lost, altered or continue? – a focus group in each city was restricted to participants I call 'post-Soviet', that is, those who were too young to be watching typically Soviet (pre-Gorbachev) news. The average post-Soviet participant was born in 1980, while old-style Soviet television was greatly changed by 1986. If there are differences, we cannot know if they are related to youth as a stage of life or to something more durable: it is a first cut at the question. Young people were also included in the other groups.

To limit variability of context, the groups were all conducted by a single experienced specialist from the Public Opinion Foundation (a Russian survey organization headquartered in Moscow).[2]

Russians watching news on the First Channel

Retrospective discussions characterizing television in abstract terms can differ dramatically from discussions of viewers' reactions to a news story they have just seen. I have opted for the latter here. During the focus group sessions, various news stories were shown; the station's logo was concealed and there were no pictures of anchors or other well-known journalists from the channel.

Here, I analyse discourse related to the story on the First Channel, which was the first story the groups watched. According to a report in *Vedomosti* (News) in September 2003, the First Channel was still the most trusted television channel, as measured by a public opinion survey conducted by a well-known Russian agency (Johnson's List, 11 September 2003).[3]

A story typical of the channel's news programmes was chosen; in fact, a good many viewers had no hesitation identifying the channel *because* they thought it so typical. The story was about the opening of a massive pipeline to carry oil from the Tengiz oilfields in Kazakhstan to the Russian port of Novorossisk and then to purchasers abroad. Why this story? First, stories like this, about economic achievement, appear very frequently on television news – and not only on channels supporting government policy. This was a big story on all news programmes. Second, given the meagre choice for viewers, whether they like them or not, these are stories they encounter repeatedly. Finally, and most importantly, this kind of story is a prime example of state broadcasters' assumptions about their public: that they will welcome and assimilate the message of upbeat trade-off-free activity.

Figure 11.2 shows the ratings pattern (calculated on an average weekday rating) for the news programmes available in each of the four cities. In all cases, it is the government-dominated First Channel and RTR (Russian Radio and Television) that show the most highly rated news programmes, and the First Channel figures at the very top, especially in Volgograd, where choice is more limited than elsewhere. Eighty per cent of the focus group participants access the news at least three to four times a week (50 per cent do so daily). When asked about news relating to Chechnya and Russia's president, over 80 per cent said they depended solely on Moscow-based networks. When asked to give their sources of news, which could be multiple, the vast majority listed the First Channel/ORT; next came RTR. NTV and TV6 were a distant third and fourth. Eleven of the 40 participants in Nizhny Novgorod listed the popular local commercial

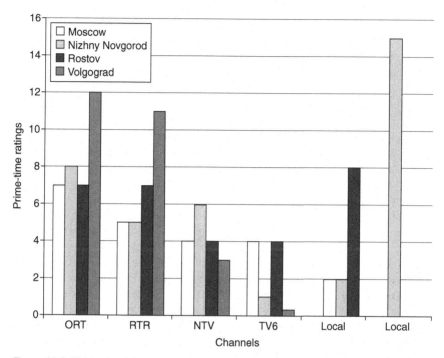

Figure 11.2 The prime-time ratings of main channel news programmes in the focus
group areas of Moscow, Nizhny Novgorod, Rostov and Volgograd.
Nizhny Novgorod's more popular local channel news is *Kstati* (By the
Way) on Seti NN, a commercial channel. It airs at 8.00 p.m. It is purely
local, mainly human interest, crime, accidents, fires, and hand-held
cameras are used. Production values are not salient to the producers; it
is not edited as professional news stories usually are (in contradistinc-
tion to the less popular local commercial channel, *Volga*). *Kstati* also
features lost and found items and includes a five-minute, not very
informative, news capsule from Ren TV in Moscow. Volgograd's local
channel, *Municipal*, is state-owned. The average daily rating for TV6
news in Volgograd is 0.3. Rostov's local channel, *Southern Region*,
replaces TV6 on its frequency after TV6 is taken off the air.

Source: Gallup

channel's news programme *Kstati* (By the Way), as part of a list that began
with ORT and RTR. For the Russian Federation as a whole, 85 per cent of
the national prime-time television audience is tuned in to one of the
Moscow-based networks, and in time of crisis it is overwhelmingly the
national television networks to which Russians turn (Mickiewicz 1999).

The First Channel news story the groups watched is framed as a thoroughly positive collection of features of an unalloyed achievement. To the
criticism that focus group members discuss topics animatedly but may not
think them important when surveyed, Lunt and Livingstone note that

'people do not talk at length or with interest about an issue on which they have nothing meaningful to say' (Lunt and Livingstone 1996: 91). The present groups engaged in lively discussions centring on the nature of trust, the meaning of facts, the quality of comprehension and the format of presentation.

Components of persuasion

Kathleen McGraw and Clark Hubbard summarize the steps necessary for persuasion: '(1) the recipients (constituents) must be *exposed* to the communication (the account); (2) they must pay *attention* to it; (3) they must *comprehend* it; and (4) they must *accept* the explanation as legitimate and credible' (McGraw and Hubbard 1996: 147, emphasis in the original). Only then would the information be stored and available for application to similar categories. Persuasion depends critically on having information or opinions at hand, ready to be applied to the next case one sees as similar or analogous, and the accessibility heuristic is one – perhaps the most powerful – of the organizing or learning shortcuts citizens use (Ferejohn and Kuklinski 1990; McDermott 2002; Mutz *et al.* 1996). As Doris Graber has noted about her research in the United States: 'Most political information is sloughed off ... because average Americans usually find it neither useful nor enjoyable. This explains why the majority of stimuli that people actually notice, including political messages, leave no long-term traces in memory and cannot be recalled even after a brief time lapse' (2001: 18).

The quality of attention

All of the focus-group participants were *exposed* to the news story. But not all paid attention. Some became mental absentees; some lapsed into boredom; some were numbed by the load of facts, as the following discourse illustrates.

High school educated, Moscow

NATASHA: I listened to half.
KATYA: I think when you watch the information, the ordinary person simply takes time out from this information.
MAXIM: Yes, you can go put the tea kettle on.
KATYA: These numbers – you can relax. There is something there, maybe, behind the picture, for whom this oil is interesting, but it's simply not interesting for us.
OLYA: No sensations.
MAXIM: In the role of the yawning listener, yes, generally...
GALYA: They bombarded us with information.
KATYA: They weighted us down.

Post-Soviet, Moscow

OLEG: It's overloaded with technical information. I don't think it's interesting for the viewer, how many millions of tons of oil are needed to fill this oil pipeline. . . . It was interesting for me.

IGOR: A little was interesting but there was a lot of water.

KATYA: Stretched out.

College educated, Volgograd

POLINA: I understood it a little distractedly . . . I didn't catch what took place.

Post-Soviet, Volgograd

EVGENY: Lots of information, badly done . . . let's say it's badly done. A bunch of information piled on.

MISHA: They just showed that it's such-and-such a length and the volume is such.

VERA: I think that the whole problem is that it simply wasn't interesting, absolutely . . . this material doesn't interest me at all and nothing was interesting.

Post-Soviet, Rostov

IVAN: If I speak honestly, for the first ten seconds I didn't understand what was going on on the screen. For example, if somebody is sitting, cutting carrots at home and watches on the side.

ANDREI: It will go right by.

ALEXANDRA: Really everything takes place in Russia basically officially. The basic part [of the story] for reporters is cutting this ribbon.

The viewers talking here were not taking much in, according to their comments. Even Oleg, a 25-year-old part-time college student who is interested in the event finds the story 'overloaded'. Watching television is often a secondary activity; it serves as background while attending to something else. In an environment such as this, television must compete with other activities and, as one viewer put it, make her 'look up' when something interesting comes on.

It was also characteristic of First Channel news that the format of the story appeared to trigger Soviet-era comparisons in the discourse:

College educated, Moscow

LENA: It's like what we had on television before – as though all data, here is so much arithmetic: so much here so much there, so much income.

IRINA: It was done as an announcement.

LENA: Yes. Some kind of information announcement.

IRINA: An announcement. They opened this thing there.

VLADIMIR: For me [it's] absolutely not interesting; however, of course, I understand that it is important.

NATASHA: Serious sums were named, therefore it can't be unimportant.

LENA: We can take this as a bulletin.

IGOR: Reminds me of the old, actually, pre-perestroika [pre-Gorbachev news].

LENA: Like a kind of accounting balance sheet.

College educated, Nizhny Novgorod

OLGA: It seems to me that it's too smooth. Too much, and it talked a lot of numbers.

ALESHA: I think it was too drawn out for a news story.

VLADIMIR: The only, the one [piece of] information was that so many tons of oil were pumped in this. There wasn't any other information.

LIUBA: So many percentages

OLGA: You don't even listen: numbers, such information.

NIKOLAI: Too many numbers; they're all empty. That is, it's necessary to separate them.

OLGA: It doesn't say anything.

ALESHA: You could state the information more quickly I think. Just say it and that's that.

OLGA: In Soviet times . . . the story itself, I have in mind, the construction [is similar to Soviet times].

High school educated, Volgograd

TAMARA: I think it's ORT [First Channel]. So much was said. It seems to me that they could even have shortened it, too much information; it was hard to stand it.

NATASHA: That's their style.

For viewers who switch their minds off or really do leave the room to make tea, it is unlikely that much will be retained. The question of others' comprehension is addressed below.

Trust, comprehension and facts

Trust involves the audience's beliefs about the credibility of the source, a process of evaluation and perhaps a certain degree of positive attitude toward the source (McGraw and Hubbard 1996). In Russian, *doveria* can be translated as both trust and confidence; its root, *vera*, means faith.

To avoid confusion, I consistently translate *doveria* as trust, but it should be borne in mind that confidence in the station or story is also intended.

The members of the Russian focus groups discussed the First Channel's pipeline story immediately after they had seen it. It was natural that the apparently fact-filled story sparked discussion of what, exactly, a fact is. I say 'apparently', because Russian viewers, used to such stories, have what might be called a graduated approach to the definition of 'fact'. At the simplest level, the discourse revealed that a fact is a narrowly delimited piece of information from a credible source for which the viewer has no means to substitute a different, equally narrowly delimited piece of information. The source is credible only in assigning a number – any number would do.

In this definition of fact, the discussion appears to conflate fact and trust, and if a survey interviewer happened by it would appear that the respondent trusts this story on this station, as the following discussion suggests. The first three comments come from participants in Post-Soviet groups: Lena, a college-educated translator, and Katya, a high-school-educated publisher's cashier in Moscow, and Nikolai, a college student in Nizhny Novgorod.

LENA: In my view something was said, facts were given: who signed what, how many tons, etc. ... is this trustworthy information or not? It was trustworthy for me.

KATYA: Trustworthy information – it's just that really it's an approach that is absolutely, purely standard and that's all.

NIKOLAI: It's objective from the technical point of view ... in principle nothing of the sort [clear contradictions] was said ... yes, they conveyed facts and that's all.

Similar comments came in the college educated groups – from Vitaly (a 24-year-old employee), Andrei (a 42-year-old entrepreneur) and Mikhail (a 48-year-old employee) in Volgograd, and from Natasha, a 50-year-old tax inspector in Moscow:

VITALY: There's no basis not to believe.

ANDREI: What's the problem? They built it or not; they're prepared to pump or not.

MIKHAIL: They're ready.

ANDREI: Then all's correct; it's pure information.

NATASHA: What does it mean: this isn't true. What? We doubt the percentages or the events? How can we judge, if we're not professional; we don't know, we are very far from it. We are average viewers; they give us information and we watch. ... The comrades [others in her focus group] say it's not true; that it's necessary to present it somehow differently, as though it's show business . . .. They move oil from one place; they received a budget, large amounts, billions of dollars, and from this money we'll do something there, we'll build, allocate, etc. Here it is concrete, purely economic.

The point was also made in the high school educated group in Volgograd by Alena, a 25-year-old artist and fashion designer, and Andrei (who did not provide his age or occupation):

ALENA: Here there's only information that doesn't elicit suspicion. Yes, a pipeline and fine.
ANDREI: They did their job.
ALENA: They just did their job – that's also good. Really, is that insufficient? I don't consider that such information can be unobjective.

How can any viewer be in a position to dispute the numbers? Who has the unmediated knowledge to draw on, when the story consists almost entirely of measurements, when the event is made up of quantified features listed in sequence? It might be logical to expect that an acknowledgment of a piece of information as fact expresses trust, but that is not necessarily the case. Much of the discourse about the story rejected this notion of fact as literally meaningless: it lacks an evaluative dimension, without which a fact – a number – has no meaning. At issue is not whether the First Channel's number or a different one is accurate, but what *any* number means, without context. As the much greater part of the discourse shows, evaluation, comprehension and retention were casualties of this mode of presentation and, with them, trust as usually understood.

For these Russian viewers, it is from the *intelligibility* of the numbers that trust and comprehension are derived. This discourse reveals that for many it is impossible to comprehend the story to which they have been exposed and paid attention. Vladimir (59 years old, unemployed and living in Nizhny Novgorod) argues that numbers by themselves have no meaning and therefore cannot be processed. If they cannot be processed, then they cannot be received and stored. Other members of his college educated group include 24-year-old teacher Liuba, 61-year-old pensioner Olga and 45-year-old company general director Nikolai:

VLADIMIR: The only, the one piece of information was that so many tons of oil were pumped in this. There wasn't any other information.
LIUBA: So many percentages
OLGA: You don't even listen; numbers, such information.
NIKOLAI: Too many numbers; they're all empty. That is, it's necessary to separate them.
VLADIMIR: I told you that a number has to be placed against something.

If in this story, they put in some comparison with some other pipeline or something we already had, then we would have watched it differently.

OLGA: Otherwise the story is not very interesting for the average viewer to watch.

VLADIMIR: Still, I'll stay with this. It is so imperative that there be numbers, if there is such information. It should always close with a number. And the number always has to be compared. One number . . . never.

OLGA: It doesn't say anything.

In Moscow, merchant marine captain Viktor, 46, and Igor, a 37-year-old engineer, discuss the same fundamental requirement for context:

VIKTOR: They said a number there: 20 billion, but if they said 30 billion, it's nothing to me – not cold, not hot.

IGOR: Yes, it's practically impossible to evaluate.

Thus, in spite of the cascade of numbers and the unremittingly celebratory tone of the story, most of the viewers in the focus groups are not able to join the party. Here, also in Moscow, are housewife Lena, pensioner Olga, engineer Igor and supplier Galina:

LENA: I'd say that I had no feeling. I'm indifferent, because really they just communicate to us what facts occurred. And maybe really they want to say that it's all good, but I don't know. I need to see a lot more factors to believe the advisability of this pipeline.

OLGA: That's what I say, insufficient information.

IGOR: Superficial information.

GALINA: I think they just gave information.

And, here, with Galina's statement, is another definition of 'fact', a conveyor of nearly nothing: facts (or information) are only a small piece of potential, but unrealized, meaning; tesserae without the full picture the mosaic makes. That is why young Igor in Moscow, a geologist and engineer, could say about the story: 'that text, it's all nonsense and I feel that they tell nothing concrete, not economically, nothing.'

It is because of the inability of viewers to evaluate a story of this kind that often very little remains afterward. Above, I noted that some said they just shut down and sat inattentively. Others watched but could remember very little shortly after the story was shown. In Volgograd, Dina, 20, a high school educated bookkeeper, said that 'literally in 2 minutes we forgot what it was about'. Others watched but did not comprehend, as the comments below indicate. The first two, Galina and Natasha, finished high school; the rest have a college education:

Moscow

GALINA: The overall purpose is not clear to me. Why did they do it? . . . Yes, to drive the oil to Europe. It's not clear to me here what's the main issue. Why is it done?

NATASHA: When I watched, it wasn't deposited into my head at all. I didn't understand it.

MAXIM: I don't understand what it's about. Is it about the storm or about some weather reports, or about oil?

Volgograd

MIKHAIL: What is all this for?

MARINA: I didn't understand and further, so they showed us this story and afterwards does this oil do something for someone?

MISHA: Why is it necessary to build [it]? I don't understand at all. They invested huge money.

Rostov

NATASHA: In general nothing's clear, really. Somebody has the main profit, how it will be divided, they said there a percent.

OLGA: Not clear at all.

VIKA: This information is simply for the average viewer, to look at it casually, to get acquainted . . . for the interested person no, it's like giving a toast [at a celebration].

Nizhny Novgorod

BORIS: Honestly speaking, it also wasn't very clear to me in general, the whole news.

College-educated viewers appear to have greater requirements for source credibility than others. It was only in their discussions that the qualifications of the reporters came into play. These viewers look for specialized backgrounds and whether or not the reporter commands sufficient expertise to explain the event with appropriate depth and accuracy, factors important to a determination of credibility in Western studies of citizen competence (Lupia and McCubbins 1998). In several conversations the story was contemptuously referred to as 'amateurish', a surprising criticism to be levelled at the oldest, richest and most widely watched channel in the country. If the story is thought to lack the necessary expertise, it cannot be trusted. Dissatisfaction with the level of knowledge displayed by the news story was expressed in better educated groups, such as the following:

College educated, Moscow

OLYA: About the people who did the story – probably they are people far from economic issues.

LENA: Maybe dilettantes.

NATASHA: A non-specialist did it.

SVETLANA: It's for the average viewer who simply sat in front of the television set and watched.

Post-Soviet, Volgograd

EVGENY: Some information was too confused, it showed some technological moments. Maybe it's not professional.

College educated, Nizhny Novgorod

VLADIMIR: In any case, this reportage is unprofessional.

All of the 158 people in the four cities where the focus groups took place were exposed by design to a news story from the First Channel, which is, according to public opinion surveys, Russians' most watched and trusted source of news. That first step in persuasion had been taken. Not all paid attention; some tuned out; some imagined themselves at home going to get something in the kitchen. Some did pay attention – the story threw out some very big investment and revenue statistics – and became candidates for the third stage in the sequencing of persuasion (accepting the frame), which is what the news was intended to accomplish. Some could not comprehend the story. They could not retain it long enough to be able to talk about it a few minutes later or, distracted by the different elements of the story, they failed to get the main point, and it was not because they had not gone to college or lived in the provinces far from Moscow. For the viewers who had tuned out, failed to pay attention, did not retain the information or did not comprehend the story, there was little likelihood that the message (the story) would be stored by the viewer and thus available for use as a future mental shortcut to interpret or understand new information and conditions.

For those who did reach the last step, when the acceptance of the frame or point of view of the story is at issue, there is an asymmetrical split in the discourse. The smaller part accepts the story's facts, but on so narrow a basis that it may be impossible to store for the future when using the availability heuristic. The larger part, at best, expresses an irritated and impatient dissatisfaction with the story for preventing them from applying their powers of evaluation. The discourse suggests that this evaluative process is something that is thoroughly familiar and ordinary for viewers, whether college or high school educated. Russians expect to exercise their powers of evaluation when watching the news and they know that to do this they require context and comparative information. Failing to find it in the story, they find themselves adrift, alienated, and, naturally, unpersuaded. It may be a big achievement of the government, but it may not. They remain unconvinced by numbers – and assertions.

Longing for positive news

The Russian public tells survey interviewers that they want positive news; they complain about the media's news menu of troubles, natural disasters and accidents. Surveys demonstrate that very large numbers of respondents say they are tired of and repelled by the dismal muck of contemporary Russian life on the television screen. In the focus groups in this study, too, in all four cities and among college educated, high school educated and post-Soviet participants, there were some who disapproved of the tone and content of the constant stream of bad news.

This discussion came early in the session, after talk about daily life. They were invited to think about what they would want in a news programme, and some expressed disapproval of bad news:

KATYA: I would try for more good, not unpleasantness or conflicts, all kinds of war, but more good. [*College student, 19, Volgograd*]

LIDIA: Today they broadcast on the radio in the news programme that in Moscow they expect acts of terrorism, chemical, all kinds. Why did they announce this? For what purpose? To pump up the situation and make people still more nervous? Why do they do this? I'd take it off altogether. [*High school educated pensioner, 63, Rostov*]

VITALY: I thought about it now, that first of all I'd take away most of the negative information, these catastrophes, sensationalism and so on. It doesn't seem to me to be interesting to the majority. I'd do sports and culture. [*College educated employee, 24, Volgograd*]

MARINA: If they gave information, for example, on vacations in various resorts or on theatrical programmes and previews of shows. I think, this, when there's such harsh information, especially negative, that's horrible – terror, Chechnya, and crime news – it's awfully hard [on us]. [*College educated employee, 43, Nizhny Novgorod*]

At first glance it appears that in focus groups, as in surveys, we find the familiar distaste for and even willingness to censor bad news. Somewhat more common is a saddened resignation that bad news reflects bad times:

LILIA: I would want less cruelty ... though I know that right now life is pretty tough, but it would be nice to have more positive emotions. [*College educated employee, 54, Rostov*]

ALEXANDER: I completely agree [that there should be more good news on television]. I watch TV and I become sober, but our life, of course, is not so simple; times have changed. [*College educated distributor, 35, Volgograd*]

Rejecting positive news on the television

That is not the end of the story. When viewers get what they appear to want – for example, when they are shown the upbeat pipeline story – instead of approving, they reject the story out of hand. They do not believe it. A positive news story undermines its own credibility by invoking three different kinds of analogies for viewers.

One comes from the new world of advertising that lends its techniques to the display of the government's achievements. Post-Soviet Mikhail in Volgograd likens the story to a public relations assignment: 'I think what we saw was simply advertising – about what money is invested and how long it is and it holds a million tons of oil. They wanted to show achievements and not what was lacking – showing everything everywhere is fine.' For Mikhail's generation, advertising and public relations businesses are commonplace; they can't recall a time before the arrival of the spin doctors. Even in his failing city deep in the Volga heartland, it is how he understands the unfolding of the benefits portrayed in the story.

The more common analogy comes from the Soviet years: a positive story cues the paradigm of Soviet-era television news, and is shunted off into the category of deliberately distorted messages serving the state. Here are college-educated Muscovites Viktor and Svetlana in one group and Lena, Igor and Vladimir in a second:

VIKTOR: Everything is good.
SVETLANA: And without depth, everything's very good … I am used to doubting everything now.
LENA: It's not realistic.
IGOR: Reminds [me] of old, really pre-perestroika [news].
LENA: Like a kind of accounting tally.
VLADIMIR: Like an accounting tally of the achievements of socialist construction.

Liuda from Nizhny Novgorod comments that 'when it all started, you know, it started so pompously, for some reason a question came up right away: what period is this? That is, in what time? I hadn't even heard the text yet, because I said to myself, it started so pompously: for me it's tied to that [time, the Soviet period].'

Finally, a positive news story can cue corruption and planted news. A thoroughly positive message may be rejected as news, because it is seen as something commissioned or ordered up (*zakazukha*), as observed in a discussion in a college educated group in Volgograd:

ANDREI: Whoever put in money into the construction of this pipeline, commissioned it [this story].

VERA: Without doubt.

SVETLANA: Because everything's fine.

MIKHAIL: Because what they said was said with such satisfaction.

POLINA: There were no difficulties in the construction.

VERA: [Saying why she didn't believe it but others might] Basically those people who maybe have high school education. Well, I have in mind old grannies and granddaddies. They believe it.

POLINA: If you compare this with elections: someone started [a rumour] that transportation will be free and naturally people, college graduates, they didn't believe it. But old grannies, they went and waited for the free rides. There were such situations.

While actually consuming positive news stories, viewers reject them as patently unbelievable. They neither trust nor recall their contents. And each population stratum says *it* isn't credulous, but *others* down the status ladder would be. Clearly, the Russian public laments the negative sides of their lives; television is only a conduit. They wish their lives were different, but they know that a buoyant portrayal lacks verisimilitude.

Conclusions

Russian viewers demand contextual information and comparisons. They do not recall or trust stories in which numbers are cited, unless there is a context in which those figures may be compared or relevant other dimensions included. Pseudo-events, which flatten the context to foreground privileged actors, are often viewed as 'ordered' or commissioned. Happy news is distrusted. Russian viewers recognize that much or even most televised news and public information is ordered (*zakazukha*); they add that information to their analytic navigational system. It is this system of navigation that has been displayed above. Some of it is a carry-over from the past; some a response to new stimuli from a new set of institutional actors. The complexity of the navigational instruments is visible in all of the cities, even where there is little political competition and slim media choice, and across the different levels of education.

External diversity – some pluralism of viewpoints on different channels – obviously assists Russian viewers as they apply their considerable effort to going beneath the surface of television news. Without according objectivity or 'truth' to any of the contending channels, viewers nonetheless clearly benefit when they are permitted to draw from a range of viewpoints on television. That option has never been safely embedded in the political system, and it was taken away with the closing of the frankly oppositionist TV6 (in 2002) and then its weaker replacement TVS, in 2003, and by the pressure to resign put on the increasingly independently minded Boris Jordan at NTV.

This dispiriting outcome does not, however, cancel out the substantial skill sets of Russian viewers and their superior ability to move outside the frame intended by the broadcaster, even without the presentation of a range of viewpoints – even with the transmission of a frame so narrow that it permits only celebratory assertions of achievements. Russian viewers weigh manipulative intent in messages. Many bring scepticism to the process, and it should not be equated with cynicism, for the viewers contribute enormous effort to squeeze information out of the news. Russians expect commercial and governmental involvement in how the news is created. They believe it is the viewer's responsibility to extract significance and correct for bias.

In producing what they intend to be persuasive messages, media elites' assumptions about reception diverge in important respects from the process by which the Russian public understands the news. Russians are aided in this by an array of mental shortcuts, salient experiences, traditions of expending effort to enlarge the context of the news and awareness of the rarity or impossibility (almost in a post-modern sense) of objectivity. They are also aided by the miscalculations elites make in constructing and disseminating messages that are intended to provide the definitive frame, but only misconstrue the public's cues, underestimate their processing capacity and fail to recognize the negotiated nature of information reception.

Notes

1 I include as commercial channels ones that broadcast entirely on a channel or share time with another channel and have audiences that are large enough to get reasonable ratings.
2 See Appendix for further discussion of methods.
3 The potential influence of newspapers, the most historically significant and respected of all media, is now much more limited in Russia. The market and economic collapse pulled out the props holding up the industry. Subsidies generally ended and circulation figures plummeted. While Moscow may now be a vigorous newspaper market, even oversaturated by publications of every kind, the national picture is much less positive (Mickiewicz 2001).

References

Bartels, L. (1993) 'Messages received. The political impact of media exposure', *American Political Science Review*, 87: 267–81.

Ferejohn, J.A. and Kuklinski, J.H. (1990) *Information and the Democratic Process*, Urbana, IL: University of Illinois Press.

Gamson, W. (1992) *Talking About Politics*, Cambridge: Cambridge University Press.

Graber, D. (2001) *Processing Politics. Learning from Television in the Internet Age*, Chicago, IL: University of Chicago Press.

Johnson's List, 11 September 2003, davidjohnson@erols.com

Lunt, P. and Livingstone, S. (1996) 'Rethinking the focus group in media and communications research', *Journal of Communication*, 46(2): 79–98.

Lupia, A. and McCubbins, M.D. (1998) *The Democratic Dilemma. Can Citizens Learn what they Need to Know?* Cambridge: Cambridge University Press.

McDermott, R. (2002) 'Arms control and the first Reagan administration. Belief systems and policy choices', *Journal of Cold War Studies*, 4(4): 29–59.

McGraw, K. and Hubbard, C. (1996) 'Some of the people some of the time', in D.C. Mutz, P.M. Sniderman and R.A. Brody (eds) *Political Persuasion and Attitude Change*, Ann Arbor, MI: University of Michigan Press.

Mickiewicz, E. (1999) *Changing Channels. Television and the Struggle for Power in Russia*, revised and expanded edition, Durham, NC: Duke University Press.

——(2001) 'Structure and exposure', *The Donald W. Treadgold Papers*, Henry M. Jackson School of International Studies, The University of Washington, no. 30.

Mutz, D.C., Sniderman, P.M. and Brody, R.A. (eds) (1996) *Political Persuasion and Attitude Change*, Ann Arbor, MI: University of Michigan Press.

Tetlock, P.E. (2000) 'Coping with trade-offs. Psychological constraints and political implications', in A. Lupia, M.D. McCubbins and S.L. Popkin (eds) *Elements of Reason. Cognition, Choice and the Bounds of Rationality*, Cambridge: Cambridge University Press, 239–63.

Wolfe, A. (1998) *One Nation After All*, New York: Viking.

Appendix: Note on methods

The Public Opinion Foundation recruited focus group participants in two stages. The first – and basic – was from the 'respondent pool', supplemented by snowball methods. This pool is constructed in cities in which the Foundation carries out surveys. As part of a regular, representative survey, information is collected on the respondents' socio-demographic (age, sex, education, occupation and other) profiles. This is necessary for quality control of interviewers and validation studies. Participants in previous focus groups are not invited again until a year has passed. Participants are given a small payment.

The same facilitator conducted all 16 focus groups reported here.

Profile of focus groups

Sex: women: 53 per cent; men: 47 per cent.

Age: 30 and under: 50 per cent (includes post-Soviet groups, which comprise 25 per cent of total groups); 31–45: 25 per cent; over 45: 25 per cent.

News consumption: daily: 51 per cent; 3–4 times a week: 20 per cent; 1–2 times a week: 20 per cent.

News sources for news of president: Moscow-based networks: 85 per cent; Moscow-based networks and other media: 87 per cent; other: 13 per cent.

News sources for news of Chechnya: Moscow-based networks: 81 per cent; Moscow-based networks and other media: 81 per cent; other: 19 per cent (60 per cent of 'other' responses refer to 'Other people' and 'People who fought there'.)

News story summary

The Novorossisk Oil Pipeline Terminal Opens (First Channel), 2 minutes, 14 seconds

CORRESPONDENT: A few hours before the ceremonial opening of the new route of export of Caspian oil, the weather in the area of Novorossisk began to worsen, and the press conference had to be postponed. The Caspian pipeline consortium is one of the most powerful and costly investment projects in the whole territory of the former USSR. The cost of just the first line was more than $2.5 billion, which will be covered by the profit. The pipeline joins the Tengiz oilfield in Kazakhstan to the sea terminal at Novorossisk port. It is 1,510 km long; it takes a million tons of oil just to fill it. From the shore the oil goes through a flexible pipeline to floating berths to which tankers are moored. This way, they can continue shipping even in an 8-point storm. The pipeline can now transport 28 million tons a year. Twenty-four per cent of the consortium belongs to Russia, 19 to Kazakhstan; and the rest to Oman and other foreign oil companies. According to specialists in the next 40 years, the Russian budget will get more than $20 billion. A good deal of it will go to the budgets of the regions the pipeline crosses.

SERGEI GNATCHENKO, DIRECTOR OF PIPELINE CONSORTIUM: The pipeline shows the investment attractions and investment opportunities in Russia. It will undoubtedly encourage other investments.

CORRESPONDENT: The pipeline will be fully functioning by summer of next year, with about 70 million tons of oil a year.

Visuals: waves breaking against rocks, tankers, guests arriving, guests in tent for ceremony; map of region, line moves from Tengiz oilfields in Kazakhstan to Novorossisk; metal pipelines; tanker at sea; pipeline and sea; guests visiting coast and pipeline; Consortium Director interviewed; guests; pipelines.

12 Politics and the media in post-communist Russia

Stephen White and Ian McAllister

Russians don't think much of the Gorbachev years. But they do value the glasnost that led to a broadening of press freedom and eventually, in 1990, the abolition of censorship itself. Censorship is still illegal, under the post-communist constitution that was adopted in 1993. Freedom of the media, however, is more fragile, partly for economic reasons – circulations have been falling, advertising revenues are uncertain, and distribution charges have been rising. Media freedom has also become more vulnerable because of political pressure, dramatically apparent over the Easter weekend of 2001, when armed guards seized the most important private television station, NTV. (In early 2002 the last remaining independent channel, TV6, lost a judicial appeal and also came under *de facto* state control.) What do Russians themselves make of all this? What do they think of the media outlets that are currently available to them, and which forms of output do they choose to consume? Does it matter that Russia's post-communist media are increasingly partisan, and can it be shown to make a difference to the electoral behaviour of ordinary citizens?

Several accounts have been published of the changes that have taken place in the Russian media over a turbulent post-communist decade (see, for instance, Egorov 1999; Mickiewicz 1999; Murray 1994; Rantanen 2002; I. Zassoursky 2001; Y. Zassoursky 2001). Our own study draws upon a different set of data and addresses somewhat different issues, many of them prompted by the unusually prominent role the media appeared to have played in Russia's parliamentary and presidential elections of 1999–2000 and 2003–04. We shall be drawing, first of all, upon two representative national surveys, in April 2001 and January 2004, in each of which 2,000 adults all over the country were asked for their opinions.[1] In addition, we conducted two rounds of focus group discussions, before and after each cycle of elections, and we gathered video evidence of political commercials and national news. One of the authors, in addition, was in Russia for the 1999–2000 elections as part of a monitoring exercise conducted by the European Institute of the Media, which provided an opportunity to interview editors, government media officials, party representatives and presidential hopefuls, and was again an official observer in December 2003.

Russian circumstances, clearly, have their own specificity. But Russia is not the only democratizing country in which a powerful executive has threatened the independence of its newly enfranchised media. Nor is it the only one in which international conventions that guarantee freedom of expression appear to have had little effect in the face of a manipulative political class, a concentration of ownership in the hands of the state or its clients, and a society that appears to show little appreciation of the values of balance and impartiality that underpin the media in Western countries. We conclude with some more general reflections on the role of the media in such partial democracies, focusing upon the conduct of formally competitive elections in which control of the media has often been used to give incumbents – or the regime itself – an undue advantage.

Patterns of media consumption

The media had a particularly important role for the Soviet leadership in the creation of a fully communist society. Lenin, after all, had declared that a newspaper should be an 'educator, agitator and organiser', and censorship had been introduced, on a 'temporary' basis, just two days after the regime itself had been established (it lasted until 1990). Newspaper circulations increased steadily through the Soviet period, and by the late 1980s they were among the highest in the world. Radio, and then television, came later: about 5 per cent of the population could receive television by 1960, but by the late 1980s more than 90 per cent of all households had a television set and the typical audience for the main nightly news programme was about 80 per cent of the adult population, including the entire armed forces (Mickiewicz 1988: 8). A decade or more later, after the social and economic changes that accompanied the end of communist rule, book and newspaper circulations had fallen sharply (journals were staging something of a recovery, but circulations per head of population were still less than one-quarter of what they had been in the last years of the Soviet Union); television, however, was still extending its reach: most of the population could receive at least three channels, and even in rural areas almost 98 per cent could receive at least one of them (see Table 12.1).

Even before the post-communist years, television had become the medium of choice of ordinary Russians – as in most other developed societies. As many as 92 per cent of our survey respondents in the spring of 2001 watched television at least several times a week, usually for two or three hours at a time, and even more on their days off. The two main state channels – *Obshchestvennoe Rossiiskoye Televidenie* (ORT, Russian Public Television, known more recently as *Pervyi kanal*, the First Channel) and Russian Radio and Television (RTR) – are the most widely watched, attracting a daily audience, on the evidence of our survey, of 84 and 71 per cent respectively of the entire adult population. The main commercial

Table 12.1 Russian media output, 1980–2003

	Year				
	1980	*1990*	*1995*	*2000*	*2003[a]*
Print media, no. of copies published					
Books (millions)	1393	1553	475	471	591
Journals (millions)	2488	5010	299	607	1164
Newspapers (billions)	29	38	9	7	6
Television coverage					
% of population	87	98	99	98	99
% of viewers receiving ≥ 3 channels	17	37	65	73	75

Source: Figures derived from *Rossiiskii* 2003: 265, 468.

Note
a Circulations in the calendar year 2002 and television reception as of the end of that year.

channel, NTV, is in third place with a daily audience of 53 per cent, disproportionately higher in urban areas (its reach in the countryside is still rather less than that of the major state channels). By contrast, newspaper circulations have fallen sharply: local papers, on the evidence of our survey, have retained a more loyal readership, but more than six times as many watch television as read a national daily (Table 12.2). Similarly, in 2004, 22 per cent 'regularly' read a national newspaper, but 82 per cent watched national television and 63 per cent watched local television on the same basis.

Reading, listening and viewing are distributed fairly evenly, but with significant discrepancies. The middle-aged are the most likely to be regular newspaper readers, on the evidence of our surveys, but there is relatively little difference in levels of viewing across age groups, or indeed across genders, occupations, educational attainments or types of settlement. There are, however, some differences between the typical audience for the First Channel and for its commercial rival. Regular First Channel viewers are slightly older than the average, but NTV viewers are considerably younger. NTV's audience is also better educated: 62 per cent of those who watched it regularly in the spring of 2001 had completed higher education, compared with 51 per cent among all other respondents. NTV's audience, most of all, is a Moscow one. In the capital, 87 per cent of our respondents claimed to watch NTV regularly, compared with 53 per cent in small towns and 36 per cent in villages (where it is less often possible to receive it). Viewers in the capital, indeed, were as likely to rely on NTV's *Segodnya* or its weekly news magazine *Itogi* as on ORT/the First Channel's long-established bulletin *Vremya*: patterns that were very different from those for the country as a whole.

Moscow apart, there is no serious challenge to the dominance of the First Channel. Not only does it attract the largest daily audience, but its

Table 12.2 Russian media consumption, 2001

	Frequency of reading/viewing (% of respondents)					
	Daily	*Frequently*[a]	*Occasionally*[a]	*Rarely*[a]	*Never*	*Don't know*
Newspapers						
National	12	24	23	16	25	0
Local	17	40	19	10	13	0
Television						
National	77	15	4	2	2	0
Local	49	22	9	5	11	4

Source: authors' survey conducted by Russian Research, April 2001 (*N* = 2,000).

Note

a 'Frequently' was defined as several times a week; 'occasionally' as several times a month; and 'rarely' as several times a year.

evening news bulletin, *Vremya*, was also the most popular with 71 per cent of our respondents (Russian Television's *Vesti* was in second place, with 56 per cent), and it was the channel our respondents were most likely to say they 'preferred to all the others', with 37 per cent (NTV came second with 26 per cent, although it was more popular than the First Channel among those who had access to both channels). The state channels, above all the First Channel, also provide the programmes that are individually most popular. The overall favourite in our 2001 survey was 'Field of Wonders' (*Pole chudes*), a word game analogous to 'Wheel of Fortune' – which was named by 47% of respondents (see Table 12.3). This was followed by *KVN* (*Klub veselykh novostei*), a team game between young people which also dates from the Soviet period. Both of these, and indeed all the most popular programmes appeared on state channels, and all but two of them on the First Channel; the presenter of 'Field of Wonders' was himself the most popular presenter on any channel.

Taking all sources of information together, state television was generally thought to be the 'most unbiased and reliable' (65 per cent), compared with 18 per cent who mentioned the national press, 14 per cent who mentioned family and friends, and just 13 per cent who mentioned commercial television. The main state channel, ORT/the First Channel, was the one respondents were most likely to see as 'trustworthy in its news coverage' (33 per cent took this view, compared with 25 per cent who opted for NTV and 13 per cent who chose RTR). Why did viewers prefer this channel? For the largest numbers, it was because it had the best news coverage (58 per cent), rather than the best films (40 per cent) or the best entertainment (32 per cent). Similarly, respondents were most likely to trust a channel because it 'presented facts' (54 per cent), although some viewers trusted a channel simply 'out of habit' (21 per cent), or more revealingly 'because it [was] a state channel' (18 per cent). At the same

Table 12.3 Most popular television programmes among survey respondents in 2001

	Channel	% choosing programme
Field of Wonders (*Pole chudes*)	ORT	47
KVN (*Klub veselykh novostei*; Club of the Merry and Ingenious)	ORT	43
My Own Producer (*Sam sebe rezhisser*)	RTR	43
Wait for Me (*Zhdi menya*)	ORT	41
How to become a Millionaire (*Kak stat' millionerom*)	ORT	39
My Family (*Moya sem'ya*)	RTR	39
In the Animal World (*V mire zhivotnykh*)	ORT	34
Traveller's Club (*Klub puteshchestvennika*)	ORT	31

Source: Authors' survey conducted by Russian Research, April 2001 ($N = 2,000$).
Respondents were asked 'What are your favourite programmes?' and shown a card listing 27 programmes with the option to add another choice; all positive responses were recorded.

Note
ORT, Russian Public Television/First Channel; RTR, Russian Radio and Television.

time there was considerable scepticism about the objectivity of news programmes as a whole, and there was a general tendency to watch more than one news programme on more than one channel: more than one-fifth (22 per cent) did so all the time and nearly half (46 per cent) did so occasionally.

Television and Russian elections

We took a particular interest in the coverage of elections to the Duma in December 1999 and December 2003, which monitoring reports and our earlier research suggested had been heavily biased in favour of the Kremlin (European Institute for the Media 2000a; Oates and Roselle 2000; Organisation for Security and Cooperation in Europe 2004: 14–17). The 1999 Duma campaign, in particular, marked a new low, with state television accusing the Kremlin's main challengers of being criminals – even accessories to murder – and accomplices of foreign powers, particularly Israel and the United States. Much was made of former prime minister Evgenii Primakov's advanced years (he celebrated his seventieth birthday during the campaign), and of his hip operation (the subject of a gory on-screen simulation). At the same time, Kremlin supporters – and those whose votes were likely to take support away from its opponents – were given disproportionate attention. (Editors themselves, in their interviews with European Institute for the Media monitors, made no effort to deny the bias in their coverage, although they added in their defence that the flamboyant nationalist Vladimir Zhirinovsky was simply good television.)

There was less *kompromat* (compromising material or 'dirty tricks') during the December 2003 Duma election campaign, but once again monitors found evidence of heavy bias in favour of pro-regime parties and candidates. 'Overall', the Organisation for Security and Cooperation in Europe mission concluded, the Russian media had 'failed to provide impartial or fair coverage of the election campaign'; this was particularly true of the 'overwhelming tendency of the state media to exhibit a clear bias in favour of United Russia [which was the main pro-Kremlin party at these elections] and against the CPRF [Communist Party of the Russian Federation]' (2004: 16). United Russia, for instance, received 19 per cent of the political and election news coverage of the First Channel, all of it positive or neutral, and went on to take more than one-third of the party-list vote in the election itself; the Communist Party received 13 per cent of mostly negative coverage, which left it in a very distant second place. There were similar patterns on the second state channel and on TV Centre, a channel controlled by the Moscow authorities, although there was a more balanced picture on NTV and the other commercial channels.

There was no doubt, over the entire post-Communist period, that television was the main source of voter information of this kind. With a national press that scarcely circulates outside the major cities and a territory that is one-seventh of the world's land surface, it could hardly be otherwise. Following the December 1999 Duma election, 43 per cent of all our respondents indicated that the national state channels had been their main source of information in choosing among the candidates and parties, and very few cited national newspapers (2 per cent), commercial television (another 2 per cent) or local state television (just under 2 per cent). In December 2003 it was again state television that had provided the overwhelming bulk of information for the Russian elector (40 per cent identified national state channels as their most important source, and another 3 per cent local state channels); only 3 per cent cited the press, and just 2 per cent mentioned commercial television. Did it matter, in these circumstances, that state television gave a disproportionate share of its attention to pro-Kremlin parties and their candidates?

The literature, so far, has taken both views. Colton, in a study that focuses on the 1995–96 electoral cycle, found that in neither election was media consumption an important determinant of electoral behaviour (2000: 65); but this was an observation that related to television in general, rather than state and commercial television respectively, which was a crucial distinction in the elections with which we are primarily concerned. Rose & Munro, in a study that centred on the 1999–2000 electoral cycle, found similarly that television ranked well behind 'none' or their own experiences as things that had helped respondents to 'decide what to do in the Duma election' (2002: 125). But television had obviously been of decisive importance in enabling Unity to secure about a quarter of the party-list vote in just three months of its foundation: so much so, indeed, that it became known as a 'broadcast party' (Oates 2003). Finally, analysts attached to the All-Russian Centre for the Study of Public Opinion found that there was a particularly high level of confidence in the mass media among Unity supporters, which in turn provided 'graphic evidence of the key role the media had played in its achievement of such a good result at the election' (Sedov 2000: 33). In this chapter we aim to take the discussion further forward, drawing upon entirely new qualitative as well as quantitative evidence, and focusing upon the Duma elections of December 1999 and December 2003.

The role of the media in the Duma elections of 1999 and 2003

Qualitative evidence

Our qualitative evidence is drawn from focus groups that we commissioned in January 2004 in four different 'middle Russian' locations: Odintsovo and Kolomna, which are both in Moscow region; Ryazan', which is a regional capital; and Novosibirsk, the capital of western Siberia. Each of the groups had eight or nine participants, nearly all of working age, and equally distributed between males and females. The interviews were conducted on our behalf by Russian associates, working to a list of prompts that had been agreed in advance. In each case we received a transcript, a floppy disk, and the comments of the moderator involved.

Focus groups, as Krueger has noted, 'provide a special type of information'; they 'tap into the real-life interactions of people and allow the researcher to get in touch with participants' perceptions, attitudes, and opinions in a way that other procedures do not allow' (1994: 238). They are particularly helpful when local cultural assumptions are different from those of the investigator, and when relatively complex and polyvalent attitudes are being examined.

We asked, in the first place, what our respondents had made of the 'teledebates' that had been a particular feature of the December 2003 Duma campaign – 45 per cent of the entire electorate were reported to have seen them (*Izvestiya*, 8 December 2003: 2).

In Odintsovo, responses were very mixed. Aleksei, a major in the armed forces, had seen none of them: 'I have no time'. Nor had housewife El'vira: 'Boring, and anyway the children don't leave me much time'. Fedor, a military pensioner, had turned immediately to another channel if he accidentally came across one of the debates – they were 'all lying'. But most of our participants had given them at least some attention. Engineer Vladimir, for instance, had 'seen a lot' of the television debates: 'At first it was very interesting, I made a special effort to see them all. But then I got fed up – they all said the same thing'. He was especially contemptuous of the 'pygmy parties' that had virtually no electoral support – why set them up at all, and give them airtime? Lyudmila, a pensioner in her fifties, was particularly dismissive of the 'democrats' and of Boris Nemtsov, Irina Khakamada and Anatolii Chubais, who were the first three candidates on the list put forward by the Union of Right Forces: 'I turn them off at once, I hate them, the windbags!' She felt that the debates themselves had been 'dishonest', with Communists marginalized.

Mariya, a schoolteacher in her thirties who was generally sympathetic to Yabloko, distinguished between the free-time programmes on the main channels and the discussion programmes on NTV. The free-time programmes, she thought, had been 'very boring': the party leaders had been poorly prepared to discuss important issues such as the budget or the taxation system, and 'got lost' as soon as they were invited to move beyond their prepared remarks. The leaders of the established parties had been much better – 'on NTV they simply dazzled'. However, it was a pity that none of them had avoided heaping abuse on their competitors. Alexander, an engineer in his forties, tried similarly not to miss a single debate. There was certainly 'too much dirt', with the radical nationalist Zhirinovsky especially offensive, but on the whole he was inclined to give the debates a positive assessment: 'Nothing wonderful, but at least people were able to say what they thought'. Boris, a tractor-driver in his sixties, shared this mixed verdict. He had seen the debates 'occasionally', but was also offended by the lack of propriety: 'The candidates conduct themselves very offensively. Call each other names as much as they can. It's even repugnant to watch it. So I tried not to see too much of it. I saw some of it all the same'.

Views in the regional city of Ryazan' covered the same spectrum. Larisa, a bookkeeper in her thirties, thought the debates were boring and hardly remembered who had taken part. Oksana, a music teacher in her forties, remembered no more than a sequence of 'boring mugs all saying the same'. Nikolai, a 40-year-old worker, wondered why the debates had been so poor: 'Did they really have no image-makers, or whatever they're called, to write good speeches for them?' One of his friends in Moscow had earned so much from the elections he had been able to buy a car. However, as in Odintsovo, there were more positive verdicts. Isaak, a researcher in his late fifties, 'listened closely to everything that the Yabloko and Right Forces representatives had said'. Lyudmila, a pensioner in her sixties, particularly liked the Yabloko leader Grigorii Yavlinsky and always listened attentively when he was on the air – 'but somehow they don't allow him to come across'. Alexander, an entrepreneur in his late forties, was another who was impressed by the representatives of Yabloko, Right Forces and *Rodina* (Motherland); Zhirinovsky, by contrast, had 'simply played the fool and been insulting, although as it turned out, many liked that'. Vera, a housewife in her forties, got so excited that her blood pressure had gone up: 'then I took a tranquilliser, but even so I wasn't able to calm down for a long time'.

In Kolomna, opinions were even more positive. Some, again, found it distasteful to see public representatives arguing with each other. Others thought the debates had at least occasionally been interesting, 'like a Mexican serial'. Even if the political arguments were of little interest, suggested Natal'ya (40 years old and temporarily unemployed), the politicians could be – for 'their criticism, and sometimes scandal'. Leonid, a commercial manager in his late forties, had little time for the free-time broadcasts in which politicians read out prepared texts, but he was another who thought the teledebates were a 'good show', particularly the programmes that brought leading candidates face to face. Vladimir, a computer programmer in his fifties, agreed: it could be more engaging than a feature film, particularly when passions were raised – 'You watch – and it's as if you've taken a shot of adrenalin'. Viktor, a manager in his late forties, 'hadn't seen anything so interesting for a long time', especially the contests on NTV in which Zhirinovsky had taken part: 'You can hardly expect to hear anything new, but what a spectacle! I just couldn't turn off'.

We were also interested in perceptions of the influence and role of television in the December 2003 election. In Odintsovo, Vladimir thought the press had been more democratic than television, which was 'under the control of the authorities'. United Russia, for instance, had taken no part in the television debates, but its leader Boris Gryzlov had all the same been on constant display. Aleksei agreed that the printed media had been more objective – perhaps because they were cheaper. He was another who had no doubt that the mass media had actively influenced the election, although he 'had the impression that only the party of power had actively exploited all the opportunities they made available'. There was particular indignation at the sight of Right Forces leaders travelling the country by air, while nursing homes and even military bases were having their power cut off: publicity of this kind had had a 'definite, negative role'. Money was certainly an important variable. 'It works this way', explained Igor, 'whoever pays the most takes part in these teledebates. They show the ones who have the most money. And those who have the most money also have better programmes'.

There were also more discriminating views. As one of our Ryazan' participants pointed out, although United Russia had taken no part in the television debates it had won a decisive victory. The influence of the media was clearly important, but so too were other factors such as 'administrative resource' – the ability of the authorities to use their control of the state machine. For Isaak, part of the problem was the audience, who weren't as interested in well-considered proposals as in empty slogans of the kind that Zhirinovsky and other nationalists put forward – ordinary people, unfortunately, took this 'crude populism at face value'. Who was to blame, asked Alexander, 'if the thoughtful words of thoughtful politicians have no real effect, and idle chatter and loutishness were successful?'

Overall, however, there was little doubt that the media had been a factor of enormous importance in shaping electoral choices. How could it be otherwise, asked Lyudmila in Odintsovo, in such a big country? How else could ordinary voters know anything about the leaders of the party lists, who almost always lived in Moscow?

Nor was there much doubt that the heavy bias in coverage reflected the advice of the Kremlin, particularly in the favourable treatment of United Russia and of Motherland (which was seen as a means of taking votes from the Communists). 'At any rate', reflected Vera in Ryazan', 'it was hard to find candidates from other parties and blocs. But all these Gryzlovs and Shoigus never left the screen'. The influence of the authorities was apparent in other ways as well: for instance, in the choice of feature films during the election period, which reflected a generally negative view of the Soviet period. And there was concern about the campaign that had been waged against the Communist Party, even by those who did not share its views. 'I didn't like the open manoeuvring of the party of power', Leonid in Kolomna told us, 'I didn't like it at all'. The entire Soviet period had been used to disparage the Communists, even when it had no direct relevance to the campaign; they had even been accused of links with the oligarchs: 'On the whole it seemed to me that the media were very unfair in relation to the Communists'.

Quantitative evidence

Together with our focus groups, we conducted two national representative surveys: one in April 2001, and another – using identically worded questions – in January 2004, immediately after the Duma vote had taken place. The quantitative evidence broadly confirms the impressions that were derived from our focus groups, and suggests that media effects were very considerable – in a variety of ways – in both parliamentary elections. The study of media effects, particularly on the basis of survey evidence, has been controversial, and we must obviously take account of flows of causation in both directions. We follow McQuail in positing that media effects are a universal and that their impact is particularly important during periods of crisis, but that the 'direction, degree, durability and predictability of effect are each uncertain and have to be established case by case' (2000: 422, 447). It would certainly be surprising if media effects were *not* apparent in the Russian elections of 1999 and 2003, given the heavy dependence of the electorate on television as a source of information and the well-documented bias in the quantity and nature of their coverage in both elections.

We asked, in the first instance, how our respondents had voted in December 1999, and compared this with the source of information that respondents said had been the most important in shaping their electoral decisions. We set out the results in Table 12.4. In the Duma election of December 1999, as we already noted, state television was the most important single source of voter information. But as Table 12.4 makes clear,

Table 12.4 Most valued sources of election news and voting behaviour for Duma elections of 1999 and 2003

% of party's voters rating source 'most important'

	1999 election							2003 election				
	CPRF	FAR	Unity	URF	Yabloko	Zhirinov-sky	Other	CPRF	United Russia	Mother land	LDPR	Other
State television	52	43	66	53	43	55	49	27	68	65	60	56
Commercial television	4	11	3	9	8	6	8	2	2	4	0	2
Newspapers	6	6	4	6	2	7	5	4	3	5	2	7
Radio	3	6	1	2	5	1	4	1	1	2	1	1
Other	35	34	26	30	42	30	34	66	27	25	36	36
(N)	(267)	(72)	(378)	(65)	(119)	(69)	(171)	(178)	(630)	(134)	(125)	(201)

Source: Authors' surveys conducted by Russian Research in April 2001 (N = 2,000) and January 2004 (N = 2,000). The question was: 'Which, for you, was the most important source of information when you decided whether or not to vote, and for whom to vote in the elections to the Duma in 1999/2003?'

Note
CPRF, Communist Party of the Russian Federation; FAR, Fatherland–All Russia; URF, Union of Right Forces; LDPR, Liberal Democratic Party of Russia.

state television was more important for the Kremlin-supported Unity party than for all of its major competitors. By contrast, commercial television was rather more important for the Kremlin's main challenger, Fatherland–All Russia, and for the liberal parties, Yabloko and the Union of Right Forces.

In December 2003, once again, there were strong and obvious associations. Supporters of United Russia, the main pro-Kremlin grouping (it competed under the slogan 'Together with the President'), were the most likely to derive the information that was most relevant to their voting decision from state television. Supporters of Motherland were also heavily dependent on state television; and so too were supporters of Zhirinovsky's Liberal Democratic Party, which has been consistently pro-Kremlin. Supporters of the Communist Party, which this time was the object of generally hostile coverage in the state media, were at the other extreme, and much more likely to be influenced by other factors entirely. These associations establish at least a strong *prima facie* case that there were strong reinforcement effects between state television and pro-Kremlin parties in both elections of a kind that seriously disadvantaged their main competitors.

Strong associations of this kind, however, are not in themselves evidence of a causal relationship. Unity and United Russia supporters may have watched more state television, and said they were guided by it in making their electoral decisions; but did state television influence their choices, or were they naturally attracted to the channel that gave the most sympathetic coverage to the party they favoured in the first place? Equally, did watching NTV make a difference to the electoral support of those who favoured Fatherland – All Russia and Yabloko, at least in 1999, or did it simply reflect the choices they would in any case have made? There are limits to the extent to which we can resolve these issues within a survey design. A regression analysis, however, allows us to show the relative importance of the various factors that appear to have contributed to voting choices, including state and commercial television. We set out the evidence in Tables 12.5 and 12.6.

Clearly, conventional factors made a difference in the Duma election, in 1999 and again in 2003. Age was likely to increase support for the Communist Party, but to reduce it for Unity, the Union of Right Forces and Zhirinovsky's Liberal Democrats. Zhirinovsky, as usual, gained rather more of his support from male voters, and the Communists drew more heavily than others on the unemployed. Media effects, however, were more readily apparent. Above all, those who gave state television as their main source in making their voting decision were much more likely to vote for Unity, net of other circumstances, and those who watched commercial television were far less likely to do so. State television was also likely to lower support for Yabloko, but commercial television to raise it, and those who relied on state television were also less likely to vote for

Table 12.5 Most important source of election information and voting, December 1999: logistic regression estimates showing parameter estimates (and standard errors)

	Parameter estimate (and standard error)					
	CPRF	FAR	Unity	URF	Yabloko	Zhirinovsky
Age	0.04**	0.01	-0.01**	-0.03**	-0.01	-0.03**
	(0.01)	(0.01)	(0.01)	(0.01)	(0.01)	(0.01)
Male	0.18	-0.23	0.06	-0.07	-0.19	0.77**
	(0.16)	(0.26)	(0.14)	(0.30)	(0.22)	(0.30)
Urban	-0.13	0.33	-0.21	0.33	0.48	0.13
	(0.18)	(0.34)	(0.15)	(0.38)	(0.26)	(0.32)
Tertiary education	-0.34	0.19	0.24	0.43	0.36	-0.72
	(0.25)	(0.33)	(0.19)	(0.36)	(0.26)	(0.45)
Employed	-0.50**	0.32	0.05	-0.34	0.01	0.70*
	(0.18)	(0.30)	(0.15)	(0.31)	(0.24)	(0.33)
Family income	0.01	0.01	-0.05	0.01	0.00	0.03
	(0.02)	(0.03)	(0.04)	(0.02)	(0.02)	(0.02)
Main media source						
State television	-0.32*	-0.43*	0.67**	0.07	-0.35**	0.07
	(0.15)	(0.23)	(0.13)	(0.26)	(0.19)	(0.26)
Commercial television	0.04	0.58	-0.83**	0.76	1.06**	-0.73
	(0.28)	(0.40)	(0.29)	(0.45)	(0.33)	(0.49)
Frequency follows politics						
On television	-0.22**	-0.04	0.05	-0.27	0.02	-0.08
	(0.06)	(0.12)	(0.06)	(0.13)	(0.10)	(0.12)
In newspapers	-0.07	0.27*	-0.05	0.29	0.04	-0.09
	(0.06)	(0.10)	(0.05)	(0.12)	(0.08)	(0.11)
Constant	-3.44	-3.99	-0.10	-1.62	-2.30	-2.22
Pseudo R^2	0.12	0.03	0.05	0.06	0.03	0.08

Source: Data from authors' survey conducted by Russian Research, April 2001.

Notes
CPRF, Communist Party of the Russian Federation; FAR, Fatherland–All Russia; URF, Union of Right Forces.
* Statistically significant at $p < 0.01$; **$p < 0.05$; both two-tailed.
Age is scored in single years, family income in thousands of roubles, and frequency of following politics on television and in the newspapers is coded from 1 (never) to 5 (daily). The remaining variables are dummy variables. Estimates exclude non-voters and don't knows; $N = 986$.

Table 12.6 Most important source of election information and voting, December 2003: logistic regression estimates showing parameter estimates (and standard errors)

	Parameter estimate (and standard error)			
	CPRF	*United Russia*	*Motherland*	*LDPR*
Age	0.06**	−0.04**	0.04**	−0.02*
	(0.01)	(0.01)	(0.01)	(0.01)
Male	0.77**	−0.46**	0.23	0.66
	(0.32)	(0.18)	(0.29)	(0.27)
Urban	−0.05	0.17	−0.17	0.36
	(0.39)	(0.25)	(0.38)	(0.42)
Tertiary education	0.34	−0.27	0.48	−0.67
	(0.38)	(0.23)	(0.34)	(0.41)
Employed	−0.08	−0.21	0.64	0.24
	(0.37)	(0.23)	(0.40)	(0.35)
Family income	0.01	0.01	−0.02	0.01
	(0.02)	(0.03)	(0.04)	(0.03)
Main media source				
State television	−1.88**	0.61**	0.34	0.16
	(0.34)	(0.18)	(0.30)	(0.27)
Commercial television	−0.33	0.09	2.04**	−0.76
	(0.82)	(0.62)	(0.66)	(0.45)
Frequency follows politics				
On television	−0.43*	0.19	0.05	−0.20
	(0.23)	(0.11)	(0.18)	(0.14)
In newspapers	−0.04	0.08	−0.09	−0.17*
	(0.10)	(0.06)	(0.10)	(0.09)
Constant	−5.59	0.35	−4.85	−1.27
Pseudo R^2	0.18	0.06	0.06	0.07

Source: Data from authors' survey conducted by Russian Research, January 2004.

Notes
CPRF, Communist Party of the Russian Federation; LDPR, Liberal Democratic Party of Russia.
* Statistically significant at $P < 0.01$; **$P < 0.05$; both two-tailed.
  Age is scored in single years, family income in thousands of roubles, and frequency of following politics on television and in the newspapers is coded from 1 (never) to 5 (daily). The remaining variables are dummy variables. Estimates exclude non-voters and don't knows; $N = 1,403$.

the Communists or for Fatherland–All Russia, who were also in opposition to the Kremlin and the media channels it controlled. Television viewing was more important than anything except age in predicting support for Unity, and more important than anything else in predicting support for Yabloko (although it had little effect on support for the Liberal Democrats).

There were similar if less pronounced effects in December 2003. Age mattered, once again: it helped the Communists and Motherland, while

United Russia and to some extent the Liberal Democrats drew disproportionately on younger age-groups. Male voters were much more likely to
opt for the Communists, and female voters for United Russia. Residence,
education, employment status and family income made little difference, at
least statistically. But, once again, the *association* between sources of
information and vote choice was a close one – and in the direction we had
predicted. Voters who drew on state television were much more likely, all
other circumstances being equal, to vote for United Russia, and not to
vote for the Communist Party; voters who drew on commercial television
were again much more likely to support Yabloko; and Liberal Democrats
were little influenced either way. Except for the Communists, a relatively
small proportion of the variance is explained by either of these models.
We have, however, sought to purge reciprocal causation in a two-stage
least-squares regression, not reported here (see White *et al.*, 2005); this
allows us to claim with some assurance that the media effects we have
demonstrated are unlikely to be spurious.

In line with our expectations, then, television had major but quite selective effects on the vote in both Duma elections. These effects remained
important even after we had controlled for a range of socio-economic
factors; indeed they were generally the *most* important of all the factors
shaping electoral choices, as we might expect in a post-Communist country
in which social structures have been rapidly changing and party loyalties
have had little time to establish themselves (Rose *et al.* 2001). The effects we
observed, moreover, were consistent with the bias that had been apparent
in the media themselves: in the case of state television, strongly pro-Unity
and pro-United Russia; in the case of commercial television, much more
supportive of the parties and candidates that were hostile to the Kremlin.

Media, elections and new democracies

Our evidence is certainly consistent with the view that post-Communist
Russia has 'free' elections, with a choice of candidates and parties. But it is
less clear that these are 'fair' elections, in which the regime confronts its
opponents on a level playing field. The state media, and the First Channel
particularly, had helped to create a pro-Kremlin party in just a few months
in 1999. The First Channel's coverage was strongly supportive of the party
it had created, extending to a smear campaign of a kind that monitors
agreed was 'unprecedented in post-Soviet general elections' (International Foundation for Election Systems 2000: 49–50). On our evidence,
Unity voters, and supporters of United Russia in 2003, were no more likely
than other voters to watch television – everyone did, whatever party they
supported – but they were much more likely to cite it as the most important influence upon their voting choices. The Kremlin had evidently
secured an extremely powerful weapon in helping it to obtain the electoral outcome it wanted.

This was a result that raised still larger issues. One of them, certainly, was further improvement of the regulatory framework. International monitors agreed that there should be better mechanisms to allow politicians to respond to attacks or unfair coverage. There might be special advisory boards for the state-controlled channels in order to protect them from the directives of their political masters. Political advertising should be clearly identified, and the concept itself should be more precisely defined. Local governors should not be allowed to shut down programmes if they disagreed with their contents. The penalties for slander and libel should be considerably increased. The Central Electoral Commission should have its own enforcement mechanism, instead of relying on the Ministry of the Mass Media and Communications. And the Central Electoral Commission should give those journalists who retained a sense of pride in their independence and impartiality the 'chance to do their jobs properly without the threat of sanctions' (see respectively European Institute for the Media 2000a: 73–5; Organisation for Security and Cooperation in Europe/Office for Democratic Institutions and Human Rights 2000: 33; International Foundation for Election Systems 2000: 134).

Recommendations of this kind, however, were not particularly new, and one of the most disturbing signs that emerged from the Russian parliamentary and presidential elections was that neither journalists nor the mass public showed much understanding of the norms of fair and impartial broadcasting to which they were all nominally committed. Journalists, monitors reported, had 'abandoned even the pretence of free and fair coverage of elections', and embraced the use of *kompromat* with considerable enthusiasm (European Institute for the Media 2000a: 75); the press had continued to provide a wider range of information and opinion, but the 'widespread practice of hidden advertising, demanded by political candidates and facilitated by willing editors, once again cast serious doubts on the ethics of the print media profession' (European Institute for the Media 2000b: 2–3). Nor had there been a single reference to the Charter of Television and Broadcasters, which supposedly committed the major stations to a common set of ethical norms, in spite of 'massive violations of taste and decency' (International Foundation for Election Systems 2000: 135).

The evidence of our focus groups, moreover, was that ordinary Russians had no better understanding of the kind of norms that underpin the media in liberal democracies, and to which their own legislation formally committed them. Many participants said they had been dismayed by the relatively novel sight of political mud-slinging on Russian television – and yet our survey results suggest that many more had been influenced by a series of programmes that were designed to undermine the reputation of politicians and their parties, and which were produced and transmitted with little regard for the election law that clearly prohibited such tactics. Some 14 per cent of our survey respondents, in fact, thought *kompromat* was 'a good way to know more about famous people' and more than one-third agreed 'there must be some truth in it or it would not be on television', while fewer than one-third thought they would not be influenced by it. Other inquiries have found that there is majority support for state ownership of the media, and for 'information control' or even censorship, with few differences across the generations – see US Department of State, Office of Research (2002), and *Izvestiya* (14 January 2004: 1), which reported that 76 per cent favoured some degree of censorship in the media.

The Duma elections of 1999 and 2003 marked a further step forward in the consolidation of Russia's electoral procedures. They marked a less positive development in the demonstration they provided, particularly in 1999, of the extent to which a determined regime could use its control over the media environment to resist any challenge to its authority and 'make anyone president'. The steps that have subsequently been taken by the Kremlin to assert its control over the channels that might have provided a genuine alternative suggest this was not a lesson they had failed to learn, and that the 1999 contest may in retrospect mark a decisive point in the Kremlin's progress towards an electoral process that is a constituent part of a 'managed democracy' over which it has all but total control.

Note

1 The survey was conducted between 10 and 26 April 2001 by Russian Research, using 110 primary sampling points and 209 interviewers. The sample was representative of the 18+ urban and rural population of the Russian Federation with control quotas for sex and age, and for education. The sample was designed using the multistage proportional representation, with random route as the method of selecting households and last birthday to select respondents within households. Questions were administered face to face, with no more than one interview in each household, and a total of 2000 interviews was achieved. Local fieldwork supervisors checked 20 per cent of completed questionnaires, and attended 10 per cent of interviews in major cities. The standard logical checks were used during data entry and cleaning. We acknowledge the support of the UK Economic and Social Research Council under grant R223133 to Sarah Oates, Stephen White and John Dunn of the University of Glasgow, and under grant RES230146 to Stephen White, Margot Light and Roy Allison for the 2004 survey, which was conducted under the same auspices and to the same specification. Support for our 2004 focus groups came from the British Academy (SG 37188) and the Nuffield Foundation (SGS 960). We are also grateful for the assistance of Gillian McCormack and Katia Rogatchevskaia.

References

Colton, T.J. (2000) *Transitional Citizens. Voters and What Influences Them in the New Russia*, Cambridge, MA: Harvard University Press.

Egorov, V. (1999) *Televidenie mezhdu proshlym i budushchim*, Moscow: Voskresen'e.

European Institute for the Media (2000a) *Monitoring the Media Coverage of the*

December 1999 Parliamentary Elections in Russia. Final Report, March 2000, Düsseldorf: EIM.

——(2000b) *Monitoring the Media Coverage of the March 2000 Presidential Elections in Russia. Final Report, August 2000*, Düsseldorf: EIM.

International Foundation for Election Systems (2000) *Parliamentary and Presidential Elections in Russia 1999–2000. Technical Assessment*, Washington, DC: IFES.

Krueger, R.A. (1994) *Focus Groups. A Practical Guide for Applied Research*, 2nd edn, Thousand Oaks, CA: Sage.

McQuail, D. (2000) *McQuail's Mass Communication Theory*, 4th edn, London: Sage.

Mickiewicz, E. (1988) *Split Signals*, New York: Oxford University Press.

——(1999) *Changing Channels. Television and the Struggle for Power in Russia*, revised edn, Durham, NC: Duke University Press.

Murray, J. (1994) *The Russian Press from Brezhnev to Yeltsin*, Aldershot: Edward Elgar.

Oates, S. (2003) 'Television, voters, and the development of the "broadcast party"', in V. Hesli and W. Reisinger (eds) *The 1999–2000 Elections in Russia. Their Impact and Legacy*, Cambridge: Cambridge University Press, 29–50.

Oates, S. and Roselle, L. (2000) 'Russian elections and TV news. Comparison of campaign news on state-controlled and commercial television channels', *Harvard International Journal of Press/Politics*, 5(2): 30–51.

Organisation for Security and Cooperation in Europe/Office for Democratic Institutions and Human Rights (2000) *Russian Federation. Elections to the State Duma, 19 December 1999. Final Report*, Warsaw: OSCE.

——(2004) *Russian Federation. Elections to the State Duma, 7 December 2003. OSCE/ODIHR Election Observation Mission Report*, Warsaw: OSCE. Online. Available HTTP in English: <http://www.osce.org/documents/odihr/2004/01/1947_en.pdf> (accessed 1 July 2004).

Rantanen, T. (2002) *The Global and the National. Media and Communication in Post-Communist Russia*, Lanham, MD: Rowman & Littlefield.

Rose, R. and Munro, N. (2002) *Elections without Order. Russia's Challenge to Vladimir Putin*, Cambridge: Cambridge University Press.

Rose, R., Munro, N. and White, S. (2001) 'Voting in a floating party system', *Europe–Asia Studies*, 53(3): 419–43.

Rossiiskii statisticheskii ezhegodnik (2003) *Statisticheskii sbornik*, Moscow: Goskomstat Rossii.

Sedov, L. (2000) 'Rol' SMI v izbiratel'noi kampanii', *Monitoring obshchestvennogo mneniya*, 1: 32–35.

US Department of State, Office of Research (2002) 'Russians not alarmed by threats to free speech', Washington, DC: Department of State, Office of Research, Opinion Analysis M-2-02, 8 January.

White, S., Oates, S. and McAllister, I. (2005) 'Media effects and Russian elections, 1999–2000', *British Journal of Political Science*, 35(2): 191–208.

Zassoursky, I. (2001) *Rekonstruktsiya Rossii. Mass-media i politika v 90-e gody*, Moscow: Izdatel'stvo Moskovskogo Universiteta.

Zassoursky, Y. (ed.) (2001) *Sistema sredstv massovoi informatsii Rossii*, Moscow: Aspekt Press.

13 New democracies without citizens?

Mass media and democratic orientations – a four-country comparison

Katrin Voltmer and Rüdiger Schmitt-Beck

When it comes to the mass media as a democratic institution there seems to be a marked contradiction between normative prescriptions, on the one hand, and the empirical contribution of the media to the functioning of modern democracy, on the other. From a normative point of view, the media are supposed to provide citizens with information about political matters that enables them to participate in a meaningful way. They are also regarded as a 'fourth estate', serving as a control mechanism that holds governments accountable by revealing possible misconduct. However, the actual performance of the media and how they present politics to their audience is a source of rising concern among political observers and scholars alike. Political coverage is increasingly characterized by sensationalism and a general hostility towards politicians rather than by factual information and rational debate. At the same time, political cynicism and apathy among citizens is spreading alarmingly. Considering the pervasiveness of the media in everyday life, the conclusion that there is a causal link between the media's negativism and political cynicism seems to be all too obvious.

The role of the media in new democracies seems to be even more problematic. In a situation where citizens lack any lasting experience of the working of democracy and where existing agents of socialization, such as political parties, churches and political mass organizations, have lost credibility, the media's performance might be of crucial importance in shaping the way in which citizens think about the new political regime. However, here, as in Western countries, the quality of political coverage seems to fall short of the normative claims. Frequent accusations include opinionated reporting, rapid 'tabloidization' and aggressive adversarialism. Thus, Bennett concludes that 'it turns out that what sustains successful revolutions, whether the armed or the velvet variety, is the same thing that can discourage the subsequent formation of stable democratic institutions. Open political communication following regime change can take on a noisy quality that confuses newcomers to democracy' (1998: 201). So, do new democracies find themselves in the paradoxical situation where 'government by the people' has been introduced without an active and supportive citizenry (Entman 1989)?

So far, the effects of mass communication on the development of democratic orientations of citizens in new democracies have not been tested empirically. This chapter aims to fill this gap. The analyses presented here are based on representative survey data from four new democracies: Bulgaria, Hungary, Chile and Uruguay.[1] These represent two different contexts of democratization – the two Eastern European countries emerging from communist rule, the two South American from a history of military dictatorship. We aim to find out whether the media matter for the emergence of democratic orientations – and, if so, in which way, and whether these effects differ according to the specific historical and institutional background in which political communication takes place.

We shall start our discussion with a brief overview of the political role of the media in the four political systems before and after these countries embarked on transition to democracy. We then examine the literature on the effects of the media on democratic orientations that have evolved from the 'media malaise' hypothesis. Finally, we will present our empirical results and discuss the implications these might have for political communication in new democracies.

Media and media policy in transitions to democracy

The history of the twentieth century has shown that transitions to democracy occur in waves – countries that share particular regional and/or structural similarities experience the breakdown of the old regime within a relatively confined period of time. According to Huntington's (1991) classification, the four countries in our sample belong to the third wave of democratization, which includes transitions from authoritarian rule in Southern Europe and Latin America as well as the demise of communist regimes in Eastern Europe in the late 1980s. Others argue that the transitions towards democracy in the former Soviet bloc constitute a distinct fourth wave of democratization (Beyme 1994; Brown 2000; McFaul 2002). Unlike transitions from military dictatorships, post-communist democracies have to tackle both political and economic transformation, which poses particular challenges to institution-building and long-term consolidation (Linz and Stepan 1996; Offe 1991).

The distinct nature of third- and fourth-wave democracies is also reflected in the different media–state relationships and the resulting conflicts over the regulation of the media, especially television, after the breakdown of the old regime. Although both types of autocratic regime imposed strict censorship on public communication, the predominance of ideology in communist regimes assigned the media a key role in the mobilization and indoctrination of the population. Hence, the media and all related industries were under direct control of the state and the ruling party. In contrast, the military dictatorships in Latin America were not devoted to a particular ideology, save the occasional use of anti-communist rhetoric. The preferred strategy to secure power was the depoliticization and acquiescence of the population rather than mass mobilization. Consequently, the media were far less politicized. On the contrary, television schedules were, and still are, dominated by cheap entertainment imports from the United States. This trend was further accelerated by a free-market approach to media regulation. The Chilean government under Pinochet was particularly active in promoting the privatization and commercialization of television (Tironi and Sunkel 2000).

It therefore comes as no surprise that the transformation of media–state relationships was a much more controversial process in fourth-wave democracies than in their third-wave counterparts. As a matter of fact, broadcast regulation became one of the most disputed policy fields in post-communist countries. Evidently, the new political leaders were not prepared to give up control over television, while the broadcast media were determined to fight for their independence from government interference. The resulting conflicts between governments and former state television companies have been dubbed 'media wars', indicating the vehemence of the controversy. In Hungary, the struggle over broadcast regulation triggered a constitutional crisis and it took five years of negotiations before parliament was finally able to agree on a new broadcasting law in 1996 (Gergely 1997). The conflict even led to mass protests when in November 1993 some 10,000 people took to the streets in Budapest after the government took a critical news programme off the air (Szilagyi 1996). In Bulgaria the 'media war' included several unsuccessful attempts to enact new legislation, and even the present compromise was subjected to revision immediately after it was passed in 1999 (Tzankoff 2002).

The role of the printed press was less disputed. In response to Hungary's rapidly growing consumer market, international media tycoons acquired large parts of the press, causing widespread concern about ownership concentration and cultural identity (Splichal 1994). In economically less successful countries like Bulgaria, the press is still highly dependent on the state for subsidies in order to survive in the marketplace. Western media companies also introduced a type of newspaper that was unknown under communist rule: the tabloid. Tabloids are especially successful in Bulgaria, but also account for about one-quarter of sales in Hungary (Gulyas 1998). Unlike the tabloids found, for example, in the United Kingdom, the popular press in Eastern Europe carries considerable amounts of political information, albeit in a sensational, polarizing and often over-simplistic style (Tzankoff 2002).

A somewhat different picture arises when we turn to the post-authoritarian countries in South America. Since commercialization of the media had taken place under the old regime, the structure of the media remained largely unchanged after transition to democracy. Consequently, the devastating conflicts over media regulation, which dominated the transformation of the media in post-communist countries, could be avoided. However, this is not to say that Latin American media today are free from state intervention. Threats against critical media and negotiated news coverage remain a recurrent problem. Further, some authors argue that the excessive commercialization of the media in Latin America's new democracies constitutes a severe obstacle to institution-building and successful consolidation (Skidmore 1993; Waisbord 1995). As a heritage of the depoliticized public sphere under dictatorship, political information is largely marginalized in today's television programming, and even news programmes devote a good deal of time to non-political topics. There is also a growing media obsession with political scandals and corruption, which according to Waisbord (1995: 221) reflects an alarming 'consolidation of a muckraking ethos' among journalists.

What are the implications of the different trajectories of transition to democracy in post-communist and post-autocratic countries for the media's impact on the democratic orientations of their audience? As Gunther and Mughan (2000) maintain, the role of the media in new democracies and their potential to affect public opinion are to a large extent dependent on the macro-structures in which they operate. We therefore assume stronger media influences in post-communist democracies for two reasons. The first relates to the traditionally high degree of politicization in these countries and the larger amount of political information available to ordinary citizens. The controversial re-organization of media–state relationships might also have contributed to a higher awareness of democratic values, such as press freedom. The second reason relates to our assumption that the complexity of system transformation, which involved both political and economic changes, resulted in an extraordinarily high level of uncertainty among citizens about the future course of their personal lives under the profoundly changed circumstances. Bulgarians in particular have suffered a dramatic economic decline and political instability, whereas in Hungary, where economic reforms had already been launched under the old regime, transition was less disruptive. According to media dependency theory (Ball-Rokeach and DeFleur 1976), the likelihood of media messages altering individual attitudes and behaviour increases the more a person relies on the media for orientation. This dependency is especially high in periods of rapid social change, erosion of values and economic insecurity. We therefore expect stronger media effects in Bulgaria and Hungary than in the two Latin American countries. Whether these effects are beneficial or detrimental for a democratic political culture remains to be seen. The discussion in the next section will provide the theoretical background to enable us to answer this question.

The political impact of the media: 'malaise' or 'mobilization'?

The question as to whether the media promote a democratic political culture of civic orientations (Almond and Verba 1963) or, rather, tend to undermine trust and political involvement is not confined to new democracies. The debate has a long tradition in both communication studies and political science, especially in the US. It was as early as 1976 that Robinson coined the term 'video malaise' to capture the detrimental effects of the media. Recently, Patterson (1998) claimed the media's portrayal of political processes as horse races and game shows creates a distorted image of politics that nurtures cynicism. Putnam (2000) considers the media to be at least in part responsible for the corrosion of social capital as they foster individualism and the tendency to withdraw from public life. However, when it comes to empirical analysis, the existing literature provides much less unequivocal evidence than these assertions suggest – and no studies have explored the relationship between the media and civic attitudes in new democracies.

The aforementioned study by Robinson (1976) suggested a negative link between political coverage and various types of democratic orientations. Based on laboratory experiments and representative surveys, he found that people who rely mainly on television for political information reveal significantly lower levels of internal efficacy (denoting an individual's capability to influence the political process) and trust in political institutions than those whose media diet is more varied. Cappella and Jamieson (1997) made similar observations. Using an experimental research design, they systematically manipulated the format in which political information is presented. They found that media frames that depict politics as a tactical power game have significant negative effects on individual political competence and on trust in political actors.

However, the 'malaise' hypothesis has not remained unchallenged. Proponents of a 'mobilization' theory assert that the media has positive effects on citizens' cognitive mobilization and political involvement. In a study based on British survey data, Newton (1999) scrutinizes the empirical evidence for 'media malaise' and 'media mobilization' – and his results largely support the latter. Following the news, whether on television or in newspapers, increases the political knowledge of the audience and encourages participation, but has no effects or only weak, negative ones on orientations towards the political system. Norris (2000) reports similar results for a wide range of Western democracies. She assumes a 'virtuous circle' at work, arguing that media information stimulates the motivation to participate in the political process, which in turn increases the appetite for more information. However, no similar circle resulting in negative reinforcement among the 'inactives' can be found.

What is the reason for the contradictory results presented in the literature? Evidently, researchers have looked at different things and thus obtained different results. In particular, as a thorough review of the field reveals (Wolling 1999), students of 'media malaise' and 'media mobilization' have focused on a wide range of different dependent variables – including internal and external efficacy, participation, knowledge, legitimacy of democracy, satisfaction with government and evaluation of candidates. However, it is plausible to assume that the impact of the media differs depending on whether cognitive, attitudinal or behavioural aspects are involved. In fact, it turns out that the 'malaise' hypothesis has mainly been proposed with reference to attitudes towards politicians and political institutions, such as political parties, government or democracy in general. The relationship between media exposure and these orientations is supposed to be a negative one due to the negativistic and superficial way in which politics is portrayed in the news media. In contrast, the 'mobilization' hypothesis is concerned with individuals' self-perceptions of their own role as citizens, including cognitive competence and political involvement. This perspective emphasizes the importance of information for mass participation. Rather than blaming the media for trivializing politics, supporters of the 'mobilization' hypothesis argue that the media provide an opportunity for 'low salience learning' (Neuman 1986: 132) that enables virtually all citizens to get involved in politics, even those who due to socio-economic disadvantages would otherwise stay away.

When it comes to the independent variable, scholars disagree on whether it is the content or the channel of media messages that is responsible for the effects observed – although this distinction is rarely spelled out systematically (Newton 1999). The distinction between newspapers and television draws on the channel quality of different types of media. Positive effects are usually attributed to the print media that may require a more active attempt at information processing, whereas television's heavy reliance on visuals is thought to discourage analytical thinking (although the emotional impact of pictures might mobilize political action, at least in the short run). A further disadvantage of television news is that it is embedded in a predominantly entertainment context that reduces political information to an interruption between the 'real' programmes (Robinson and Levy 1986). This is particularly the case in highly commercialized broadcasting systems. The content dimension, in contrast, refers to the substance and quality of the information conveyed by the media. In Western media systems there is a clear distinction between public service television and broadsheets that carry a large amount of political information including in-depth analysis and background information, and the tabloid press and commercial television that provide only rather superficial information in a colloquial linguistic style and increasingly in a format borrowed from entertainment programmes.

Overall, the existing empirical literature can be said to provide fairly consistent evidence for the 'mobilization' hypothesis, whereas support for the 'malaise' hypothesis is mixed at best. However, all these studies have been conducted in the context of established Western democracies, so it remains an open question whether the same pattern will appear in new democracies. On the one hand, it can be argued that citizens in new democracies lack a consistent history of experiences to support the belief that, in the long run, democratic institutions do work in spite of occasional failures such as scandals or economic decline. The lack of first-hand experience might make citizens in new democracies more vulnerable to the negativistic and adversarial style of political reporting than has been found in established democracies. On the other hand, one can plausibly assume that independent – or largely independent – media provide more meaningful information and a larger range of different viewpoints than the propaganda that media citizens have been exposed to before, which should enable them to improve their cognitive competence and get actively involved in politics. Further, the role of particular types of media remains uncertain. Public service broadcasting, where it exists in new democracies, may be discredited by its past as state television and its role as the mouthpiece of the government. Thus, it might be less effective in promoting democratic attitudes than its West European counterparts, most of which are better able to preserve their political independence in order to serve the public interest.

Research design and data

The data used for this study are representative national samples that were collected in the context of recent elections. The data set includes the 1996 Bulgarian presidential election (N = 1,216), the 1998 Hungarian parliamentary election (N = 1,500), the 1993 Chilean presidential election (N = 1,305) and the 1994 parliamentary election in Uruguay (N = 1,005). The same questionnaire was used in all countries to ensure comparability. Minor deviations are confined to national particularities or additional questions. The wide range of variables included in the surveys allows us to test the 'malaise' and 'mobilization' hypotheses simultaneously, thereby avoiding the shortcomings of much of the existing literature in the 'media malaise' tradition.

As *dependent* variables we chose four variables: two capturing each of the competing assumptions about the relationship between the news media and democratic orientations (for question wording and details of operationalization see Appendix pages 244–5). The two variables that relate to the 'mobilization' hypothesis are 'political knowledge' and 'political participation'. Knowledge is an indicator of an individual's cognitive competence on political matters, which is an important precondition for effective democratic citizenship. We measured respondents' knowledge about politics by questions testing their ability to correctly identify key political officeholders. Our participation variable measured the respondents' willingness to take part actively in the political process by focusing on voting and various other activities related to elections. Electoral and election-related participation is by far the most widespread form of participation, even in established democracies (Milbrath and Goel 1977). Its relevance derives from the fact that elections are the key institutional difference that distinguishes democracy from authoritarian rule, endowing citizens with the right to choose their political leaders themselves in free and fair elections.

The next two dependent variables refer to the assumptions of the 'malaise' hypothesis and comprise various orientations towards the political system and its normative foundations. First, we constructed a variable that captures a respondent's 'evaluation of political parties'. It is important to note that our measure does not refer to electoral support for a particular party but to the general legitimacy of parties and party conflicts as an institutionalized part of democratic politics. After decades of dictatorship or one-party rule, with political communication characterized by the display of false harmony among political elites, many citizens in new democracies might experience party conflict as a new, and often disturbing, element of political life. Political parties are also the main targets of journalistic criticism in coverage of day-to-day politics. Finally, we consider the respondents' 'support for democracy'. Following Easton's (1975) concept of 'diffuse support', our measurement refers to the general evaluation of the abstract notion of a democratic political order, regardless of possible deficiencies of the particular way in which democratic rule has been implemented in one's society, the present state of the economy or other performance-related criteria. The points of reference are the norms and values of democracy as opposed to non-democratic forms of government.

Moving on to the *independent* variables, we measured 'exposure' to media messages by classifying the particular media to which the respondents are exposed to according to the amount and quality of political information they provide. In contrast to most large-scale surveys, which generally capture media exposure in very general terms, our respondents were asked to provide the name of the newspaper and television programme they most frequently turn to for political information. For each country, we consulted several national experts[2] to assist us in the precise classification of individual media outlets. Newspapers were categorized into the three well-known categories of quality, middle-market and tabloids, reflecting different degrees of information quality. Most of the newspapers in our sample adhere to some kind of partisan leaning. However, insofar as this concerns only their stances on current issues, we do not assume that this will affect the more general democratic orientations of their readers. Only in those cases where a paper's dominant position is linked to the transformation conflict itself, either by promoting democratic change or by favouring the *status quo ante,* do we take political leaning into account. This applies to Bulgaria, where *Duma* stood close to the Bulgarian Socialist Party and represents nostalgic support for the old regime, while at the other end of the political spectrum *Demokratia* promoted pro-democracy ideas. Similarly, in Chile, the daily *La Epoca* played an important role during the democratization process, while *El Mercurio* continued to sympathize with Pinochet's autocratic system.[3]

With regard to television, the distinction between public and private broadcasters can be expected to be of some consequence to the quality of political information. Even in post-communist countries, public service channels are, in spite of their state-television past, better able to provide comprehensive and substantive political coverage than their commercial counterparts. Due to a higher dependence on audience and advertising markets, commercial television is usually more entertainment-oriented and devotes less resources and airtime to political information. As mentioned above, this is particularly true in Chile. A further particularity of Chile is that a number of television channels are operated by universities rather than the state or private investors. In addition, in some countries we find private broadcasters operating at a local or regional level in a legal 'grey zone': for example in Bulgaria, where broadcasting has not yet been formally opened up for private investors.

When looking at the level of media exposure (numbers not presented here), one general pattern appears across all four countries: only a small proportion of citizens turns to the printed press for political news. Overall, only half or fewer of the respondents turn to the daily press for political information. Newspaper readership is particularly low in Uruguay, where only about one-third of respondents obtain their political information from the printed press. In most countries the most popular type of print medium is the middle-market press, comprising mainly local or regional titles, followed by highbrow outlets. The relevance of tabloids varies considerably. In Bulgaria readership of tabloids exceeds that of any other type of newspaper. Television, by contrast, reaches far more citizens. In all countries large majorities of citizens – three out of four in Bulgaria and even more in the other countries – are exposed to at least some political information through television. Thus, once again, television appears to be an almost all-pervasive medium, which for a significant number of citizens constitutes the only source of information about current affairs. However, the role of public service broadcasting differs greatly across countries. In Uruguay, it plays only a marginal role, whereas in the other three countries it is the dominant source of information.

Media exposure and democratic orientations – a multivariate analysis

In the following section we report findings from multiple regression analyses that we used to examine the effects of media exposure on democratic orientations in each of the four countries. This technique enables us to identify the total impact of media exposure as well as the specific contribution of each medium in shaping our respondents' democratic orientations, while holding other possible influences constant. It has to be kept in mind that the capability of this kind of correlational analysis to clearly establish causal relationships is limited. Only long-term observations can unequivocally identify causes and effects. Nevertheless, for logical and theoretical reasons we believe that the causal relationships presented in our regression models reflect the predominant processes involved in linking media exposure and democratic orientations.

The most obvious factors that need to be taken into account as potential alternative sources of influence – and thus included as control variables – are socio-demographic characteristics such as age, gender and formal education. These variables stand for different experiences of socialization and world views that may shape an individual's political attitudes independently of media exposure. Furthermore, we take into account whether a respondent has favoured the winning or losing side in the previous election. It can be assumed that supporters of the governing parties are more favourably disposed not only to the current government, but also to the more general aspects of governance, while supporters of the minority parties feel more alienated from politics. This is again of particular relevance in new democracies where citizens cannot look back to a sufficiently long history of alternations between government and opposition for reassurance that in the long run their own party might have a reasonable chance of getting into power (Wessels and Klingemann 1998). Finally, it can be assumed that, particularly in new democracies, a citizen's satisfaction with democratic rule depends to some extent on the ability of the new government to ensure a sufficient level of economic wealth. We therefore augmented the models predicting respondents' diffuse support for democracy with their evaluation of the state of the national economy as well as their personal economic situation.

Table 13.1 presents the results of a series of regression models that are designed to represent the pattern of media influences in each of the four countries. The models were run blockwise with the full set of control variables entering the model first, followed by the media variables. The increase of the overall explanatory power of the models (incremental R^2) after all control variables have been taken into account can be interpreted as a measure of the total impact of media exposure on the respective dependent variables. The individual β-coefficients that are computed for each type of media in each country reveal more fine-grained patterns of influence, testing the role of different media types with regard to democratic orientations. The positive or negative signs of these coefficients indicate whether these effects are beneficial or detrimental to democratic orientations, supporting either the 'malaise' or the 'mobilization' hypothesis.

Table 13.1 Media exposure and democratic orientations

		Political knowledge	Political participation	Evaluation of political parties	Support for democracy
Uruguay					
Press	Quality (*El Observador*)	0.08*	0.03	−0.03	−0.05
	Middle market	0.11**	0.25**	0.05	−0.01
	Tabloid (*El Diario*)	0.04	−0.03	0.02	0.03
TV news	Public	0.00	0.16**	−0.06	0.05
	Private (national)	0.07†	−0.06	0.06	−0.00
	Private (local)	−0.08*	−0.02	0.10*	0.01
Adjusted R^2	Full model	0.134**	0.093**	0.055**	0.007†
	Increment media	0.031**	0.091**	0.007†	−0.005
(*N*)		(662)	(417)	(648)	(555)
Chile					
Press	*El Mercurio*	0.16**	0.06†	0.03	−0.09*
	La Epoca	−0.01	0.08*	0.06	0.03
	Middle market	0.12**	0.04	0.06†	−0.02
	Tabloid (*La Cuarta*)	0.02	0.09**	0.00	0.03
TV news	Public	0.05†	0.06†	0.10**	0.08*
	University	0.10**	−0.07*	0.06†	0.00
	Private	0.02	−0.01	0.06†	−0.02
Adjusted R^2	Full model	0.289**	0.054**	0.082**	0.067**
	Increment media	0.058**	0.024**	0.024**	0.008*
(*N*)		(897)	(897)	(892)	(890)
Hungary					
Press	Quality	0.20**	0.15**	0.10**	0.05†
	Middle market	0.09**	0.15**	0.11**	0.01
	Tabloid	0.02	0.03	0.04	0.05*
TV news	Public	0.15**	0.18**	0.25**	0.19**
	Private (national)	0.10*	0.10**	0.21**	0.09**
	Private (local/ regional)	0.02	−0.01	0.10**	0.08**
Adjusted R^2	Full model	0.216**	0.150**	0.177**	0.155**
	Increment media	0.076**	0.087**	0.118**	0.037**
(*N*)		(1441)	(1431)	(1397)	(1405)
Bulgaria					
Press	*Demokratia*	0.07**	0.09**	0.09**	0.09**
	Duma	0.05†	0.24**	0.10**	0.06*
	Quality	0.17**	−0.04	0.07*	0.04
	Middle market	0.05†	−0.05†	0.07**	0.05†
TV news	Tabloid	0.12**	−0.02	0.11**	0.07*
	Public	0.27**	0.19**	0.25**	0.03
	Private (local/ regional)	0.08**	0.00	0.04	0.02
Adjusted R^2	Full model	0.303**	0.148**	0.156**	0.220**
	Increment media	0.168**	0.123**	0.131**	0.018**
(*N*)		(1174)	(1175)	(1162)	(1155)

Notes
** $p < 0.01$; * $p < 0.05$; † $p < 0.10$.
Entries are standardized β-coefficients; coefficients for control variables not shown.

Our first hypothesis maintained that, according to media dependency theory, media effects should be stronger in countries where the transition to democracy has affected more aspects of the socio-political structure, resulting in a stronger sense of insecurity on the individual level. This assumption is clearly supported by the data. The incremental R^2 is highest by far in Bulgaria, where the transformation process was highly problematic and frequently put back by political and economic crises. A similar pattern can be found in Hungary, the other post-communist country, albeit at a lower level. The overall strength of media effects in the two Latin American countries is much lower. Here, regime change was confined to political changes and did not trigger an economic crisis. In addition, in both countries a vivid democratic past is still part of the collective memory, interrupted only by comparatively short periods of military dictatorship (16 years in Chile and 11 in Uruguay).

Our second hypothesis was that media effects are not uniform. Rather, the degree to which political orientations are vulnerable to media influences differs depending on the kinds of orientations involved. Across all four countries, orientations related to an individual's own role as a democratic citizen tend to be more affected by the media than attitudes to the political system, especially those relating very generally to the notion of democracy as such. Citizens' cognitive competence in political matters and their willingness to take part in electoral politics are significantly shaped by their pattern of media use. In contrast, support for democracy is hardly affected by the media – as indicated by small R^2 increments. This is certainly good news, as it shows that beliefs in democracy are rooted in fairly stable value preferences rather than the day-to-day reporting of current political events. The evaluation of political parties is clearly more sensitive to the media, particularly in the two post-communist countries. In Chile and Uruguay, in contrast, political parties were not eliminated altogether during the dictatorship, so parties were able to preserve both their organizational structure and the loyalty of their core supporters. Hence, attitudes to political parties are considerably less affected by media coverage.

Our discussion of the empirical findings so far suggests that the mass media are indeed important for citizens' orientations in new democracies. However, the crucial question is whether this influence is beneficial or detrimental, in other words whether the name of the game is 'malaise' or 'mobilization'. The β-coefficients displayed in Table 13.1 indicate that – with only few exceptions, most of which hardly reach conventional levels of statistical significance – the direction of media effects tends to be positive. Only a few media seem to affect democratic orientations negatively. Most noteworthy, Chilean readers of *El Mercurio*, a right-wing outlet with persisting sympathies for the old regime, express less support for democracy, although at the same time they appear particularly knowledgeable about political affairs. Similarly, university television in Chile seems to demobilize citizens in elections. In Uruguay, watching local commercial television news apparently decreases rather than increases citizens' political knowledge. However, while these negative effects are statistically significant they are rather small, with β-coefficients below -0.10.

In contrast to the widespread belief that television has a superior capacity of moving public opinion, empirically there is less support for such a clear-cut distinction between the printed press and broadcasting. Only in the two post-communist countries does television, in particular public service broadcasting, play a significant role in supporting democratic orientations; in the South American countries the picture is more ambiguous. In Bulgaria and Hungary exposure to public television increases political knowledge, mobilizes people into electoral action and even contributes to a positive evaluation of political parties. Most notably, it has strong positive effects ($\beta = 0.19$) on support for democracy in Hungary, the scene of a fierce 'media war'.

In our theoretical discussion we further distinguished between public and commercial broadcasters, arguing that the latter provide lower quality of information and therefore have less beneficial effects on the development of democratic orientations. This assumption can be confirmed by our data. Exposure to the news on private channels has some positive effects, but there is no clear pattern across the countries. Again, Hungary is an exception: both national and regional private television have positive effects on all four dependent variables, but in all instances these effects are weaker than the ones found for public service broadcasting.

Turning to the role of the printed press in promoting democracy, we find that, as with television, the quality of information provided makes a difference. In the two post-communist countries, due to the generally stronger relationship between media usage and democratic orientations, clearer patterns emerge than in the two Latin American countries. Reading highbrow papers – and also middle-market ones, but to a somewhat lesser degree – significantly increases political knowledge and stimulates political participation. At the same time, orientations towards the political system generally appear to be less affected by exposure to newspapers. The pattern in the two post-communist countries is again somewhat different in that exposure to the daily press tends to increase favourable evaluation of political parties.

A surprising finding concerns the effects of the tabloid press. This type of paper is often treated with suspicion because its sensationalist and emotional style is feared to have detrimental consequences for the democratic attitudes of their readers. Our results do not justify such worries. They suggest that consumption of tabloids is rarely related to citizens' political orientations in either a negative or a positive direction. This finding is very much in line with research from established democracies, including Britain with its notorious tabloid press, suggesting the political irrelevance of this type of paper (Brynin and Newton 2003; Schmitt-Beck 1998). We did, however, find one exception: the Bulgarian tabloid press has a significant effect on political knowledge, evaluation of political parties and even support for democracy – and it is a positive one. A possible explanation could be that, unlike many Western tabloids, these papers consist for the most part of political information rather than entertainment and celebrity gossip, albeit packaged in the usual tabloid style. The Bulgarian tabloid press can be regarded as a good example for the benefits of 'low salience learning', providing easy access to politics for about one-fifth of the Bulgarian population.

Conclusions

In this chapter we have sought to explore the role of the media in the development of political culture in new democracies, using survey data from four countries. Our findings alleviate worries that the media might undermine the development of a healthy public climate. With only minor exceptions, the overwhelming majority of our findings support the 'mobilization' hypothesis, which posits positive media effects on individuals' own role as democratic citizens. In particular, the media seem to play an important part in enhancing political knowledge and encouraging electoral participation. What is more, in spite of their critical, often adversarial, coverage, the media seem to foster positive attitudes towards political parties and – to a lesser extent – the notion of democracy itself. The allegation that the media are responsible for citizens' political apathy and cynicism does not find empirical support in our data. This is not to deny that there is widespread disenchantment and alienation among citizens in new democracies, but this is obviously not caused by the media.

Although the pattern of media effects is very similar across countries, we find clear differences between the countries in the extent to which the media have an impact on citizens' orientations. While the media in Chile and Uruguay exert only moderate to weak influence, citizens in the post-communist countries of Bulgaria and Hungary appear to be highly susceptible to media messages. These differences seem to suggest that the extent to which the media are capable of shaping political orientations is not a constant but depends on situational circumstances. The dramatic changes involved in transition from communist rule, affecting both the political and economic order, create an increased need for orientation on the part of citizens. Here, in contrast to the two Latin American countries, the weakness of the intermediary system of political parties and associations leaves the media as the main agents of political socialization. As Dalton concludes in a recent review of the state of comparative political behaviour research, '[p]erhaps the most important lesson that has been learned so far is that the political legacy of Communist regimes for citizen politics is much different from the legacy of right-wing authoritarian regimes' (Dalton 2000: 934). Our findings confirm this diagnosis with regard to the role of the media in these countries' political cultures.

Our findings leave us with a puzzle as to the normative expectations about the media's role for the functioning of democracy and their actual performance. Fierce battles about media policies have been fought in the post-communist countries. And most of the media included in our analysis have frequently been accused of deviating from professional norms in various ways. And yet, exposure to exactly this kind of political coverage evidently contributes to a strengthening of an audience's democratic orientations. How could this apparent paradox be explained? It seems that the media are frequently criticized for fulfilling what is actually their prime function: providing accessible information and holding those in power accountable. What critics might regard superficial and inadequate coverage could in fact be 'low cost' information that requires only little time and effort to be processed and integrated into existing cognitive structures. Even though, from an expert's point of view, this information might lack analytical depth and precision in detail, it equips citizens with sufficient knowledge to be mobilized to become engaged in public life. Further, it is difficult to draw the line exactly between (democratically desirable) watchdog journalism and (harmful) muck-raking journalism. The present study cannot give an answer to this problem. However, our data suggest that the cognitive processes of de-coding and re-constructing media messages on the part of audience members are more complex than 'media malaise' theorists presume. The fact that negative and critical reporting is not mirrored in negative and critical evaluations indicates that media effects are filtered through complex processes of individual and social interpretations. It might well be the case, therefore, that after years of oppression of freedom of expression and freedom of the press citizens value open and critical debate as an indicator of the functioning of their new democracy rather than its failure.

However, it has to be noted that some of the media that are associated with the observed positive effects reach only relatively small audiences, while the tabloid press and commercial television that do not contribute greatly to democratic culture are rapidly gaining popularity. Hence, the availability and quality of 'mobilizing information' (Lemert 1981) is still of concern for the viability of democracy, both old and new.

Notes

1 The data were collected in the context of the Cross National Election Project (CNEP2). Principal investigators are Richard Gunther, Jose Ramon Montero and Hans-Jürgen Puhle. The project is funded by the Mershon Centre, Ohio State University, USA, and the Volkswagen Stiftung, Germany. An extended version of this analysis will be published in Gunther, Montero and Puhle, *Political Intermediation in Old and New Democracies* (forthcoming). We thank the principal investigators of the project for the permission to report on selected findings in the context of the present volume.

2 We are greatly indebted to the following colleagues for sharing their expertise

with us: Georgi Karasimeonov and Plamen Georgiev for Bulgaria; Tamas Fricz, Csilla Machos and Gabor Toka for Hungary; Eugenio Tironi, Markus Moke and Hans Blomeier for Chile; and Pablo Mieres and Christoph Wagner for Uruguay.
3 It has to be kept in mind that the description of the media given here relates to the time when the surveys were carried out. The situation might have changed in the meantime: for example, the papers *Demokratia* and *La Epoca* have now disappeared from the market.

References

Almond, G.A. and Verba, S. (1963) *The Civic Culture. Political Attitudes and Democracy in Five Nations*, Princeton, NJ: Princeton University Press.

Ball-Rokeach, S.J. and DeFleur, M.L. (1976) 'A dependency model of mass-media effects', *Communication Research*, 3: 3–21.

Bennett, W.L. (1998) 'The media and democratic development. The social basis of political communication', in P.H. O'Neil (ed.) *Communicating Democracy. The Media and Political Transitions*, Boulder, CO: Lynne Rienner, 195–207.

Beyme, K. von (1994) *Systemwechsel in Osteuropa*, Frankfurt: Suhrkamp.

Brown, A. (2000) 'Transnational influences in the transition from Communism', *Post Soviet Affairs*, 16: 177–200.

Brynin, M. and Newton, K. (2003) 'The national press and voting turnout. British General Elections of 1992 and 1997', *Political Communication*, 20: 59–77.

Capella, J.N. and Jamieson, K.H. (1997) *Spiral of Cynicism. The Press and the Public Good*, New York: Oxford University Press.

Dalton, R.J. (2000) 'Citizen attitudes and political behavior', *Comparative Political Studies*, 33: 912–940.

Easton, D. (1975) 'A re-assessment of the concept of political support', *British Journal of Political Science*, 21: 285–313.

Entman, R.M. (1989) *Democracy without Citizens. Media and the Decay of American Politics*, New York: Oxford University Press.

Gergely, I. (1997) *Understanding the Media in Hungary*, Düsseldorf: The European Institute for the Media.

Gulyas, A. (1998) 'Tabloid newspapers in post-communist Hungary', *Javnost/The Public*, 5(3): 65–77.

Gunther, R. and Mughan, A. (2000) 'The media in democratic and nondemocratic regimes. A multilevel perspective', in R. Gunther and A. Mughan (eds) *Democracy and the Media. A comparative perspective*, Cambridge: Cambridge University Press, 1–27.

Huntington, S.P. (1991) *The Third Wave. Democratization in the Late Twentieth Century*, Norman, OK: University of Oklahoma Press.

Lemert, J.B. (1981) *Does Mass Communication Change Public Opinion After All? A New Approach to Effects Analysis*, Chicago, IL: Nelson-Hall.

Linz, J. and Stepan, A. (1996) *Problems of Democratic Transition and Consolidation. South Europe, South America, and Post-communist Europe*, Baltimore, MD: Johns Hopkins University Press.

McFaul, M. (2002) 'The fourth wave of democracy and dictatorship. Noncooperative transitions in the postcommunist world', *World Politics*, 54: 212–44.

Milbrath, L.W. and Goel, M.L. (1977) *Political Participation. How and Why Do People Get Involved in Politics?* 2nd edn, Lanham, MD: University Press of America.

244 *Katrin Voltmer and Rüdiger Schmitt-Beck*

Neuman, R.W. (1986) *The Paradox of Mass Politics. Knowledge and Opinion in the American Electorate*, Cambridge, MA: Harvard University Press.

Newton, K. (1999) 'Mass media effects. Mobilization or media malaise?' *British Journal of Political Science*, 29: 577–600.

Norris, P. (2000) *A Virtuous Circle. Political Communications in Post-industrial Democracies*, Cambridge: Cambridge University Press.

Offe, C. (1991) 'Das Dilemma der Gleichzeitigkeit. Demokratisierung und Marktwirtschaft in Osteuropa', *Merkur*, 45: 279–92.

Patterson, T.E. (1998) 'Time and news. The media's limitations as an instrument of democracy', *International Political Science Review*, 19(1): 55–67.

Putnam, R.D. (2000) *Bowling Alone. The Collapse and Revival of American Community*, New York: Simon and Schuster.

Robinson, J.P. and Levy, M.R. (1986) *The Main Source. Learning from Television News*, Beverly Hills, CA: Sage.

Robinson, M.J. (1976) 'Public affairs television and the growth of political malaise. The case of "The Selling of the Pentagon"', *American Political Science Review*, 70: 409–32.

Schmitt-Beck, R. (1998) 'Of readers, viewers, and cat-dogs', in J.W. van Deth (ed.), *Comparative Politics. The Problem of Equivalence*, London: Routledge, 222–46.

Skidmore, T.E. (ed.) (1993) *Television, Politics and the Transition to Democracy in Latin America*, Baltimore, MD: Johns Hopkins University Press.

Splichal, S. (1994) *Media Beyond Socialism. Theory and Practice in East-Central Europe*, Boulder, CO: Westview.

Szilagyi, Z. (1996) 'Hungary has a broadcast media law, at last', *Transition*, 19 April: 22–5.

Tironi, E. and Sunkel, G. (2000) 'The modernization of communication and democratization. The media in the transition to democracy in Chile', in R. Gunther and A. Mughan (eds) *Democracy and the Media. A comparative perspective*, Cambridge: Cambridge University Press, 165–94.

Tzankoff, M. (2002) *Der Transformationsprozess in Bulgarien und die Entwicklung der postsozialistischen Medienlandschaft*, Hamburg: Lit Verlag.

Waisbord, S.R. (1995) 'The mass media and consolidation of democracy in South America', *Research in Political Sociology*, 7: 207–27.

Wessels, B. and Klingemann, H.-D. (1998) 'Transformation and the prerequisites of democratic opposition in Central and Eastern Europe', in S.H. Barnes and J. Simon (eds) *The Postcommunist Citizen*, Budapest: Erasmus Foundation, 1–34.

Wolling, J. (1999) *Politikverdrossenheit durch Massenmedien? Der Einfluss der Medien auf die Einstellungen der Bürger zur Politik*, Opladen: Westdeutscher Verlag.

Appendix

Dependent variables

Political knowledge: additive index, based on count of correctly answered knowledge questions regarding names of political office-holders (chairpersons of trade unions or interest organizations, ministers, chairpersons of national parliaments, and others).

Political participation: additive index, counting number of election-related activities actually performed by respondents, out of the following three: voting; attending party campaign meetings; actively participating in a party's campaign activities.

Evaluation of political parties: additive index, counting pro-party orientations out of the following list: agreement with statement 'Without parties there can be no democracy' positive evaluation of at least one party on closeness scales; party identification.

Support for democracy: in Chile and Uruguay, agreement with the statement: 'Democracy is the best system for a country like ours'. In Hungary and Bulgaria, this was an additive index, additionally including agreement with the statement: 'Democracy is preferable to any other form of government'.

Independent variables

Exposure to daily newspapers/television news: additive indices based on frequency of habitual reading of newspapers/watching of television news in days per week. Initial measurement was at the level of specific newspaper titles/channels. These were classified by information quality and editorial stance towards democratization.

14 Conclusion

Political communication between democratization and the trajectories of the past

Katrin Voltmer

Throughout this book it has been argued that if we are to understand the dynamics of transitions to democracy and the functioning and quality of the emerging institutions of the new regime we need to take the mass media as a central mediating structure into consideration. Without fair access to the media political actors – be it governments, political parties or civil society groups – would be unable to mobilize support, and elections as a democratic mechanism of allocating power would be meaningless. However, the ideal of an open 'marketplace of ideas' is difficult to achieve, and the chapters of this book, which cover a wide range of emerging democracies from around the world, demonstrate in various ways the constraints and impediments involved in the transformation of political communication.

In the introduction to this volume it has been argued that political communication emerges from the interaction between the media, politicians and citizens which entails a complex set of rules, normative expectations and routines that govern the day-to-day business of producing and disseminating messages to the wider public. Hence, democratizing political communication requires more than the transformation of media institutions and journalistic practices; it also involves a change of behaviour and orientations of political actors and citizens in this process. The aim of this book is to locate the role of the media in this web of interdependencies. The experiences of countries as different as Russia, South Africa, Chile and Taiwan – to name but a few that have been covered in this volume – reveal striking similarities with regard to the problems and challenges facing the democratization of political communication. At the same time there are also significant differences that prohibit over-generalized conclusions about the relationship between media and politics in new democracies.

What could the explanation be for the apparent similarities and differences? To begin with the similarities, all countries discussed in this volume can be subsumed in the 'third wave' of democratization and as such have to manage transition under similar historical circumstances (Huntington 1991). The most recent democracies that emerged in the aftermath of the demise of Soviet-style communism underwent extremely rapid changes that left little time for careful consideration before making decisions about the future structure of the new institutions. Everything had to be done at the same time. The obvious solution for making decisions under extreme time constraints was to adopt institutional models from the West. With regard to the media this usually meant wide-ranging privatization and commercialization not only of the printed press, but also of broadcasting. Some countries in Eastern Europe implemented public service broadcasting with some degree of independence from both the state and market competition. However, in most new democracies central parts of broadcasting remained firmly in the hands of the state. The most obvious example of this is Russia, but the same applies to numerous Latin American and Asian countries. The juxtaposition of untamed market forces and the heavy hand of the state has serious implications for the performance of the media, as it makes it difficult for balanced and thorough reporting to flourish (Splichal 1994).

Another important difference that distinguishes the recent wave of democratization from previous ones is that building the new institutions is taking place in a media-saturated environment, where television is a pervasive part of political life. From the outset the newly elected political leaders have to act in the limelight of the media, and more often than not find themselves the target of fierce public criticism. As a consequence, counter-strategies of news management and 'spin' quickly became a dominant part of the political process, propelling political communication in new democracies immediately into what has been labeled 'media democracies' (Meyer with Hinchman 2002). Oates (see Chapter 9) argues that in Russia the powerful media system inherited from the Soviet era prevents the formation of a stable party system. Elsewhere Waisbord (1995) has demonstrated that the close alliance between populist leaders and the media in Latin America works as an impediment both to the development of democratic institutions, and to their consolidation.

Apart from these similarities, the specific characteristics of the old regime are an important factor that accounts for significant differences between new democracies. Different autocratic regime types constitute specific path dependencies, resulting in particular structural and cultural conditions in the new democratic era that affects the way in which the media operate and how both political actors and audience members use the media for their own purposes. Literature on the significance of different pathways to democracy for the performance of the new regime usually distinguishes between departures from communist oligarchies, military dictatorships and one-party rule (Hollifield and Jillson 2000; Linz and Stepan 1996), each of which have dominated particular regions, namely Eastern Europe, Latin America and Southern Europe in an earlier phase of the 'third wave', and Asia and Africa respectively.

In communist regimes the media played a central role as a propaganda instrument for re-educating the masses and disseminating extensive party messages across the country. The highly politicized role made the media an indispensable part of the power structure. Needless to say, both television and the printed press were owned by the state or associated mass organizations. From this brief, and to some extent simplistic, description of the media's role under the old regime it becomes clear how complex the transition to a democratic system of political communication is. It requires restructuring the entire media system, both with regard to its relationship to the government and its economic structure.

In contrast, military dictatorships were more concerned about depoliticizing, rather than mobilizing, the masses. Accordingly, the principal communication strategy was censorship, that is keeping certain topics out of the public realm, rather than propaganda. Hence, with the exception of some core outlets that served as direct mouthpieces of the government, most media remained in private hands. This allowed the media to preserve at least some degree of independence, especially, as was the case with the majority of the media, programming was largely dominated by entertainment. So it seems that, with the demise of censorship, media transformation in post-authoritarian countries should be a relatively straightforward task. However, a persisting legacy of the past is the marginalization of politics in an overwhelmingly entertainment-oriented media. Even political coverage itself is characterized by entertainment related features, such as personalization and sensationalism.

Finally, democracies that grew out of one-party rule inherited a unique set of problems that still shape the relationship between the government and the media. One of these is a tradition of a strong state that is regarded as agent and protector of development (Clark 2000; Potter *et al.* 1997). In fact, managing economic development was – and still is – frequently used as a justification for the denial of democratic liberties such as press freedom. Another historical factor that shapes democratic politics in this group of emerging democracies is the colonial past. In many countries, especially those with deep ethnic or religious divisions, nation-building is still an unfinished project so that social integration and national unity appear as primary values above individual liberties and open debate. From its comparatively late introduction about three decades ago television has been placed in the context of these societal goals and has been used by autocratic governments to serve development and national unity. Since these problems persist after transition to democracy the media, especially broadcasting, encounter strong resistance from the side of the government to loosen control over public communication.

While this typology allows us to identify patterns of differences between groups of new democracies, it disguises a high degree of variation within groups. The duration of the old regime is an important factor that has implications for the new political order and the performance of the media, regardless of the particular pathway to democratization. If the autocratic regime was an interruption of an already existing democratic tradition then governments and the media will find it easier to negotiate rules of their relationship that are conducive to open and critical political reporting than in countries that are implementing democratic politics for the first time in their history. Partly related to the duration of the old regime is the extent to which political parties and civil society groups were able to hibernate. A situation of 'flattened landscape', where parties and candidates are forced to mobilize public support without relying on effective organizational structures is more likely to result in massive instrumentalization of the media for electoral purposes than in countries where at least parts of the intermediary system could survive. Furthermore, from the perspective of the media the economic situation of a country is of crucial importance. The existence of a substantial consumer market enables the media to draw on revenues from advertising, while dependency on subsidies from the state exposes them to political pressure that impairs their capability of independent reporting.

The chapters of this volume present cases from each of the three different pathways that are assumed to shape the pattern and quality of political communication in the subsequent democratic regime. Six chapters focus on post-communist countries and include analyses of Russia, Ukraine, Bulgaria and Hungary. Democracies that emerged from military dictatorship are the subject of four chapters and include Spain and various Latin American countries. Finally, three chapters cover the pathway from one-party rule and include Taiwan and South Africa. Since almost all chapters of this volume deal with a particular country or area the following summary aims to take a comparative perspective. Each set of actors involved in the process of political communication – the media, political actors and the audience – will be discussed across countries and pathways in order to identify similar patterns and differences.

The media

The contributions by de Smaele (Chapter 3) on Russia and Wasserman and de Beer (Chapter 4) in this volume, as well as evidence from previous research (Hankiss 1994; Paletz *et al.* 1995; Randall 1993; Skidmore 1993), suggest that more often than not transition to democracy triggers fundamental conflicts between governments and the media over the meaning and practice of a free press. Is freedom of the press in a democracy an absolute value or limited by certain higher, or competing, objectives, such as protection of social and cultural values, national security or public order? It would be wrong to dismiss these conflicts as purely instrumental, either serving as a Trojan horse to justify political interference in the operation of news organizations or as an attempt to boost circulation rates by sensationalism and muck-raking. As has been discussed in the introduction, the nature of press freedom is an equally contested issue in the philosophical and democratic theory literature. However, genuine concerns and strategic utilization of higher principles are difficult to disentangle, as is indicated by the fact that governments' references to 'democracy' or 'national interest' are obviously aimed at silencing public criticism.

In contrast, the Spanish case stands out as a unique example of consensus between the government of the young democracy and the media, which included even those outlets that over the last decades had supported Franco's regime. As Barrera and Zugasti (Chapter 2) show in their historical study of the early years of Spanish democracy, the media unanimously supported the government's democratization policy of civil liberties, reconciliation and national integrity. The authors emphasize that this consensus was based on voluntary, not imposed, collaboration and disappeared after a couple of years to give way to a pattern of government – media interaction that resembles the pattern in established democracies. Why is Spain so markedly different? One explanation is the dark shadow of the civil war, which led all participants to work toward a resolution and avoid a relapse into violent division at all costs. Yet this would also apply to South Africa; however, a similar consensus across political and media elites could not be achieved. A possible reason for the probability of conflict between governments and the media could be the particular elite constellation in the immediate post-transition period. In Spain, each of the elite groups included supporters of both sides of the political conflict. In contrast, the situation is prone to fundamental disruptions when political and media elites can be clearly identified as old and new elites. South Africa can serve as an example for this constellation as the government represents the new (black) elite whereas the media elite is still predominantly composed of the old (white) elite and therefore regarded with hostility.

An important step for the media to achieve independence from the political power holders is to adopt their own mode of selecting and framing political news. Waisbord's study of Latin American journalism (Chapter 5) and the chapter by Krasnoboka and Brants on Ukraine (Chapter 6) allow us to compare the professionalization of journalism in the aftermath of different regime types. Obviously, the communist legacy is a significant impediment to the development of independent journalism that is not paralleled by the Latin American situation. One could argue that at the time of writing Ukrainian democratic transition was still incomplete. However, studies on journalism in other post-communist countries have shown a similar lack of professionalism and exposure to political instrumentalization (O'Neil 1997; Voltmer 2000). But what would be appropriate standards to evaluate journalistic professionalism? Waisbord rightly argues that the American model of neutrality and objectivity is not universally applicable. In Latin America partisan journalism coexists with a modern, detached style of reporting. Both forms are important and, as has been argued in the introduction, are legitimate ways of establishing trust and credibility between journalists and their audience. However, in most new democracies (with the exception of a few east-central European countries) it has been impossible to implement an independent and neutral medium, similar to the public service broadcasting model, to serve as a forum for all voices of the political spectrum in order to counterbalance an otherwise fragmented and deeply divided public sphere.

Political actors

The main reason for conflicts arising between the media and political actors is the vital importance of access to audiences for surviving in a competitive political environment. In established democracies political parties and governments have adopted sophisticated methods of news management and political marketing, often referred to as 'Americanization' of political communication, in order to keep, or regain, control over the public agenda (Kavanagh 1995; Pfetsch 1998; Swanson and Mancini 1996). Numerous political parties and candidates in new democracies have been eager to apply the principles of modern political marketing or have bought the services of international political consultants. There seem to be striking similarities between the conditions under which political parties and candidates in established democracies campaign and those of their counterparts for whom competitive elections are a new experience. Coming from opposing trajectories, they both find themselves in a situation where they have to find an effective response to low levels of voter loyalty, declining membership and an overpowering media environment.

According to the assumption that the trajectories of the past affect political communication in post-transition circumstances, one would expect a higher degree of 'Americanization' where political parties have been radically suppressed under the old regime and therefore were unable to preserve at least some rudimentary organizational structures. The Russian case (see Oates, Chapter 9) seems to provide strong evidence for the argument that the lack of social ties with relevant groups of the electorate fosters a 'postmodern' style of politics with 'spin' and media manipulation being the key to electoral success. The striking victory of so-called 'broadcast parties' and their candidates in recent Russian elections may have been a success for political marketing, but not for the quality of the democratic process. However, Russia might be a special case even within the group of post-communist countries. In most east-central European countries political parties, in particular those that have their roots in the pre-communist past or in opposition movements against the former communist regime, have been fairly successful over the last 15 years in building sustainable organizational structures (Olson 1998).

Taiwan, a young democracy that emerged from decades of one-party rule, might serve as an interesting example that a weak party system does not necessarily result in a media-driven style of political communication (see Rawnsley, Chapter 8). As recent election campaigns demonstrate, the key to success here is a combination of modern marketing techniques and reliance on traditional patterns of social loyalties and clientelism. These ties cannot be effectively mobilized through mediated communication. Instead, they require grassroot canvassing and participation in local social life. Even though these practices have their downside, as they frequently involve favoritism and vote buying, they seem to ensure that politicians maintain a viable communicative link with their voters.

In contrast, in many Latin American countries political parties were to some extent able to hibernate during the years of dictatorship, in particular in Chile and Uruguay (see Espíndola, Chapter 7). Political parties in Latin America are highly efficient machines, with considerable mobilizing capacity during election time when thousands of people join the campaign trail. However, the overall pattern is again that professional campaign strategies and grassroot campaigning coexist and complement each other. Interestingly enough, modern media-centred campaigning is not necessarily more effective for winning the election than traditional, labour-intensive canvassing.

In the long run, the package offered by Western consultants may bear its own risks as marketing strategies weaken the consolidation of an effective party organization even though they promise to compensate for actual structural deficiencies. First, professional campaigns are primarily media-centred and as such cost-intensive. In less developed countries in particular this can be an unaffordable option. As a consequence, corruption as a means of raising the necessary capital is widespread, which seriously damages the party's credibility in the eyes of potential voters. Second, professional campaigning is highly centralized around the 'war room' of the campaign strategists, resulting in a vicious circle of further alienation from ordinary voters and in turn intensification of campaign expenditures. The studies in this volume demonstrate that more imaginative ways of communicating to voters that employ indigenous cultural traditions and non-mediated communication can be better ways of establishing viable party–voter relationships.

The citizens

Given that most citizens in new democracies lack the durable party identification that has developed in Western democracies over a long period of time (Lipset and Rokkan 1967), it is easy to conclude that they must be extremely vulnerable to political messages and media bias. They are also assumed to be badly equipped for dealing with the sudden flood of negative news, muck-raking and contradicting messages disseminated by the media after the end of state censorship. As the political reality is changing, the cognitive schemata that were perfectly suitable for reading between the lines of propagandistic media texts seem to be outdated for processing information in a democratic environment of open debate. However, this view underestimates citizens' ability to learn and to adapt to their new role.

Qualitative research shows (see Mickiewicz, Chapter 11) that the experiences from the past are an effective tool for decoding the hidden purpose of political messages and classifying them as partisan or biased. The main difference between the information imparted to citizens in the old regime and the new democratic order is not so much a shift from persuasive to neutral information, but from monolithic, one-sided messages to a diversity of competing truth claims. It is also remarkable to see that citizens are willing to accept the predominance of negative news even though they are longing for positive and reassuring stories. Yet, knowing the manufactured nature of the news of the past that praised the achievements of the system even when it was already apparently eroding, citizens remain deeply suspicious about positive news. This paradox of individual information perception could be an explanation for the empirical finding that exposure to the news media has predominantly positive effects on citizens' democratic orientations (see Voltmer and Schmitt-Beck, Chapter 13). Following the news encourages individuals to take on an active role as a citizen and increases their positive evaluation of democratic politics in spite of the fact that political reporting is typically characterized by an aggressive and polemical tone. The general pattern found in this study is largely similar across countries from post-communist and post-authoritarian pathways, but the effects are significantly stronger for respondents from the former. This pattern can be interpreted as an indicator for the higher level of politicization in communist countries that still persists after regime change. In contrast, the marginalization of politics in the Latin American media makes political information more elusive and hence less effective in moulding political orientations.

Although Chapters 11 and 13 draw a positive picture of the relationship between the media and democratic citizenship, it would be premature to conclude that the media's impact is a positive one throughout. Obviously, content does matter, though the crucial factor is lack of diversity rather than negativism. Empirical findings from recent Russian elections (see White and McAllister, Chapter 12) highlight the devastating effects of a manipulated media. The results from representative survey data corroborate that the media had a decisive impact on electoral choice. These effects were largely consistent with the pro-Kremlin bias apparent in the political coverage of the media, especially the main television channels. This study dramatically emphasizes the crucial importance of plurality and a fair representation of existing viewpoints in the media – if not in individual outlets, then at least in the system as a whole. For without fair competition of alternative options, the meaning of democratic elections will be reduced to an acclamation of the power elites who have the manipulative skills and financial resources to get the media under their control.

Taken together, the contributions of this volume demonstrate both similarities and differences in the way in which political communication and the mass media shape the course of politics in new democracies. While the countries covered in this book bear their specific patterns of transition and unique cultures of public communication, they also share particular problems in establishing an open public sphere of political debate that fosters the consolidation of the new political order. The extent to which the media are able to actively shape the political process or, on the contrary, remain in the subordinate position of being subjected to the interests of political elites depends on the effectiveness of the new political institutions. At the same time, the quality of the democratic process is highly contingent on the performance of the media in creating a circle of success or failure that underlines the complexity and interdependence of the relationship between political communication and democratization.

References

Clark, C. (2000) 'Modernization, democracy, and the developmental state in Asia. A virtuous cycle or unraveling strands?' in J.F. Hollifield and C. Jillson (eds) *Pathways to Democracy. The Political Economy of Democratic Transitions*, New York/London: Routledge, 160–77.

Hankiss, E. (1994) 'The Hungarian media's war of independence', *Media, Culture and Society*, 16: 293–312.

Hollifield, J.F. and Jillson, C. (eds)(2000) *Pathways to Democracy. The Political Economy of Democratic Transitions*, New York/London: Routledge.

Huntington, S. (1991) *The Third Wave. Democratization in the Late Twentieth Century*, Norman,/London: University of Oklahoma Press.

Kavanagh, D. (1995) *Election Campaigning. The New Marketing of Politics*, Oxford: Blackwell.

Linz, S. and Stepan, A. (1996) *Problems of Democratic Transition and Consolidation. South Europe, South America, and Post-Communist Europe*, Baltimore, MD: Johns Hopkins University Press.

Lipset, S.M. and Rokkan, S. (1967) 'Cleavage structure, party systems, and voter alignments', in S.M. Lipset and S. Rokkan (eds) *Party Systems and Voter Alignments. Cross-National Perspectives*, New York: Free Press, 1–67.

Meyer, T. with Hinchman, L. (2002) *Media Democracy. How the Media Colonize Politics*, Cambridge: Polity Press.

O'Neil, P. (ed.)(1997) *Post-Communism and the Media in Eastern Europe*, London: Frank Cass.

Olson, D.M. (1998) 'Party formation and party system consolidation in the new democracies of Central Europe', *Political Studies*, 46: 432–64.

Paletz, D., Jakubowicz, K. and Novosel, P. (eds)(1995) *Glasnost and After. Media Change in Central and Eastern Europe*, Cresskill: Hampton Press.

Pfetsch, B. (1998) 'Government news management', in D. Graber, D. McQuail and

P. Norris (eds) *The Politics of News. The News of Politics*, Washington, DC: Congressional Quarterly Press, 70–93.

Potter, D., Goldblatt, D., Kilon, M. and Lewis, P. (eds.) (1997) *Democratization*, Cambridge: Polity Press.

Randall, V. (1993) 'The media and democratization in the Third World', *Third World Quarterly*, 14: 625–46.

Skidmore, T.E. (ed.) (1993) *Television, Politics and the Transition to Democracy in Latin America*, Baltimore, MD: Johns Hopkins University Press.

Splichal, S. (1994) *Media Beyond Socialism. Theory and Practice in East-Central Europe*, Boulder, CO: Westview Press.

Swanson, D.L. and Mancini, P. (eds) (1996) *Politics, Media, and Modern Democracy. An International Study of Innovations in Electoral Campaigning and their Consequences*, Westport, CT: Praeger.

Voltmer, K. (2000) 'Constructing political reality in Russia. Izvestiya – between old and new journalistic practices', *European Journal of Communication*, 14: 469–500.

Waisbord, S.R. (1995) 'The mass media and consolidation of democracy in South America', *Research in Political Sociology*, 7: 207–27.

Index

Printed in the United States
by Baker & Taylor Publisher Services